Ian McFetridge

LOGICAL NECESSITY AND OTHER ESSAYS

Aristotelian Society Series

Volume 1
COLIN MCGINN
Wittgenstein on Meaning

Volume 2
BARRY TAYLOR
Modes of Occurrence

Volume 3
KIT FINE
Reasoning with Arbitrary Objects

Volume 4
CHRISTOPHER PEACOCKE
Thoughts: An Essay on Content

Volume 5
DAVID E. COOPER
Metaphor

Volume 6
DAVID WIGGINS
Needs, Values, Truth: Essays in the Philosophy of Value

Volume 7
JONATHAN WESTPHAL
Colour: Some Philosophical Problems from Wittgenstein

Volume 8
ANTHONY SAVILE
Aesthetic Reconstructions:
The Seminal Writings of Lessing, Kant and Schiller

Volume 9
GRAEME FORBES
Languages of Possibility: An Essay in Philosophical Logic

Volume 10
E. J. LOWE
Kinds of Being: A Study of Individuation, Identity and the Logic of Singular Terms.

I. G. McFetridge

Logical Necessity and other essays

Aristotelian Society Series

Volume 11

edited by

John Haldane and Roger Scruton

Aristotelian Society

First published 1990
by the Aristotelian Society
Birkbeck College, Malet Street, London WC1E 7HX

British Library Cataloguing in Publication Data

McFetridge, I. G. (Ian Graham) *1948–1988*
Logical necessity : and other essays. – (Aristotelian
Society series, v. 11).
1. Philosophy
I. Title II. Haldane, John III. Scruton, Roger
IV. Series
100

ISBN 0-907111-24-6

Photoset and printed in Great Britain by
The Longdunn Press

Contents

Preface

At the time of his death, aged 40, in 1988, Ian McFetridge was lecturing at Birkbeck College in the University of London, where he taught almost every branch of philosophy, from symbolic logic (which was his first love) to the philosophies of Plato, Berkeley and Kant. He was also working on various papers, concerned with modality, *a priori* knowledge and metaphysical realism. He had planned to write a book on these topics, and sketches for various chapters survive among his papers. Although none of this work was in a finished state when he died, much of it, in our view, is sufficiently interesting and pertinent to justify publication in this collection of his papers. We have therefore done our best to edit those essays which seemed to be of lasting value, and to present them here to the reader. Altogether five of the ten papers in this volume have been retrieved from McFetridge's *Nachlass*.

We have also included the two memorial addresses that we delivered at a service held on December 8th 1988, in the University Church of Christ the King, London. These addresses, although prepared for a specific occasion, were written under the immediate impact of his death, and testify, however inadequately, to the great loss which prompted them. It is difficult to exaggerate that loss. The least that we can say, in retrospect, is that the range and fertility of McFetridge's mind went far beyond what can be gathered from the essays contained in this volume. Partly through diffidence, but partly also from a conviction that academic philosophers write too much and too carelessly, McFetridge wrote only when he believed that he had a genuine contribution to make. Nevertheless, even in these essays, glimpses are offered of the range of historical reference, and the intellectual competence (in logic, mathematics and science, as well as in philosophy) which informed his thinking, and which made him such an inspiring colleague and teacher.

John Haldane
University of St Andrews

Roger Scruton
Birkbeck College, London

Acknowledgements

We are grateful to Jennifer McCarthy for unearthing the drafts from which the posthumous papers were reconstructed and for compiling the index, to Andrew Jack for help in editing essay X, to Dorothy Edgington for assisting us in editing and seeing this volume through the press; and to the following editors and publishers:

The Aristotelian Society, for permission to reprint essays I and III; the editor of the *Philosophical Quarterly* for permission to reprint IV and V; and Oxford University Press for permission to print VII.

A Memorial Address

John Haldane

I

In her biography of G.K. Chesterton, Maisie Ward writes of Chesterton's general kindness and charity. She then continues with the following words:

> Even more attractive to most of us was his fashion of making us feel that we had contributed something worthwhile. He would take something one had said and develop it till it shone and glowed; not from its own worth but from what he made of it. Almost everything could thus become a starting point for a train of his best thought.

Those of us who had the very considerable privilege of having been taught by Ian McFetridge or having been a professional colleague of his, or indeed of having been both, will immediately recognize in these words written of one brilliant man a description that exactly fits that other gifted thinker for whose life we have come here to give thanks.

II

My own first memory of Ian is of him conducting a logic class in a building opposite the student union in Malet Street. The surroundings were somewhat at odds with our purpose in being gathered there. Very many of those drawn to study philosophy at Birkbeck have (quite properly) a romantic attachment to the idea of abstract speculation conducted in a university setting. Perhaps they dream to see themselves in Gothic or neo-classical cloisters or, by contrast, in small dark rooms withdrawn from the world in concentration on ancient questions of truth and value. Such images are not to be derided or discouraged, for the best philosophy as well as the worst philosophy is the product of curiosity sustained by emotional attachments. However, the reality of evening study in Central London – at the end of a day's work, often after a rush hour journey, under the numbing glow of neon lights – can be very discouraging for all concerned. Yet it was in these circumstances that Ian was often at his best: presenting abstract ideas and giving them an almost visible structure, filling them with colour and texture, moving them around to show better the relationship between them until, as I say, one's sense of their character became almost visual.

His capacity to make one 'see' the essence of an idea and the formal structure of an argument depended as much upon his expressive and engaging personality as on his analytical skills. In fact here we may be reminded of a philosophical point about the way in which *form* and *content* can be inseparable. For my own part, I recall associating the significance of certain philosophical views with Ian's expression of them, and then reflecting on how difficult it would be to capture that significance in any other way. That is to say, it seemed that there were distinctively 'McFetridgean' thoughts.

One unforgettable aspect of his lively style which immediately struck and amused me was the manner in which taking up, lighting and smoking a cigarette (and in later days the process of rolling one of his own liquorice-paper creations) became part of the expression of an idea. Striking a match, inhaling and so on, were elements in the extended syntax of his speech. I have a very vivid image of a type of situation when someone would have been reading a philosophical paper. At some point in the proceedings, not having yet spoken, Ian would light a cigarette, or put one out, with a deliberation that indicated an objection had become clarified in his mind. When he then went on to present it – again with draughtsmanlike precision – he would as often proceed to suggest how the objection might be replied to.

This was perhaps his greatest philosophical skill: to see and effectively communicate to others the structure of a problem, striking just the right balance between abstract generality and the specifics of the topic, and then, having done this, to show what possibilities were available on various sides of the issue. Sometimes people capable of such comprehension are intolerant of its absence in others and will not take time to help them understand. But I never knew this to be so of Ian. Indeed, it is a commonplace among his friends and former students that he was an exceptionally patient, generous and helpful teacher and always one who made us 'feel that we contributed something worthwhile'. This is not at all to say that he was tolerant of anything. He hated pretension, especially among professional philosophers, such as high moral tones, or claims to substance and profundity on behalf of lightweight gas.

III

Chesterton once wrote that 'one cannot find truth with logic unless one has first found truth without it'. Otherwise put, the point is that although one may reason with the intellect of an angel one's conclusions will only be as good as one's premisses. I have referred to Ian's analytical and teaching skills. His appetite for the truth, and his capacity to discern it, were likewise concentrated within the philosophical aspect of his nature. But he also had an appreciation of the possibility that things significant and valuable may be revealed by non-philosophical exploration.

Roger Scruton will speak of Ian's general aesthetic and religious sensibilities. I first became aware of the latter by way of his interest in music, in particular opera. While a student at Birkbeck I wrote a shortish article concerned with 'education and the spiritual in art' in which I discussed several religious paintings and considered the possibility that these might not so much *illustrate* beliefs, as *present* religious truths. I was surprised by Ian's enthusiasm for this idea, since while we had often discussed religious doctrines from an abstract point of view I had not previously heard him voice religious feelings. He then explained that what most consistently elicited these was opera, and that the idea that an aesthetic response might be intelligible only on the assumption of a belief in the religious significance of its object was one which his experience seemed to confirm.

The story of Ian's spiritual life would be long and complex and would have to take account of the darkness as well as of the light, of unreasoning euphoria and of considered reflection, of pessimism and disbelief, of optimism and hesitant faith, of animated and of lifeless agnosticism. I shall not even attempt to sketch its outline or assess its significance. I offer no interpretation of these matters but it is appropriate – especially given the circumstances of Ian's death and the setting of this memorial – to say something about this increasingly dominant feature of his last years. I presume to do so also because religion was the subject of many conversations and of much correspondence between us. Indeed, it was implicated in his last communication with me – a postcard which I received several days after his death.

Roger Scruton will mention Ian's moral sensibilities and his longstanding interest in the aesthetic spirituality of the Oxford movement, in particular his appreciation of Cardinal Newman. In a letter in which he reflects back upon these interests, and other school and university days' attitudes to religion, Ian writes as follows:

> I was quite explicit: that to accept that Christ taught the moral truth was not to have Christian faith. And I suppose I've always more or less explicitly known that (hence my oft-repeated conditional: if I were a Christian I'd be a Catholic – meaning then *Roman* Catholic). But, in fact, [among] my grounds for then asserting that conditional my admiration for the logical rigour of what little I knew of Roman theology is not something I now feel.

The point here is not that Ian's attraction to Christianity had waned. Quite the contrary. Rather, one reason – admiration of argumentative rigour – had been replaced by another more important for this kind of faith, *viz*., a sense of sacramental presence and more generally of the immanence of the divine.

Let me again quote Ian's own words, this time from an earlier amusing letter written when he was absorbed with the ideas and culture of Orthodox Catholicism. I should stress that in reading this and being moved by it, it is important to note that it was written during a phase in which he was given to bouts of euphoria that later came to be replaced by periods of depression and rejection. I offer it, therefore, not as unambiguous evidence of a religious conversion, for given the darkness and despair that followed it could not be that. Rather, it serves to bring in to the partial and personal sketches offered in this and Scruton's memorials a distinctive feature of Ian's later life which should not be ignored; and more importantly it lets us hear again the characteristic excitement of Ian's voice. He writes:

As you will understand just now is an exciting, sometimes disquieting but joyful time for me. For some of my friends, however, it seems rather to cause them worry . . . but also anger . . . [Two things] 1) I am pretty sure I shall become a communicant member of a Christian church; 2) I am pretty sure (as sure as I am of the first) that it will be the Orthodox Catholic Church. From 1) it follows that I need both guidance and the fellowship of other Christians but (from 2) some at least must be Orthodox. I participated this morning in my first collective act of Orthodox worship but knowing little Greek and the service being particularly long – I foolishly went at the beginning 10.00 am and at 11.30 they were only up to . . . the end of the offertory – I felt I had to go somewhere I understood the words. I managed to catch the end of matters at St. Paul's. (These peripatetic devotions only being made financially possible by The Bus Pass!).

So one thing I didn't read till I got home this evening was the creed. I ought perhaps to have worried about that before . . . but reading it now I think I can say I find no difficulty with it. What I mean is: I could, I feel, express my faith in these words.

IV

In the months and years following the date of this letter we talked and corresponded much more on matters religious as on topics philosophical. Ian's thoughts developed, changed, broke off, were resumed and became both more and less complex in different respects. But the religious sensibility continued to move him if in less excited and committed ways. He was a regular, if infrequent, visitor to Westminster Cathedral on the occasions of going there with my mother, of whom he had become a kind and affectionate friend. In the weeks before his death he spent some days at a Carmelite Priory in Kent and it was during this time that he visited the shrine of St. Jude in Faversham. The postcard mentioned earlier was a photograph of the Saint—the Patron of Lost Causes. That reflects Ian's sense of irony and tells us something we all already know about the painfully depressed state of Ian's mind in his final days, but it may also suggest an idea of where he thought all hope might possibly come to rest. Those for whom this makes sense should pray, therefore, that Ian is now where restless yearnings cease, while others might simply remember with affection and gratitude an unusually gifted and generous man—one who had the capacity and the wish to make others feel that they had contributed something worthwhile.

Ian McFetridge

A Tribute by Roger Scruton

Ian was a teacher who loved his subject and his students equally. Happy or troubled, idle or busy, drunk or sober, at any time of the day or night, he would jump into dialogue just as soon as anyone showed the wish for it. The thoughts of others—however lame and uninstructed—were as valuable to him as any thought of his own, and he would strive to rephrase them in the words which gave them the greatest intellectual credit. He placed even his slowest pupils on a par with the great philosophers, not so as to flatter them, but because he saw no reason to prefer the thoughts of the famous to those of the obscure, until each had been granted a hearing. His mind was like a court of law, dealing impartially with every idea, examining, cross-examining and lending the best defence to all. To be taught by Ian was to step from the ordinary world of opinion into a realm of peace and understanding. It is the glimpse of this realm, far more than any doctrine, that has been the ancient promise of philosophy.

Ian will be remembered with a gratitude all the deeper for the tact and modesty with which he dealt with everyone who knew him. He died young. But he gave more of himself and to more effect than most of those who enjoy their three score years and ten. Diffident in all his ways, he nevertheless brought strength to those around him, and imbued them with an immense intellectual confidence.

When I first knew him, I was a graduate student in Cambridge, giving tutorials in order to supplement my grant. Ian came to me at the beginning of my second year, and, within a week of meeting him, I realized that this unassuming person was to be the most important of my teachers. I had set him an essay on the topic of personal identity, recommending him to read a book by Sydney Shoemaker which I was currently studying, and whose subtle thoughts had quite defeated me. Ian's essay, pushed through my door the night before the tutorial, was a revelation. Patiently, modestly, and with extreme economy, he destroyed Shoemaker's arguments, rephrased in his own words the question which they had been designed to answer, and then left it hanging. I read the essay with sinking heart. What could I possibly teach this man, and how could I find enough to say during the next day's tutorial?

I stayed up late, re-read the book (understanding it for the first time), and studied Ian's essay. I made some notes, tore them up and made some more. The next morning my feelings resembled those ascribed by Shakespeare to the usurping princes who, having scratched together their faithless armies, awake to the day of battle that will decide their fate. Here was the living proof of my inadequacy, in this shy but eager Scot, who sat in my study looking not at me but to one side of me as though embarrassed by the situation in which he had inadvertently put me.

It is no exaggeration to say that it was Ian and not I who conducted that tutorial. But what was most remarkable, and what afterwards stayed vividly in my memory, was the fact that, by the end of the hour, he had entirely restored my confidence, replaced me on my teacher's pedestal, and taken grateful leave as though it were he and not I who had derived the greatest benefit. His technique was simple: so simple that 'technique' is hardly the word for it. He merely listened, with eager anticipation of my every word, adding finishing touches to my thoughts, and sometimes rephrasing them in words that left him silent and impressed, as though it were I and not he who had uttered them. My hesitant objections to his essay emerged from our dialogue as equal partners in a collective enquiry; what had seemed to me thin apologies for argument became, thanks to Ian's extraordinary intellectual empathy, genuine answers to his more interesting thoughts. And by the end of the hour I realized that I had been granted not only a brilliant pupil, but also the teacher who would show me how to teach, and who would give me the confidence for which I had hitherto searched in vain.

Ian was difficult to know. His essays were rigorous, abstract, giving away nothing personal. His diffidence—which never left him, and indeed which seemed to grow as the years went by—created a barrier to intimacy, while his sheer brilliance as a student kept me in awe of him. Only by accident did I discover that we had interests in common outside philosophy. One day he came early for a tutorial, when I was listening to Schubert's *Schwanengesang*; he sat down quietly, and, when the record was over, unexpectedly remarked that there was more truth in such music than in any abstract philosophy. Schubert, he told me, was his favourite composer; and more and more, as time went on, I associated Ian with Schubert, whose music seems to contain so much of the warmth, the gentleness and the tragic sense of being cast adrift which were also Ian's. Like Schubert, Ian lived under a shadow, and even his brightest days were darkened by it. Perhaps he knew that he would not live out the span of human life. And perhaps this knowledge worked on him to compel a sense of urgency—a need to live as much as he could in the time available. Perhaps, then, we owe to his early death many of those qualities as a teacher for which he will be remembered, so that if we can accept his death now it is also because we have benefited from it—as Ian's favourite music benefited from the premonition which caused Schubert to concentrate a lifetime's passion into a few urgent years.

I discovered, as time went on, that we had other interests in common. Ian was a lover of Brahms and Wagner, of English poetry, and of the poetry of Eliot in particular. He had a passion for useless knowledge—for history, customs, liturgies and literatures. He had a discreet and wayward spiritual life, which would break out in unexpected acts of devotion, in periods of religious melancholy and studious guilt, and sometimes too in anger on behalf of a world which cries out for justice and which receives from heaven only obscure and ambiguous replies. Ian was an admirer of Cardinal Newman, and found in the Oxford Movement a precursor of his own spiritual journey, away from the worldly certainties of the established Protestant church, towards those sensual southern rituals, in which the ancient gods of the Mediterranean live on and lend their mysterious force to the Christian morality of love.

This morality of love ran deep in Ian; but it was a source of anguish. In this too he was diffident, believing himself unworthy of his own ideals, and unfit either to give the charity which welled up in him, or to receive it in turn from others. His self-doubt was compounded by a sensitivity to the modern world, and a knowledge of its spiritual dangers. He suffered the darkness of our times both outwardly and inwardly, and this darkness could all but extinguish the light of life which burned in him. He would sink, on occasion, to the bottom of the human world, seeking the unloving and the unlovely in the belief that he deserved no better, and could relate only to them. And then—by a miracle, for it could happen in no other way—he would right himself, float upwards to the light, and live once again in charity and humour. As I grew to know him I became more conscious of this fatal strife within him, and more anxious for him, knowing that it was his excess of sympathy—his ability to enter and appropriate the minds of others—that led him to decry himself, and left him so exposed to delusions of unworthiness.

If I mention the dark side of Ian's character, it is because I believe he would have wished us to remember it. He had no patience with people who pretend that the abyss does not exist, or who are always filling it with trivia. Ian was never trivial, never shallow, never willing to deceive himself or others. His favourite authors were those—such as Eliot, Cavafy and Seferis—who had stared into the abyss with unblinking eyes, and given form to its nothingness. He saw himself faced at every step by ultimate choices, in a world which remains deaf to our cries. His was the experience captured in a poem by Seferis, the Greek of which he memorized. It is called *Arnese*—'Denial':

In the secret shore
White as a dove,
We thirsted at noon:
But by brackish water.

On the golden sand
We wrote her name;[1]
But the sea-breeze blew
And the writing vanished.

With what heart, what spirit,
What desire and passion
We lived our life: a mistake!
So we changed life.

[1] γράψαμε τ'ὄνομά τησ: but who is 'she'? The poet does not say.

Ian changed life many times, moving restlessly through the gamut of emotions in search of peace; peace came to him, however, only when life was over.

But of course, it is not the dark side that we principally remember. We are here to pay a debt of gratitude, for a man who gave to the world far more than he took from it, and whose loss is irreparable. My own debt to Ian is enormous. From the very first years he would read my work and give his lucid comments, leading me to perceive what I *really* meant, and how I was *really* arguing. His performance was the more remarkable in that he rarely agreed with my conclusions. So great were his imagination and his sympathy that even ideas that he found repugnant elicited from him as many arguments in their favour as arguments against. Almost the last time I saw Ian, two weeks before his death, it was in order to discuss an article which I had been writing over the summer, on a subject far from any which he had previously considered. As always, he saw my meaning more clearly than I did, sketched for me the principal objections, how I might reply to them, and what issues they raised. As always, too, I left him with my self-confidence and interest restored. Scarcely a day has gone by since then, when I have not wanted to turn to him and ask for my meaning.

It was a remarkable feature of Ian that, while his sufferings were solitary, his joys were shared. He made a large space in his life for those who were dearest to him: for his parents, to whom he was so deeply devoted; for his sister Lilian, who was his pride and joy and for whom he wanted every good thing; for his dear friends Martin, Alex and Costas; and for Mary, who knew him as teacher, counsellor, friend and husband, and who was the light for which he reached in his greatest darkness, the focus of all his hopes and the brief promise of their fulfilment.

All our students will remember Ian's good humour: his songs at the piano, his wild and zany conversations, his lively sense that life should be permitted in all its forms, and his constant chiding of the grim, cold hand of puritanism. When I think of him now, three images come before me: I see the shy undergraduate, who taught me to teach. I see the Ian of those later years, searching, repudiating, throwing all that he possessed away. And I see that concentrated force of life, that generous and cultivated heart, which, even in its deepest anguish, was open to every sympathy and which poured out its charity alike on the weak and the strong. These three Ians were one Ian, and in their unity each is justified. Thinking on his life I feel how good it was, and how the path of thorns which Ian trod was also a way of redemption.

It took uncommon gifts to do what Ian did: to light a lamp of truth in every place he passed through, however dark. His were not the gifts of the teacher only, nor only those of the philosopher; they were the gifts of the friend. Few people I have known have come as close as Ian came, to embodying that eternal Greek ideal, of the lover of wisdom, whose wisdom is the love of friends.

I

Propositions and Davidson's Account of Indirect Discourse*

Consider the following dialogue:

> *A*: The earth moves.
> *B*: Galileo said that.
> *A*: The earth moves.
> *B*: That's *another* thing Galileo said.

This dialogue, which could continue indefinitely in the same vein, is, I take it, absurd. More precisely, the use of 'another' in *B*'s second remark is mistaken. Yet on Davidson's account of indirect discourse, as we shall see, *B*'s comment would be perfectly in order. Davidson, I shall argue, has given a mistaken account of *things said*, and I shall suggest an alternative. But first the question arises: are there such things as things said?

I

(1) Galileo said that the earth moves. Hence
(2) Galileo said something *i.e.*, there is something which Galileo said.

We produce and seemingly understand sentences such as (2) and infer them from sentences like (1). The theorist of natural language, as opposed perhaps to the constructor of a regimented idiom for certain scientific purposes must, it would seem, allow that there are things said, stated, asserted and so on. More generally that there are things propounded, in various modes. Uncommitted as yet to any account of their nature, he must allow that there are propositions.[1] If his

* From *Proceedings of The Aristotelian Society*, 1975–6, pp. 131–145.

[1] *The Shorter Oxford Dictionary*: '*Proposition* . . . that which is propounded.' The entry, of course, gives other senses of 'proposition'. This though is the one which interests me. It can be treated, if one wishes, as mere shorthand for 'that which is said, asserted *etc*'.

account of our linguistic resources is to proceed by providing, for each sentence of our language, a formal representation amenable to inclusion in a finite theory of truth, then such a representation of (2) must, it would seem, contain a bound variable ranging over things said. While to account for the entailment of (2) by (1) the representation of (1) must contain after the verb of saying a position accessible to such a variable, hence a position accessible to a singular term referring to something said.

Two objections may be raised at this early stage. Both agree that (2) is to be represented using a variable bound by an existential quantifier. The first denies that this requires a domain of objects—things said—to serve as values of such a variable. The account is Prior's.[2] Represent (2) as (3)

(3) $(\exists p)$ (Galileo said that p)

and explain such a form by saying that it is true if there is a true sentence obtainable by dropping the initial existential quantifier and replacing the variable thereby left free by a sentence. But this substitutionalist account is, at best, incomplete. It makes free use of the notion of the truth of sentences obtained by placing arbitrary sentences in such contexts as 'Galileo said that . . .'. Until we are shown that an account of *this* is available which does not reintroduce the notion of things said, the objection is quite worthless. In any case, if the objection to things said is, as it seems to be in Prior, an essentially nominalist one, then little has been achieved by the substitutionalist account. We are not, I presume, to take it that substitution is an operation performed on concrete objects, on sentence-*tokens*.

The second objection would be to point out that we cannot make the simple connection suggested above between the English expressions 'something', 'there is something which', and the category of singular terms. In English as we have it, such expressions can be used to express quantification into positions accessible to predicates, and sentences containing them can formally be represented by second-order quantification. This objection is correct and shows two things: first, that it is

[2] A.N. Prior, *Objects of Thought* (Oxford 1971) Chapters 2, 3, esp. pp. 35–6.

unnatural to attempt a formal account of the linguistic resources we actually possess within a purely first-order language; secondly, that the existential generalisation test we in effect used to identify first-order quantification in (2) and the occurrence of a singular term in (1) needs supplementation. We need at least criteria for distinguishing idiomatic first- and second-order quantification. Such tests can be devised[3] and I here merely report that, as might be expected, they reveal the quantification in (2) as clearly first-order. Hence, I suggest, a straightforward account of (1) will locate therein a singular term whose referent is something said—a proposition—and an account of (2) will require a variable ranging over such things.

To see (1) and (2) thus is, *ipso facto*, to see them as containing an expression 'Galileo said' which would be represented as a predicate, true or false of things said, and hence, plausibly as locating an at least two-place predicate, 'said', relating persons and things said.

II

Objections to propositions spring from at least two sources: (a) that they are intensional objects; (b) that they are abstract objects.

I shall first look briefly at (a). On the traditional view of the matter, the singular term I claimed we ought to find in (1) would be the complex expression 'that the earth moves'. This might certainly be called an *intensional singular term* where this means: substitution within this term of co-extensional expressions may change the reference of the whole term. For example, substitution for 'the earth' of a different singular term with the same reference may change the reference of the 'that' clause. And the ground for this claim, of course, is that such substitution may alter the truth-value of (1). To see (1) as containing the predicate 'Galileo said'—true or false of propositions —is to commit ourselves to seeing changes in the truth-value of (1) under substitution within the alleged singular term as explicable only on the supposition that the proposition referred to has shifted. Thus, on the traditional view, such expressions as 'that the earth moves' are intensional singular

[3] See Michael Dummett, *Frege: The Philosophy of Language* (London 1973) Ch. 4.

terms the referents of which are propositions.

But while we can thus classify singular terms as, in this sense, intensional, it is difficult to see how we can move from this to a classification of their referents as intensional: difficult to find a property which *objects* must possess if and only if they are intensional.[4] Such a classification could be derived from the notion of an intensional singular term in only two ways, it would seem. We could say either (i) an object is intensional if every singular term referring to it is intensional or (ii) an object is intensional if there is at least one intensional singular term referring to it.

No entities meet the condition in (i). Thus, cleaving to the present case of propositions, if there ever are singular terms referring to propositions, then, in sentences such as 'John said what Mary said yesterday' or 'Galileo asserted the theory of Copernicus', there are extensional singular terms referring to propositions.

If substitution of co-referring singular terms can ever change the truth-value of a sentence in which they occur (and it was only this possibility which could force us to treat any singular terms as intensional) then any entity for which we possess a singular term meets the condition in (ii). Let '$C(\ )$' be a context completable by a singular term to yield a sentence which can change from true to false under substitution, for the contained singular term, of a co-referring one. Suppose 't' be a term such that '$C(t)$' is true. Let a be an arbitrary object for which we possess a singular term 'a', and 'b' a singular term for an object b, where $a \neq b$. Then the following, (4), is an intensional singular term for a:

(4) $(\iota x)[C(t) \supset x = a \ \&\ {\sim}C(t) \supset x = b]$

All this is merely to say, what is in any case obvious, that problems about intensionality are merely problems about, among other things, ways of referring, not particularly about the objects allegedly referred to: that objections to so-called intensional objects are often simply objections to, among other

[4] For arguments against moving from grammatical features of sentences ascribing mental states to alleged properties of mental states see Roger Scruton 'Intensional and Intentional Objects' *Proceedings of the Aristotelian Society* 1970–71.

things, intensional singular terms. I shall not rehearse such objections.

Now a necessary condition of a singular term's being, in the above sense, intensional is that it contain semantically significant parts. We defined the intensional character of a singular term *via* the notion of substitution within it of expressions having the semantic property of extension or reference. Thus a sufficient, and rather radical, condition of avoiding intensional singular terms for things said is to see singular reference to propositions as being standardly made by means of expressions which lack semantically significant parts. But singular terms for propositions have a potential infinity of distinct referents. Thus if the semantic properties of singular terms for propositions were themselves sufficient to determine their referents they would needs possess a potential infinity of distinct semantic features which, under the present assumption, they would not derive from their possession of parts with semantically significant properties. But, as Davidson has repeatedly argued, no learnable language, and no language amenable to a finite theory of truth (which may not be the same thing) could contain expressions meeting this specification.[5] Thus on the present hypothesis the referent of a term picking out a proposition must be determined by something more than the semantic properties of the term alone. And the only plausible candidate for that which, in addition to the semantic properties of a term, can determine its referent is, speaking broadly, the context of its utterance. If we call a singular term, the referent of which on an occasion of utterance is thus in part determined, a demonstrative singular term, then, on the present hypothesis, things said will standardly be referred to by means of demonstrative singular terms. This is, of course, Davidson's proposal.

III

To say that the referent of a demonstrative singular term *is determined by* some feature of the context in which it is uttered is not to say that its referent, on a particular occasion, *is* some

[5] For the beginnings in Davidson of this argument, see D. Davidson 'Theories of Meaning and Learnable Languages' in Y. Bar-Hillel (ed.) *Logic, Methodology and the Philosophy of Science* (Amsterdam 1965) pp. 383–394.

feature of that context, some object, for example, present in that context. I shall argue that by moving from something like the former to the latter, Davidson has given an absurd account of things said, one which, within a framework broadly like his, can only be avoided by maintaining the second allegedly undesirable feature of propositions, *viz.*, that they are abstract objects.

Davidson's proposal concerning the logical form of sentences such as (1) should by now be familiar. It is that

> . . . sentences in indirect discourse . . . consist of an expression referring to a speaker, the two-place predicate 'said', and a demonstrative referring to an utterance. Period. What follows gives the content of the subject's saying, but has no logical or semantic connection with the original attribution of a saying.[6]

Thus in his and our favoured example, *viz.*, (1), the expression 'that' has the logical rôle of a demonstrative singular term standardly used to perform an act of demonstration to the ensuing utterance of 'the earth moves'. Given that it has such a rôle, the position it occupies is open to first-order quantification. A sentence such as (5)

(5) $(\exists x)$ (Galileo said x)

is thus quite legitimate on Davidson's account and may seem to provide a reading for 'Galileo said something' *i.e.*, for (2). Moreover, as Davidson notes[7] if, in uttering 'Galileo said that' the speaker does succeed in referring, by means of the demonstrative, to an utterance, then one can deduce that Galileo said something. We thus find an explanation of the plausibility of the inference from (1) to (2).

Davidson does, then, locate in (1) and (2) respectively singular reference to, and quantification over, things said *i.e.*, propositions in the minimal sense. They are utterances.

It is to be noted, though, that the things said, on Davidson's account, by Galileo are not (or at least not necessarily) *his* utterances but utterances of mine, yours or possibly anybody's. And it certainly seems odd to say that among the things said by

[6] Davidson 'On Saying That' *Synthese* 19 (1968–9) p. 142.
[7] *Ib.* p. 144.

Galileo is an utterance of mine. While odd, it is difficult to see in this fact an actual error.

Nevertheless the theory does have a consequence which is, surely, a mistake. Suppose we ask: *how many* things did Galileo say (possibly on some particular occasion which interests us)? The answer must be given: as many distinct things as he came, by his utterance on that occasion, to stand to in the saying relation. But if the things to which he stands in that relation are utterances, possibly of anybody's, this number can be indefinitely extended. For example, each appropriate utterance of 'The earth moves' is a distinct thing to which Galileo stands in the saying relation *i.e.*, a distinct thing said by Galileo. Producing more and more such utterances we can multiply at will the number of things said by Galileo, which is absurd. This, of course, is just the absurdity graphically illustrated in our opening dialogue.

It has frequently been urged that there is, intrinsically, no answer to the question, how many distinct things a man said on an occasion. For some, this alleged fact is, of itself, sufficient reason to give up the notion of things said. But, as I argued, no account of our actual linguistic resources can do that.[8] The grounds for saying that there is no determinate answer to this question have typically been that there is no unique or determinate standard of correctness in the reporting of another's speech. Tightening the match required between reporting and reported speaking will yield more stringent conditions on the identity of things said, whatever they are, and thus multiply the number of distinct things said, on an occasion, by a speaker. Variation in our interests in, hence in our standards of, speech attribution, may thus vary the degree

[8] Indeed doctrines of this sort have been held about entities other than things said. See, for example, D. Wiggins *Identity and Spatio-Temporal Continuity* (Oxford 1967) pp. 39–40 on oily waves and crowns. Such doctrines may just be that *we* cannot give an answer to the question 'How many *F*'s?'. But the move from this to the view that there *is* no answer to the question requires hard work. If we retain the predicate '*F*' and standard quantification theory with identity then we can formulate, for each finite number *n*, a sentence stating that there are exactly *n F*'s. Under a realist semantics each of these sentences will be determinately true or false, and at most one true. Perhaps then the doctrine is, at least, that all are false. But then we need a way of distinguishing the cases where the ground for this is that there is a determinate, but non-finite number of *F*'s, from the present alleged sort of case.

of match required. Hence there may be no determinate answer to the question 'How many things were said?'. My objection to Davidson can ignore such points. Even if we could fix on a determinate degree of match between reported and reporting utterance, the number of things said cannot depend on how many subsequent matching utterances are made. On Davidson's account it does so depend.

Another problem for Davidson's account, and hints towards a solution, emerge by considering sentences of a sort we had occasion to mention briefly before, *e.g.*, 'Galileo asserted Copernicus' theory'. If verbs of saying typically relate speakers to utterances then Copernicus' theory is an utterance. But this is absurd. If Copernicus' theory were an utterance then there would be an utterance which Copernicus' theory was (identical with). And clearly there is no utterance of which we can say that it (and hence it alone) is identical with Copernicus' theory. What is not absurd is to say, of many distinct utterances, that they are each *of* Copernicus' theory. Thus we should regard the referent of 'Copernicus' theory' as being the sort of entity that different utterances can be of. Similarly, if we wish to see a sentence such as 'Copernicus' theory is that the earth moves' as an identity judgment containing a demonstrative 'that', then likewise we should see the referent of 'that' not as the ensuing utterance but as something which it, and other utterances can be of.

Given that expressions such as 'Copernicus' theory' can occur after verbs of saying, such entities *viz.*, those which utterances can be of, can be the second terms of those two-place relations which, on Davidson's account, verbs of saying express. Uniformity would better be served, then, by seeing such entities as, in general, the second terms of such relations, hence by seeing the demonstrative 'that' which Davidson has located in standard attributions of sayings as referring not to the ensuing utterance, but to something which it, and other utterances, can be of. Likewise the variable in '$(\exists x)$ (Galileo said x)' ought to be seen as ranging over such things and not over utterances themselves.

Such a move would solve the counting problem mooted above. The number of distinct things said by Galileo on an occasion would not depend on the number of distinct utterances to which he stood in the original saying relation but on how many distinct things these utterances were of. Old-fashioned writings remind us to distinguish sayings, and what is said, utterances, and what they are of. The counting problem within a programme committed to locating things said would seem to provide a telling reason for such a distinction.

IV

Things said, then, must be things utterances can be of, not utterances themselves. To give an account of such entities within a broadly Davidsonian framework we shall find it necessary to look not merely at his account of the logical form of (1) but at the analysis proposal which it abbreviates. This runs:
The earth moves.

(6) $(\exists x)$ (Galileo's utterance *x* and my last utterance make us samesayers)
(6) is the analysis of (7).
(7) Galileo said that.

The analysis introduces a primitive predicate 'make . . . samesayers'—a four-place predicate relating two speakers and two utterances. Implicit in the use of the predicate is the idea that utterances *a,b,* can only make speakers *p,q,* samesayers when *a,b,* are utterances made by, respectively, *p* and *q*. Given that two utterances *a,b,* are by speakers *p,q,* what more is required for *a,b,* to make *p,q,* samesayers? Simply that a certain relation *R*, as yet unspecified, hold between the utterances in question.

Now the first thought here, *viz.*, that the utterances in question must be by the relevant speakers (implicit in the notion of *making-samesayers*) is, elsewhere in the analysis, made explicit—namely in the allusion to *Galileo's* utterance, and to *my* last utterance. So this first thought is, needlessly, caught twice over. We can drop its implicit occurrence in the notion of *making-samesayers*, replacing this four-place predicate by what then remains of it, *viz.*, a two-place predicate holding between utterances. Davidson himself makes such a move in his analysis of 'Jones asserted that Entebbe is equatorial' where a two-place relation between utterances is introduced by the expression 'has the content of'.[9]

The syntax of 'has the content of' is a little suggestive for our purposes. For one thing, it suggests rather strongly that the relation is symmetrical. (If *a* has the content of *b* must not *b* have the content of *a*?) It would be rash to assume this. If we wish an expression for the relation, other than the aseptic '*R*', then I shall use 'reports'. This will be a relation which an utterance *a* must have to an utterance *b* in order that *a* could be used to report *b*, a relation which can hold between *a* and *b*, in the usage I shall adopt, even when *a* is not, in fact, being so used. Nothing I say should be taken to imply that we are here dealing with a single relation, or with something which may not vary with our interests, standards of fairness, judiciousness and so on. As I said above, even if all these were fixed, the present counting problem would still arise.

Embodying our two-place predicate 'reports' (or rather its converse) into the analysis as it stands yields:

(8) $(\exists x)$ (Galileo's utterance x is reported by my last utterance).

An oddity of this is that the bare demonstrative 'that' in the logical form proposal has yielded to the much more explicit demonstrative 'my last utterance'. All that is essential to Davidson's account is that reference be made demonstratively to an utterance (or, of course, to an inscription) and Davidson himself begins his paper with a case where demonstrative reference is allegedly made to an utterance of one other than the speaker.[10] So we can best capture the spirit of Davidson's account by retaining the demonstrative 'that' and merely making it clear that it is intended to refer to an utterance. Thus by something like:

(9) $(\exists x)$ (Galileo's utterance x is reported by that utterance).

The counting problem then is that if we derive a reading for 'Galileo said something' from (9) by existential generalisation with respect to the demonstrative singular term, construed as it there is, distinct utterances reporting Galileo's utterance will be distinct things said by Galileo.

[9] *Loc. cit.* p. 143.
[10] *Ib.* p. 130 where Wilde allegedly refers to an utterance of Whistler's.

I suggested that we ought to find, rather, for things said, entities which distinct utterances could be of *viz.*, propositions, and that these should be the referents of the demonstrative 'that' and the values of the variables in the representation of 'Galileo said something'. Thus (9) should yield to something like (10):

(10) $(\exists x)$ (Galileo's utterance x is of that proposition).

Within the present framework the most plausible candidates for propositions will be classes of utterances *i.e.*, a certain sort of abstract object. To say that an utterance of Galileo's is *of* a proposition will be to say that it is a member of it.

Some writers, *e.g.*, Dummett, have seen it as typical of at least some abstract objects that they are not possible objects of ostension, hence, presumably, not of demonstrative reference.[11] Nevertheless, whatever the deeper roots of this doctrine, abstract objects can be introduced into discourse, and singular terms for them explained *via* what Quine has called *deferred ostension*.[12] I point to a concrete inscription and say 'That is alpha'. Relative to our standard grammatical apparatus, subsequent utterances of 'alpha' can make it clear that 'alpha' is to be construed as a singular term. It was to just such apparatus, in particular the accessibility of certain positions to first-order quantification, which led us to seek singular terms after verbs of saying. In the case of 'alpha', appeal to our apparatus of individuation, in particular to our notion of identity, can make it clear that 'alpha' (and hence the demonstrative used in its introduction) is not to be construed as referring to the concrete inscription in the presence of which the demonstrative utterance was produced. Different utterances of 'That is alpha', in the presence of different concrete inscriptions, are to be taken as involving reference to the same thing *viz.*, alpha—a letter which different inscriptions can be of. Likewise, it was such an appeal to our apparatus of individuation, embodied in such devices as the expression 'another' and in counting, which showed that the demonstrative

[11] Dummett *op. cit.* Chapter 14, esp. p. 481.
[12] W.V.O. Quine *Ontological Relativity and Other Essays* (New York and London 1969) pp. 40ff.

reference located by Davidson in utterances of 'Galileo said that the earth moves' could not be to the particular utterances of 'the earth moves' therein produced, but to a single thing, a proposition, which these distinct utterances could be utterances of.

As Quine notes, it is plausible to regard a letter as the class of its inscriptions, *i.e.*, a set of inscriptions '. . . variously situated in space-time but . . . classed together by virtue of a certain similarity of shape.'[13] Aiming to pick out such a class, then, we perform an act of demonstration in the presence of one of its members. While the presence of the inscription aids in determining the referent of the demonstrative, it itself is not the referent.

Analogously, then, could we not see such deferred ostension occurring in attributions of saying, regarding the thing said, thereby picked out, as the class of its utterances? Not quite analogously. We said, following Quine, that a letter was a class of inscriptions like in shape, meaning like in shape to each other. This requires that *like in shape* be an equivalence relation. But there is no reason to think that the corresponding relation *reports*, which we might use to construct propositions along similar lines is an equivalence relation.[14] Indeed there is good reason to think that it is not. In the first place, we can often correctly report another's utterance by means of an utterance of a sentence which is logically weaker than that which he uttered, but not conversely. Thus I could report the Galileo utterance in question by means of an utterance of 'A planet moves', *i.e.*, I could say that Galileo said that a planet moves. But his stronger utterance might well not be usable to report mine. Thus the relation *reports* is not symmetrical.[15] Secondly, if *reports* were an equivalence relation, then propositions would be equivalence classes of utterances, hence disjoint classes. Thus each utterance, if it was of any

[13] The quotation is actually a proffered account of expressions in general, one rejected by Quine basically on the ground that some distinct expressions, lacking instances, would be identically the empty class. But he does accept the account for *letters*.

[14] A point made by Mr. John McDowell in a talk he gave at Birkbeck College.

[15] An example suggested by Mark Platts. I am indebted to him, and to Roger Scruton, for discussion of these matters.

proposition at all, would be of exactly *one* proposition. Each saying would be a saying of exactly one thing. And this seems just wrong.

Propositions, then, cannot be classes of utterances which report each other. Rather, I think, we must say that a proposition is a class of utterances sufficiently alike for there to be at least one utterance which reports all and only the members of the class. Such an utterance binds the utterances it reports into a unity, so I shall call it a *binder* of the proposition. Now it seems plausible to maintain that if an utterance reports any utterance then it reports itself, *i.e.*, the relation *reports* is reflexive. Thus the binders of propositions will be members of the propositions they bind.

My claim, then, is that the demonstrative 'that' in attributions of sayings is characteristically uttered in the presence of an ensuing utterance, but that its referent is not that utterance but the set of utterances bound by that utterance, a set of which that utterance will be a member. Note therefore that each attribution of a saying will have the same truth conditions as those given by Davidson. In attributing a saying we shall be stating that the reported utterance is a member of the class of utterances bound by the ensuing utterance. But the reported utterance will be a member of this class if and only if it is reported by (*i.e.*, matches in content) the ensuing utterance, which is just what Davidson said.

But our proposal, unlike Davidson's, avoids the counting problem. Distinct utterances of the demonstrative 'that', in the presence of distinct ensuing utterances, need not usher in distinct things said. At least this will be so if distinct utterances can bind the same proposition. It is easy to state the conditions necessary for distinct utterances so to do. If *a,b,* bind the same proposition *P*, then *a* is a member of a set all and only the members of which are reported by *b*, and *vice versa i.e.*, *a,b,* report each other. And while we agreed that *reports* is not in general symmetrical, there is no reason to think this situation never occurs. If it never occurred, then, for example in our initial dialogue the two utterances of *A* would not report each other. And if this were so then, on the present account as on Davidson's, it would have been incorrect for *B* to have said, after *A*'s first utterance, 'You are just about to say that again', and to have said, after *A*'s second utterance 'You said that a moment ago'. And both these remarks seem perfectly in order.

Whether the fact that *a,b,* report each other is a *sufficient* condition for them to bind the same proposition, hence to be usable to introduce by deferred ostension the same proposition, is not to me clear. It would require that whenever *a* reports *b*, and *vice versa*, that *a,b,* report, in general, exactly the same utterances. I have no proof that this must be so, hence no general account of what is sufficient for deferred ostension in the presence of distinct utterances *not* to be used to ascribe distinct things said to the speaker whose speech we are reporting. But surely, again, it would be implausible to think that distinct utterances which report each other can *never* report exactly the same utterances. Again, returning to our original dialogue, if the mutually reporting utterances of *A* did not in general report exactly the same utterances, then it must be possible to find something of the form '*X* said that' which *B* could truly utter after *A*'s first utterance and falsely utter after *A*'s second utterance. And I can find no plausible example of this.

V

I end with what might seem an obvious objection. On the current view, a proposition is a set of utterances such that there is an utterance which reports all and only the members of the set. Given that 'reports' is reflexive such an utterance will be a member of such a set. There are thus no unuttered propositions. More precisely: for any proposition *P* there is an utterance of *P*.

But I do not find this consequence in the least objectionable. Certainly we can say: there are things which might have been said but haven't and won't. Equally we can say: there are things which might have happened but haven't and won't. Perhaps a construal of such sentences will require an ontology of things which might have been said, things which might have happened. But things which might have been said are no more things said (*i.e.*, propositions) than things which might have happened are happenings (*i.e.*, events). Perhaps we do need an account of things which might have been said, or things which might have happened *i.e.*, of possible propositions and possible events, perhaps even of possible *F*'s in general. But if we need such a theory, then this need must surely be met by a general doctrine of possible objects, not piecemeal. It is no criticism of a theory of what *F*'s are that it does not, by itself, constitute a theory of what possible *F*'s are.

This objection, though, may be pursued in a more interesting way by pointing to the fact that things said can be identical with things believed. And that some things believed may never be said. But the present theory leaves no room for such believed but unuttered propositions.

This thought certainly points to a real gap in the theory, but one which I think, in principle, could be filled. The present account of reports of speech requires an ontology of particular events—utterances —which can stand in certain relations to other such particulars, and be members of the propositions of which they are utterances. Its extension to, say, belief, would require an ontology of particular believings (which might be states rather than events) which could stand in analagous relations to each other, to utterances, and be members of the propositions they were beliefs in. I shall not here embark on an attempt to show that such an ontology is required, and for purposes other than preservation of the theory under consideration.

II

Truth, Correspondence, Explanation and Knowledge*

I

'When a statement is true, there is, *of course*, a state of affairs which makes it true. . . .' (Austin).[1] 'When I speak of a fact . . . I mean the kind of thing that makes a proposition true or false' (Russell).[2] '. . . a statement is true only if there is something in the world *in virtue of which* it is true' (Dummett).[3]

Austin and Russell, in the works from which the above quotations are taken, write as defenders of (different versions of) something called 'the correspondence theory of truth'. And Dummett remarks that his dictum captures an important feature of the concept of truth which was expressed by the correspondence theory, and which we retain despite our (justified?) abandonment of that theory.

What *is* the connection between these three very similar remarks and the correspondence theory of truth? In this section I follow what I ultimately take to be a quite mistaken path—one which has been, if only implicitly, much-travelled. I hope, nevertheless, that there is still something to be learnt *en route*.

To what enterprise are correspondence theories of truth meant to be a contribution? I suppose the answer which springs to mind is: to the enterprise of *defining* truth (or 'true', or 'is true') or of *explaining*, *analysing* or *explicating* (the concept or notion of) truth. This answer serves, at best, merely to locate, in the vaguest way possible, a perhaps empty class of putative

*This paper was written *circa* 1977 for the Birkbeck College Philosophy Society Magazine *Phi*. It is here published for the first time.

[1] J.L. Austin, *Philosophical Papers* (Oxford: The Clarendon Press, 1961), p. 123, and in George Pitcher (ed.), *Truth* (Englewood Cliffs, N.J.: Prentice-Hall, 1964), p. 23.

[2] Bertrand Russell, *Logic and Knowledge: Essays 1901–1950* edited by R.C. Marsh (London: George Allen and Unwin, 1956), p. 182.

[3] Pitcher *op.cit.* p. 106, and P.F. Strawson (ed.) *Philosophical Logic* (Oxford: O.U.P., 1967) p. 63.

philosophical projects. For we have, I think, no clear view of what the task, peculiarly philosophical, of defining, explaining, analysing or explicating words, notions or concepts, actually *is*: no single unchallenged account of the constraints to which either here, in the case of truth, or in general, a project thus delineated, should be subject. One very minimal requirement might be (in the present case) that we find, for any sentence containing the word 'true', another sentence not containing 'true' which is in some sense equivalent to the original one. This is presumably not a sufficient condition of success. It would be met (under certain not implausible assumptions) by an account which explained '. . . is true' as: 'the negation of . . . is false', to which a variety of completely vague retorts might be offered e.g. that the notions of negation and falsehood *presupposed* or had to be *elucidated in terms of* the concept of truth; or that they were less clear than that of truth, or equally in need of explication. Presumably, then, a definition (*etc.*) of truth, in this peculiarly philosophical sense, must use notions which don't presuppose (*etc.*) that of truth, or which are clearer than, or less in need of explication the concept of truth. We might demand too that the definition be 'non-trivial' or 'illuminating'.[4] Unless these appealing remarks can be spelt out, I don't think we should have any confidence that in talking of 'defining truth' we are succeeding in picking out exactly one project. Indeed, on one classical account of the constraints on philosophical analysis, we have good reason to think that we are not picking out even *one* project: for, on that account, the constraints are jointly unsatisfiable.[5] In speaking, then, of correspondence theories as aiming to define or analyse truth, I am merely telling you which unhappily characterised project(s) I am, for the moment, concerned with.

Our question was: what do our opening dicta have to do with the correspondence theory of truth? This can now be put: what do they have to do with the project of defining, correspondence style, the notion of truth?

[4] *Cf.* Donald Davidson, 'True to the Facts', *Journal of Philosophy* 66 (1969), p. 758. Reprinted in Donald Davidson, *Inquiries into Truth and Interpretation* (Oxford: Clarendon Press, 1984).

[5] I allude to the once-notorious 'Paradox of Analysis'; see, e.g., Arthur Pap, *Semantics and Necessary Truth* (New Haven: Yale University Press, 1958), pp. 275ff.

Concentrating on Dummett's way of putting it, we might follow out the ensuing (as we shall see, quite misleading) train of thought. Let us write out his remark in the following quasi-canonical notation:

(1) S is true $\supset (\exists x)(S$ is-true-in-virtue-of $x)$.

'S' here is supposed to range over what we might call 'truth-bearers'—things which are true. 'x' is to range over what I shall label 'truth-makers'—things which make truth-bearers true. The hyphenated phrase appears to introduce a relation which can hold between a truth-bearer and a truth-maker (indeed the converse of the relation of *making-true* apparently introduced by Austin's and Russell's remarks). The dictum seems to say, then, that a necessary condition of a truth-bearer's being true is that it stand in the relevant relation to at least one truth-maker. Given the way we have (following Dummett) expressed the apparent relation, this condition would seem also to be sufficient for a truth-bearer's being true: for if there is something in virtue of which S is true then, surely, S is true. We can, therefore, strengthen (1) to a biconditional *viz.*:

(2) S is true $\equiv (\exists x)(S$ is-true-in-virtue-of $x)$.

This, as it stands, hardly meets even our minimal condition on a definition of truth. The expression 'true' occurs, apparently all too significantly, on the right-hand side. But we might derive from (2) (and hence from the initial dicta which it mirrors) something like a general *schema* for correspondence-style definitions of truth, *viz.*:

(3) S is true $\equiv (\exists x)(SRx)$.

We would locate the correspondence element in the fact that we are invited to find, in an explication of the notion of truth, a two-place relation which can hold between truth-bearers and truth-makers. Presumably the traditional tasks of correspondence theories are to elucidate, in ways meeting whatever constraints are thought appropriate to the definitional project:

(a) the range of 'S'. (Sentences, statements, propositions. . . .)
(b) the range of 'x'. (Facts, states of affairs, concatenations of objects. . . . And what *are* these entities?)

(c) the relation *R*. (Corresponds with, pictures, . . . And can this relation be elucidated subject to the constraints?)

It might be held, then, that Dummett's dictum (and Austin's too) captured not merely a residual element of the correspondence theory of truth, but the very *form* of such a theory.

It is worth noting, in passing, that the account Austin gives of truth does not, apparently, conform to the pattern which his own remark suggests, *viz.* the pattern of (3). For Austin doesn't say that a statement is true if and only if *there is* an historic state of affairs (his preferred locution for truth-makers) related in a certain way to the statement. Rather, his definition runs along the lines: a statement is true if and only if *the* state of affairs with which it is correlated (in one sort of way) stands in a certain (complex) relation to the words used in making it (and hence, indirectly, in a certain relation to *it*).[6] And it was just this departure from the *form* of definition adumbrated in (3) which laid his theory open to (what I take to be) a decisive objection by Strawson, put forward in his final paper in that prolonged controversy.[7] For Austin's account seems committed to finding, for any statement, true *or* false, *the* state of affairs with which it is correlated (in the first way), concerning which there arises the further question as to whether it stands in a second, complex, relation to the statement. And Strawson, in the work cited, claims to find insuperable difficulties in this commitment. I think that Strawson is right about this, but that is not the subject of the present paper.[8] The point here is rather that the failure, on this count, of Austin's version of the correspondence theory of truth cannot show anything about the impossibility of a definition of truth meeting the structural requirements of schema (3); for *this* failure arises precisely from Austin's departure from those requirements.

A more recent defender of a correspondence theory of truth is Donald Davidson.[9] Relating his claims to our discussion so

[6] For details see Austin *op.cit.* pp. 121–2 or Pitcher *op.cit.* p. 22.

[7] P.F. Strawson, 'Truth: A Reconsideration of Austin's Views' in his *Logico-Linguistic Papers* (London: Methuen, 1971). See esp. pp. 241ff.

[8] For an attempted, but to my mind unsuccessful, rebuttal of Strawson see Honderich, 'Truth: Austin, Strawson, Warnock' in Rescher (ed.), *Studies in Logical Theory* (Oxford: Blackwell, 1968).

[9] Davidson *op.cit.*

far, we might say: he finds comfort for the correspondence theory by locating, within Tarski's account of truth for first-order languages, a 'natural interpretation' (Davidson's phrase) of our schema (3). Familiarly enough, Tarski utilizes, in his definitions of truth for such languages, a two-place relation—*satisfaction*—holding between sentences (open or closed) of the languages in question, and certain non-linguistic entities, *viz.*, (denumerable) sequences of objects.[10] The connection between satisfaction and truth is this: that a closed sentence *S* of some such language *L* is *true* if and only if every denumerable sequence *s* of objects is such that *S* (as a sentence of *L*) is satisfied by *s*. This doesn't quite match the form of our (3). But we can easily make it do so by replacing the initial universal quantifier ('*every* denumerable sequence') by an existential one ('*some* denumerable sequence'). The result is equivalent to the original; for, since closed sentences are satisfied either by every or by no sequence, if satisfied by at least one they are satisfied by all, and *vice versa* (on the necessary assumption that there exists at least one denumerable sequence of objects). We have thus, it seems, located in a formula of the required structure, truth-bearers (closed sentences), truth-makers (sequences of objects), and a relation (satisfaction) between the latter and the former.

But what has this to do with the alleged definitional project at which correspondence theories were supposedly aiming? And what has it to do with the initial dicta from which we derived the definitional schema (3)? In both cases, not much, I think. Concerning the first issue I shall make the following, on the whole boringly familiar, points.

(1) These remarks are *ad hominem* against Davidson: Davidson, in the paper currently under consideration, clearly wishes to locate, in Tarski's work, a correspondence-style contribution to the vague project we have so far been discussing. He talks of 'explaining truth', 'explaining the property of being true' and of 'explaining what it is to make a true statement'. The claim that Tarski's work can, for Davidson, be thus seen is quite

[10] For more details see, e.g., Davidson *op.cit.* or Quine, *Philosophy of Logic* (Englewood Cliffs: Prentice-Hall, 1970), Ch. 3. Tarski's original paper, 'The Concept of Truth in Formalized Languages', is in his *Logic, Semantics, Metamathematics* (Oxford: Clarendon Press, 1956).

inconsistent with other (better) writings of his.

(a) Davidson, familiarly, wishes to find in a *theory* of truth for a given language, one which uses Tarskian devices (and from which a Tarski-style *definition* of truth can easily be constructed) the form of a theory of meaning for that language. As he says elsewhere:

> Our outlook inverts Tarski's: we want to achieve an understanding of meaning or translation by assuming a prior grasp of truth.[11]

But, as we saw, he seems to want, in 'True to the Facts' to use Tarski's work to elucidate the concept of truth. And one surely cannot have it both ways.[12]

(b) Our last quotation from Davidson suggests that Tarski's aim was something like a philosophical elucidation of the concept of truth. I think it is fairly clear that this was not at all how Tarski saw his project.[13] More importantly, given my scepticism about the nature of the alleged task of elucidating the concept of truth, I find it fairly uninteresting to make or deny claims concerning Tarski's work as a contribution to *that*. And Davidson, elsewhere, would seem to share this attitude. In 'Truth and Meaning'[14] he alludes to the 'question whether the concept Tarski has shown how to define is the (or a) philosophically interesting conception of truth or the question whether Tarski has cast any light on the ordinary use of such words as 'true' or 'truth': and he goes on to deprecate discussion of these issues as 'confused and confusing battles'. I can only applaud, and point out how ill this accords with the confident claims, on precisely these issues, of 'True to the Facts'.

(2) If we *are* to enter into these confused and confusing battles,

[11] 'Belief and the Basis of Meaning', *Synthese* 27 (1974), at p. 138. Reprinted in Davidson *op.cit.*, 1984.

[12] For this thought see Strawson, 'Meaning and Truth' in his *op.cit.* at page 180.

[13] For the start of an account of what Tarski was really up to see Hartry Field, 'Tarski's Theory of Truth', *Journal of Philosophy* 69 (1972). I owe a considerable debt to the perspective on semantic theory afforded by this and other papers of Field. Unfortunately there will not be space to itemize debts and (some) disagreements.

[14] In J.W. Davis *et al.* (eds.), *Philosophical Logic* (Dordrecht: Reidel, 1969), p. 7 reprinted in Davidson, *op.cit.*, 1984.

then I am prepared to make one, hypothetical, claim: that if there *is* a coherent project of providing a philosophically illuminating definition or analysis of the concept of truth, then Tarski's work does not provide it. Two points might be made here.

(a) The first, familiar, thought is to note that Tarski provides a method of constructing, for any given language *L* which has a certain structure, a 'definition' of *true sentence of L*; but provides no means (and could provide none) of extending this to give a quite general definition of *true sentence.* (I leave this vague and crude: the point needs much more careful handling than I can here give it.)[15] But the traditional correspondence theory was an attempt to give such a general definition. So the fact, if it were one,[16] that for each language *L* a definition of *true sentence of L* threw up a formula having the structure of (3), would provide no comfort for that traditional theory. Providing such comfort would, rather, require that we locate such a formula in the (very different) project of giving a general definition of truth. And there is no reason to think that we will be able to do that.[17]

(b) Suppose, though, that we did not demand such generality in a philosophical elucidation of truth, but were content with different definitions of 'true sentence of *L*' for each different *L*. Even if we *were* content with philosophical elucidation of this series of notions, it is perfectly evident that the technical sense of 'define' in which Tarski is able to define, for a variety of particular *L*, 'true sentence of *L*', has little to do with that sense, if there is one, in which philosophers seek to 'define' words, analyse concepts *etc.* What Tarski's methods enable us to do, for each language of the kind in question, is to find an open

[15] One major difficulty is to state, exactly, what the generality allegedly lacking in Tarski's account consists in, or is with respect to. For more careful handling, and diverging views on *this* issue, see Strawson, 'Meaning and Truth', in his *op.cit.* and Peacocke, 'Truth Definitions and Actual Languages', (esp. Section 1) in Evans and McDowell (eds.), *Truth and Meaning: Essays in Semantics* (Oxford: Clarendon Press, 1976).

[16] Which it isn't. The issues here are technical: for an exhaustive account see Kripke, 'Is There A Problem About Substitutional Quantification?', in Evans and McDowell *op.cit.*, and references therein.

[17] *Cf.* Strawson *op.cit.* and Peacocke *op.cit.*

sentence of enormous complexity,[18] containing no semantic terms, which has the same *extension* as the open sentence '*S* is a true sentence of *L*'.[19] But most philosophers who believe in the existence of an activity of analysing or elucidating concepts or notions would, as we noted above, regard such extensional equivalence as quite insufficient to ground a claim to have elucidated the concept in question. It would normally be demanded that our grasp of the concept to be elucidated could be seen as, at least implicitly, constituted by a grasp of the concept expressed by the analysis (whatever all that means!). But in the present case it is simply absurd to think that our grasp of the concept *true sentence of English* (if we have such) even implicitly consists in our grasp of the concept expressed by the enormously complex open sentence which a Tarski-style 'definition' of 'true sentence of English' (if we had one) would provide.

Our second question was: what has the occurrence, in Tarski's account of truth, of a version of schema (3) to do with the initial platitudes from which we derived, apparently, that schema? The lack of connection can be brought out by noting, as Davidson himself does,[20] two differences between the truth-makers here invoked—*viz.* sequences of objects—and such traditional candidates as facts.

(a) Given the all or nothing nature of satisfaction for closed sentences, every true sentence, on the present account, relates in the relevant way to (*viz.* by being satisfied by) exactly the same truth-makers (*viz.* every sequence of objects). Whereas, of course, the initial dicta suggest that what makes a sentence true will, in general, vary from sentence to sentence.

(b) As Davidson notes, sequences of objects don't seem much like facts. We could present Tarski's theory in such a way as to make the finite sequence <Dolores, Dagmar> the (particular) satisfier of, say, 'Dolores loves Dagmar'. But this ordered pair, as Davidson remarks, is very unlike traditional accounts of

[18] For a hint as to its complexity see Quine *op.cit.* p. 43.

[19] The extension of the latter being taken as fixed by the totality of T-sentences for the language L: i.e., sentences of the kind: S is a true sentence of L iff p (where 'S' is replaced by a name of a sentence and 'p' by (a translation of) that sentence).

[20] Davidson *op.cit.* pp. 758ff.

what would make such a sentence true: a traditional truth-maker would 'somehow include the loving'. Putting it in terms of our initial dicta, what would make 'Dolores loves Dagmar' true, or that in virtue of which it would be true, would be not simply Dolores and Dagmar, but the fact that Dolores loves Dagmar.

These remarks certainly point to *differences* between the theory under consideration and traditional correspondence theories. But we are in no position to assess the significance of these differences until we have a better grasp of the force of our opening platitudes. It should, though, by now be clear that whatever their force *is*, it is not one which can be captured merely by producing a definition of truth fulfilling the requirements of schema (3). For if the Tarski-Davidson line had been successful in meeting the other demands on the definitional enterprise, it *would have* embodied a version of schema (3) while failing, as the last two paragraphs make clear, to connect with the ideas that seemed to lead to that schema. Putting it another way: if, as Davidson remarks, 'correspondence theories rest on what appears to be an ineluctable if simple idea'[21] and if, as Austin, Russell, Dummett and myself appear to think, that simple idea is expressed in our opening dicta, then it is an idea not caught by our structural demand on definitions of truth. Indeed, as I shall shortly argue, I don't think that simple idea ought to be connected with *definitions* of truth (in our vague sense) at all.

II

What makes a sentence (or utterance or statement) true? Davidson, in another paper,[22] deplores this question, claiming that it is a confused reformulation of the vague—'What is it for a sentence (or utterance *etc.*) to be true?'. This latter question is, I take it, an invitation to embark on the definitional project which we have so far considered. Davidson, as we have seen, is in some moods sympathetic to *that*. Why then does he think that the former way of pressing the definitional demand is

[21] *Ibid.* p. 748.

[22] 'In Defence of Convention T', in H. Leblanc (ed.), *Truth, Syntax and Modality* (Amsterdam: North-Holland Publishing Co., 1973). Reprinted in Davidson *op.cit.*, 1984.

confused? Because, he claims, it prompts one to think that truth is to be defined in terms of a relation between a sentence as a whole and some entity, perhaps a state of affairs or a fact—leads one to embark, that is, on the project we apparently elicited from our opening dicta. But why should the request for a definition of truth, phrased as the question 'What makes a sentence true?' prompt, in particular, a response in the style: 'its correspondence with a fact'? If we adhere purely to the definition-seeking interpretation of the allegedly misleading question, it surely cannot, of itself, suggest an *answer* of that form in preference to one of any other kind that might be offered—'its coherence with other sentences', 'its satisfaction by every sequence' or whatever.

The question can only confuse us (and has confused both proponents and opponents of traditional correspondence theories) if we run together the above, definition-seeking, interpretation of the question with another, quite different, one. Let me introduce this second interpretation of the allegedly confused question by noting that our initial dicta can be derived from an answer to the question 'What makes a sentence true?': not from the answer—'its correspondence with a fact', but from the answer—'a fact'. However, if 'a fact' can be an appropriate answer to the question 'What makes a sentence true?', then this question cannot, *here*, be seen as a version, even a confused one, of 'What is it for a sentence to be true?' For the sequence of question and answer which runs 'What is it for a sentence to be true?'—'A fact', is simply gibberish. If 'a fact' can be the appropriate answer, then question and answer here must rather be seen as generalisations of questions and answers of the following form:

(4) 'What makes the (English) sentence "Snow is white" true?'
'The fact that snow is white.'
(5) 'What makes the (English) sentence "Grass is green" true?'
'The fact that grass is green.'

And these questions, and their generalisation into 'What makes a (any) sentence true?' are not requests for *definitions* (etc.) of 'true' (the concept of truth etc.); but rather requests for (partial) *explanations* of *why* certain particular sentences are true. And only confusion between these two very different projects could suggest that dicta, such as our opening ones, derived by generalising a series of explanation-seeking questions and answers should be somehow convertible into a definition (the project we considered in Section I).

Talk of facts enters into the answers to the explanation-seeking questions (4) and (5), not because what we are particularly explaining is why certain sentences are *true*, but simply because such talk enters naturally into answers to *any* explanation-seeking questions put in the idiom 'What makes. . . .?' or 'In virtue of what is. . . ?'. Thus if one were asked—'What makes salt soluble in water?', the most natural answer would be something of the style, '*The fact that* it has such-and-such structure'.

If this kind of talk does require an ontology of facts or states of affairs, and if, hence, our opening remarks should be seen as quantifying over such entities, then this will not be because facts are required for a definition of truth; but because they are required to make sense of our talk about explanation (somewhat as Davidson has argued that we require an ontology of events to provide a coherent construal of our everyday talk of causation and action).[23] Here is not the place to adjudicate on whether our explanatory discourse does indeed have to be seen as invoking such an ontology—even if I knew the truth on this (which I don't). I shall make a few remarks, though.

Encouragement for the foes of facts might be found by noting that many apparent singular terms for facts can be readily paraphrased away. Thus 'The fact that salt has such-and-such structure makes it soluble in water', with its apparent singular reference to a fact, can be seen as a mere periphrasis for 'Salt is soluble in water because it has such-and-such structure', which contains no such singular reference. But this thought gives no long-term comfort unless we are convinced that a serious theory of the 'logical form' of sentences of the

[23] See, e.g., 'Causal Relations', *Journal of Philosophy* 64 (1967), 'The Logical Form of Action Sentences', in Rescher, N. (ed.), *The Logic of Decision and Action* (Pittsburgh: University of Pittsburgh Press, 1967) and 'The Individuation of Events' in Rescher *et al.* (eds.), *Essays in Honor of Carl Hempel* (Dordrecht: Reidel, 1969). All reprinted in Donald Davidson, *Essays on Actions and Events* (Oxford: Clarendon Press, 1980).

latter type will not reintroduce the ontology of facts.[24] Further, there are things we might want to say about explanation where the apparent reference to facts is not so readily eliminated: an example might be the claim that Einstein's theory explains all the facts which Newton's theory explained.

If we are eventually forced to take facts seriously as part of our ontology, then we shall equally have been forced to find in our *ideology* (Quine's term) properties of, and relations involving, facts. If I'm right in claiming that talk of facts enters most importantly in our talk of explanation, then one central relation involving facts will be a two-place relation between facts *viz.* that of explaining. We might put this canonically: fact A explains fact B. We should then be committed to locating in (4) and (5) above a genuine relation between a fact and something else. But this relation would not hold between (*e.g.*) the fact that snow is white and the English sentence 'Snow is white': rather between the former and *the fact that* this sentence is true, the relation being that the former (partially) explains the latter. Again, this relation would have nothing particularly to do with truth: the same relation would hold between the fact that salt has such-and-such structure and the fact that salt is soluble in water. Nor would it be sensible to try to *define* truth in terms of this relation: no more sensible than the analogous attempt in the case of solubility.

An austere philosophical view of explanation, one apparently requiring no ontology of facts, is the famous deductive-nomological account.[25] At its simplest, the theory runs: to explain why *p* is to deduce that *p* from premisses meeting certain conditions—most importantly that they be true and that at least one be a 'law'. A Tarski-style theory of truth for a particular language can be seen as a party to the enterprise of explaining, within the constraints on explanation imposed by

[24] *Cf.* a similar dispute about events. Geach ('Some Problems about Time' in his *Logic Matters* (Oxford: Blackwell, 1972) argues that apparent singular reference to events can always be paraphrased away. But Davidson would locate, in the resulting sentences, (implicit) quantification over events (see refs. at n. 23).

[25] For an exhaustive exposition, by its most distinguished adherent see Hempel, 'Aspects of Scientific Explanation', in his book of that title. For the beginning of a discussion as to whether this account does require an ontology of facts see Israel Scheffler, *The Anatomy of Enquiry* (New York: Alfred Knopf, 1963), 'The Problem of Ontological Interpretation'.

the deductive-nomological account, why the true sentences (or utterances) of that language *are* true. Such a theory will consist of a series of 'laws' governing the expressions of that language: laws stating, for example, the conditions under which certain predicates are satisfied by (sequences of) objects, and how the satisfaction conditions of certain complex expressions are determined by the satisfaction conditions of their parts. Of course no scientist would be inclined to apply the term 'law' to such axioms of truth theory. But this is merely a special case of the (trivial) fact that the notion of 'law' employed in the deductive-nomological account of explanation is a term of art, not essentially connected with the much narrower notion of 'law' employed by scientists.[26] In the deductive-nomological theorists' usage, 'law' means, very roughly, 'non-accidental general statement'. The axioms of truth-theories are essentially general (generalising over, among other things, such entities as sequences of objects and sentences) and by most of the standard tests 'law-like' as opposed to 'accidental' generalisations. They will, for example 'support counterfactuals'. Thus, for example, the satisfaction axiom for the English predicate 'is red' would not merely license the thought that every object which, as it happens, is red satisfies that predicate, but the counterfactual thought concerning any object that if it had been red, it would have satisfied that predicate.

The axioms of a truth-theory for a given language are, famously, designed to have as logical consequences, for any sentence *S* of the language in question a T-sentence: *i.e.* a sentence of the kind exemplified, for the English sentence 'Snow is white' by

> 'Snow is white' is a true sentence of English if and only if snow is white.

(I ignore, for the moment, complexities introduced by the existence, in natural languages, of sentences whose truth varies with speaker, time of utterance *etc.*)

On the deductive-nomological account of explanation, then,

[26] For this thought, mistakenly employed as an argument against the deductive-nomological account, see Peter Achinstein, *Law and Explanation* (London: Oxford University Press, 1971).

the axioms of such a truth-theory will explain why (*i.e.* explain the fact that) 'Snow is white' is a true sentence of English if and only if snow is white. To explain further why 'Snow is white' is a true sentence of English we need only add one further premiss to the deduction (invoke one further fact) *viz.* the premiss (fact) that snow is white. The complete deduction, then, constitutes, in accord with the deductive-nomological account, an explanation of why 'Snow is white' is a true sentence of English. Our naive way of putting it, at (4) above, is justified by the point that the premiss that snow is white is an essential constituent of an explanation of the truth of 'Snow is white'. (Putting it in terms of facts, we need to invoke, in explaining the truth of this sentence, not merely certain facts about English (stated in the axioms of the truth-theory) but also the fact that snow is white.)

Our initial dicta, then, should have been seen as expressing the thought that for every sentence which is true there must be some explanation of why it is true. And a Tarski-style theory of truth, for a particular language, seems to yield the essential materials for the construction of such explanations. Tarski himself, notoriously, thought that his theory captured something of the traditional correspondence theory: but not (*cf.* Davidson) because it defined truth in terms of the relation of satisfaction. He thought it was rather because of the presence, as logical consequences of his 'definitions', of a T-sentence for every sentence of the language in question. Certainly if the essence of the correspondence theory of truth is the project, considered in Section I, of defining truth in terms of some relation, then Tarski was quite wrong to think that: for nothing of that sort emerges from reflection on T-sentences. But if the roots of the correspondence theory lie in the dicta from which we started, then Tarski was basically right about this.

III

I have tried to detach our opening platitudes from the project of *defining* truth and to relocate them as comments on the enterprise of *explaining*, concerning particular sentences or utterances of sentences, why they are true, *viz.* as expressive of the thought that for any true sentence or utterance, there must be an explanation of why it is true. But this latter thought may seem to lack two kinds of interest which our initial dicta (and hence the 'correspondence theory' insofar as that arose from these) possessed.

1. I have so far located the fulfilment of the explanatory enterprise demanded by our platitudes, on the current interpretation, within a formal theory of truth of the kind which Tarski showed us how to construct. Hence, for all that has been said so far, the project of explaining why sentences are true is one carried out within, and of concern only to, the technical discipline of formal semantics. Our dicta would then seem to be, as it were, (rash?) predictions concerning the future success of that discipline. But, as Dummett notes, the thought expressed by his remark seems to embody something important about our concept of truth, and hence ought to connect with our *everyday interest* in that concept, and not merely with a certain highly technical enterprise. If our interpretation of these initial remarks is to preserve for them that role, then we must find a connection between the task of explaining, concerning certain sentences and utterances why they are true, and our everyday interest in the concept of truth. This I attempt to do in Section IV.

2. Our initial platitudes were to the effect that if a sentence is true there must be something which makes it true. We might be concerned, as philosophers, to employ this dictum contraposed; to argue, that is, that just because, for certain sentences, there could be nothing of the sort relevant to make them true, they were not really, despite appearances, capable of truth. As Putnam remarks:

> One interest of the correspondence theory might be to provide a construal of the thought that certain 'assertions' (or sentences having the form of assertions) are neither true nor false. (A correspondence theorist would presumably say that neither they nor their negations bear the appropriate relation C to suitable extra-linguistic facts.)[27]

(As a matter of irrelevant autobiographical fact, my own initial interest in the correspondence theory was precisely that.)

[27] Putnam, 'Do True Assertions Correspond with Reality?', in his *Philosophical Papers, Volume II* (Cambridge: C.U.P., 1975), p. 71.

Have we, on the current account, left any room for a construal of such a thought? I shall attempt to find room for this in Section V.

IV

To make the connection suggested at 1. above, I shall press into service a remark of Hartry Field and, somewhat opportunistically, an account of knowledge developed by Gilbert Harman.[28] (These will also be of use in answering the question raised at 2. above.)

Field remarks:[29]

> The notion of truth serves a great many purposes but I suspect that its original purpose . . . was to aid us in utilizing the utterances of others in drawing conclusions about the world.

Let us consider a simple example of thus utilizing an utterance of another. In a conversation with Fred I hear him utter certain sounds—sounds plausibly taken as a token of the English sentence 'She's just had two'. As a result, I come to know that Mary, my next-door neighbour, has recently given birth to twins. How do I, as a result of hearing these sounds, come to know *that*? Better put: can we give an account of the nature of my resultant belief that Mary has had twins which will make sense of our willingness to say, in some circumstances of the general kind just sketched, that this belief constitutes knowledge (and make sense of our unwillingness to say this in other cases)?

Field talks of 'drawing conclusions' from the utterances of others. And Harman, in such a case, would claim that I had 'made inferences' from Fred's utterance. A familiar retort to such ways of speaking is that these would have to be inferences

[28] Gilbert Harman, *Thought* (Princeton, N.J.: Princeton University Press, 1973). I say 'somewhat opportunistically' for two reasons: i) I'm not sure I really believe the views on knowledge which Harman puts forward. I certainly could not defend them adequately. ii) I utilize the simplified theory which Harman develops up to Ch. 8 of the book. He himself, in Ch. 10, cogently criticises it, and develops a rather more sophisticated version to accommodate these objections. But I can make my points more perspicuously within the framework of the unmodified version, while feeling fairly sure that they could be developed also within the final version of Harman's theory.

[29] Field *op.cit.* pp. 370–371.

of which I was quite unconscious: I could give no report of any such process of inference, nor of the intermediate beliefs I might allegedly pass through during this process. I simply heard Fred tell me that Mary has had twins.

Harman thinks this familiar line of thought not to be a conclusive objection to the view that, nevertheless, inference is going on. He remarks[30] that such a retort requires the '. . . assumption that we have an independent way to tell when inference has occurred and when it has not'. (Independent, I take him to mean, from our views about the items of knowledge which are the outcome of the alleged inferences.) And this is an assumption Harman is prepared to reject. Rather, he wants to say '. . . the only way to discover when a human makes inferences is to discover what assumptions about inference are needed to account for his knowledge'.

The most important kind of 'accounting for' knowledge to which Harman alludes, derives from a problem about traditional definitions of knowledge which was raised by Edmund Gettier.[31] As Harman succinctly puts it:

> Gettier demonstrates that the ordinary concept of knowledge cannot be analysed as justified true belief. He describes a pair of situations in which a person believes something. In both situations, what he believes is true: and he is equally justified in believing as he does in the two situations. However, a speaker of English is inclined to say that the person would know something in the one situation but not in the other. Any such pair of situations can be called a *Gettier example*.[32]

(I shall be giving, later, some Gettier examples relevant to the cases of knowledge here in question.)

Harman (in the simple version of the theory to which we are here confining ourselves) wants to account for our intuitions about Gettier examples by appeal to what he calls Principle P:

> P. Reasoning which essentially involves false conclusions, intermediate or final, cannot give knowledge.[33]

[30] Harman *op.cit.* p. 20.

[31] 'Is Justified True Belief Knowledge?', *Analysis* 23 (1963), reprinted in A. Phillips Griffiths, (ed.), *Knowledge and Belief* (Oxford: O.U.P., 1967).

[32] Harman *op.cit.* p. 21.

[33] *Ibid.* p. 47.

But of course we cannot use this principle to rationalize our judgments concerning Gettier examples unless we make assumptions concerning the occurrence in such cases of processes of (unconscious) reasoning or inference. We are to postulate, then, the occurrence of those inferences (and intermediate conclusions) which, combined with the use of Principle P, will account for our views concerning which situations in Gettier examples *are*, and which are *not*, to be seen as giving rise to *knowledge*.

For Harman, in the simple version of the theory, the major kind of inference involved in the acquisition of inferential knowledge is what he calls 'inference to the best explanation'.[34] Inference will typically move (inductively) from a premiss that *p* to a conclusion of the form: *p* because *q* (from which we could move (deductively) to the conclusion that *q*).

Let us now apply this (simplified) model to the case of knowledge acquisition from an utterance of another which we sketched above. I come to that situation with a considerable body of knowledge about the English language, about Fred, and about the immediate context (linguistic and extra-linguistic) of Fred's utterance: 'She's just had two'. I would wish to suggest, within the simplified Harman model, that I might make inferences which proceeded via the following series intermediate conclusions. I start from the premiss, supplied by hearing, that Fred has made an utterance of that sentence. I might infer

(a) He uttered that sentence because he believed that utterance of it to be true. So
(b) He believes that utterance to be true
(c) He believes that utterance to be true, in part, because it *is* true. So—
(d) That utterance is true. But—
(e) That utterance (of that English sentence in that context) is true because Mary has just had twins. So—
(f) Mary has just had twins.

If this account of the acquisition of knowledge from the utterances of others is roughly correct, then a crucial inter-

[34] *Ibid*. Ch. 8.

mediate conclusion in such a process, *viz.* (e), would be of precisely the kind comment on which I located in our initial dicta; *viz.*, a claim concerning the *explanation why* a given sentence or utterance is true. And, on the present account of such knowledge-acquisition, only if there is such an explanation, for a given utterance or sentence (only if there is something which makes it true) will one be able to acquire knowledge from that utterance, or from an utterance of that sentence, of another. And enabling us to do this is, *pace* Field, a primary function of the concept of truth. So we have sketched what was demanded above: a connection between the initial dicta, on our interpretation, and our everyday interest in the concept of truth.

But is there any reason, even given the (bold) assumption of the approximate correctness of Harman's account of knowledge, to locate intermediate conclusions of the above sort in the process of acquiring knowledge from the utterance of another? I think so. For Principle P predicts that if the above intermediate conclusions *did* occur in this process, then the falsity of any one of (a)–(f) would incline us to deny that I *knew* that Mary had just had twins. And I think that this prediction is borne out.

Clearly this is right about conclusion (f). Consider now the case where (b) (and hence also (a)) is false, the others remaining true. Fred doesn't believe his utterance to be true: he was trying to mislead me but accidentally told the truth. I think we should be inclined to say that I did not then know that Mary had had twins. Suppose now that although (b) *etc.* are true, (a) is false. Fred, although he does believe his utterance to be true, didn't make it because of that but because, say, he wanted to make a remark on the subject of conversation (Mary's confinement) which rhymed with my question. (I asked 'How did she do?' If I'd asked 'How has she done?', Fred might have replied 'She only had one.') Again I feel inclined to deny that I would then know that Mary had had twins. Consider now the falsity of (c); everything else remaining true: no part of the explanation of Fred's believing this utterance to be true is that it *is* true. He picked up the remark from that old racist Mrs. Smith who, knowing nothing of Mary's condition, wished to convince him of the (dangerous) fecundity of West Indians. Again it seems to me plausible to say that I do not know that Mary has had twins. Finally, and crucially for our present purposes, suppose that (e) fails and everything else remains true. Fred's utterance is true, not because Mary has had twins (although she has) but because Sheila has had twins (Fred's utterance of 'she' referred to Sheila), or because Mary has just had two whiskies (Fred's utterance of the predicate 'has just had two' is satisfied by an object if and only if that object has recently consumed two drinks of a contextually indicated kind). Again, I think, we should be inclined to say that I did not know that Mary had had twins.

I suggest, then, that if Harman's treatment of Gettier examples is correct, it is not absurd to say that we could locate the above intermediate conclusions in this typical case of acquiring knowledge from the utterances of others. (I realise that, even under the assumption of the correctness of Harman's account, the above example could be accounted for quite differently. I lack the space to discuss alternatives.)

A connection worth noting between the preceding and the (very different) approach to truth-theory and its role in a 'theory of interpretation' advocated by Davidson, is this. In a number of places[35] Davidson has made the claim that it suffices to 'interpret' the utterances of others that one knows certain T-sentences for their utterances and knows that they are entailed by an (adequate) theory of truth for their language; but one does not need to know the theory which does entail these T-sentences. Suppose that, in the above example, one knew that an adequate truth-theory for Fred's language (plus certain premisses about the context of utterance) entailed that his utterance was true if and only if Mary had had twins. Then one would know (if the deductive-nomological account of explanation is right) that the only further premiss required to explain the truth of Fred's utterance (if it is true) is the premiss that Mary has had twins: i.e. one would know, on the present account of explanation, exactly what one needs to know to know that Fred's utterance, if true, is true *because* Mary has had twins. And this latter explanatory claim is just what, on the present account, one needs to know (among other things) in order to acquire knowledge from Fred's utterance.

[35] See, e.g., *Dialectica* (1973) at p. 326, or in Evans and McDowell *op.cit.* at p. 34.

V

What now of the problem raised at 2. in Section III above? Can we give our initial platitudes, under the present interpretation, any teeth? Can we find room for the thought that certain sentences of natural languages are not capable of being true or false, there being nothing which could make them, or their negations, true?

The problem, of course, is that on the present interpretation, for there to be nothing which could make a sentence true or false would require that it not be possible to construct an adequate explanation of why it was true (if it was) or its negation true (if it was false). And for all that has been said so far, it is not obvious how that could not be possible. For if we were able to construct, for the natural language in question, a theory entailing, for *each* sentence of the language a T-sentence (*i.e.* a sentence of the form: *S* is true if and only if *p*)—and the difficulties here seem to be technical rather than ones of principle—we have, on the deductive-nomological account of explanation, the materials from which to construct an explanation of the truth of *S* (if it is true) or the truth of its negation (if *S* is false), *viz.*, in the first case, add to the deduction of the T-sentence the premiss that *p*, and in the second case, the premiss that not-*p* (which, with the standard axioms for negation, will yield that the negation of *S* is true). If the result is not to count as an adequate explanation of the truth (falsity) of *S*, hence not to count as there being something in virtue of which *S* is true (false), it must be because we are placing constraints on what counts as an adequate explanation which are supplementary to the bare requirements of the deductive-nomological account.

One such constraint, of global application to explanations, might be provided by a doctrine of 'physicalism'. This might be phrased as the claim that (ultimately) the only acceptable explanations were those provided by 'physical' laws or theories, or by laws and theories 'reducible' to those of physics (in some sense). Clearly such a doctrine would require a great deal of spelling out (what do 'physical' and 'reducible' come to here?) and considerable argument to render it plausible. Here is not the place for that. The points I wish to make here are these. First, physicalism is often expressed as the doctrine that there are only physical *facts*. Hence the physicalist way of giving teeth to our initial dicta would take the form: a sentence is true only if there is a physical fact which makes it true. But, in accord with the views of this paper, I think physicalism should be expressed (as in the second sentence of this paragraph) as being, in the first instance, a doctrine about explanation. Of course, if talk of explanation has to be seen as invoking an ontology of facts, then physicalism as a claim about explanation will, in turn, license the ontological claim; but I think the argument should proceed in *this* direction. I shall not here treat of physicalism as a constraint on adequate explanation of the truth of sentences, for two reasons. First, its plausibility derives from its plausibility as a general requirement on explanation, and hence is not peculiarly relevant to discussions of truth. Secondly, a discussion of this requirement on semantic theory would have to take into account an already substantial literature.[36]

I shall rather discuss two constraints which derive peculiarly from the nature of, or interest of, the enterprise of explaining why certain sentences are *true*. Discussions of truth, belief *etc.* frequently have resort to the image of a mirror, of language or belief attempting to 'reflect' reality.[37] Clearly, such metaphorical talk is not, ultimately, very illuminating. But it is worth taking one aspect of it seriously. To say that a mirror 'reflects' reality is in part to make a claim about explanation, *viz.*, that part of the explanation of why certain things 'appear' in the mirror will allude to things 'outside' the mirror, things which would be there even if the mirror were not. It would destroy the claim that the mirror was 'reflecting' reality if, in attempting to explain why things appeared in the mirror as they did, we were forced to invoke entities whose only role was to appear in mirrors. The 'theory of reflection' should not require, as it were, objects not required elsewhere in our science of nature. Applying this to the theory of truth (the 'theory of reflection in language') we might say: it would seem illegitimate to invoke, in explaining why certain sentences are true, categories of

[36] See, e.g., Hartry Field *op.cit.*

[37] See, e.g., Bernard Williams, *Problems of the Self* (Cambridge: C.U.P., 1973), p. 203: '. . . the basic requirement that a man's words, and his belief, should reflect things as they are . . .'

objects not otherwise needed in our explanatory projects. For if the only ground for invoking such objects were to explain why certain sentences were true, this would undermine our view that the role of true sentences is to reflect a reality which would be there even if they were not. An apparent case of this would be the invoking, on one fashionable approach to semantic theory, of possible worlds. For it might appear that in invoking such entities to explain, for example, the truth of certain counterfactuals, we are appealing to an ontology which has no other role than that, within semantic theory, of explaining truth. Unfortunately, the possible-world theorist has a reply. For, he might claim, the ontology of possible worlds explicitly introduced by him, within semantic theory, is already, implicitly, employed, outside semantic theory, in our use of sentences whose truth is to be explained by invoking possible worlds: thus that in using, for example, the sentence, 'If the match had been struck, it would have lit' we are (implicitly) making a claim about possible worlds, which can thus not be seen as entities invoked merely within semantic theory. So this line of thought provides no obvious objection to, for example, possible worlds truth-theory (nor, therefore, to the claim that they give an account of what makes counterfactuals true). It does, however, suggest, that the possible-world theorist is committed not merely to the claim that by appeal to possible worlds we can *explain the truth of* certain sentences but to the stronger claim that by such an appeal we give, in some sense, *the (real) meaning of* those sentences.

The second point I'd like to make, which can give our interpretation of the dicta some force, concerns not so much an additional constraint on the explanation of the truth of sentences, but arises rather from the kind of interest I tried to find for that project within our everyday employment of the concept of truth (Section IV above). In giving an account of how we used the utterances of others to acquire knowledge, a key role was played by an intermediate conclusion to the effect that the speaker's believing the utterance to be true was to be (partially) explained by its being true and hence (in turn) by that in virtue of which it was true. We can thus predict that matters will become problematical in cases where this latter thought fails: that is, in cases where the truth of an utterance arguably has no role to play in explaining the making of the utterance. A possible case here might be moral utterances. Suppose, in our earlier example, Fred had rather said: 'She ought to marry Bill'. Let us take it that nothing stands in the way of our explaining why, it is true, if it is, *viz.* because she ought to marry Bill (*i.e.* we can allow the analogue of our intermediate conclusion (e)). What is problematic is rather the analogue of conclusion (c) above, *i.e.* the thought that Fred believes this utterance to be true because it is true (and hence, in turn, because Mary ought to marry Bill). For one might well think that one could give a complete account of why Fred held this sentence to be true which did not allude to its truth but merely to, for example, certain non-moral beliefs of Fred's (and hence, in turn to the non-moral 'facts' explaining his possession of these) plus some attitudes, feelings or whatever of Fred's. But lacking (c), the notion of the *truth* of Fred's utterance plays no role in explaining Fred's utterance. Hence even if the notion of that in virtue of which a moral utterance is true is quite unproblematic, it plays no part in an account of our acquiring knowledge from the moral utterances of others, *i.e.* (*pace* Field) does not play its standard role. And if we were, on the basis of a (non-truth-invoking) explanation of Fred's utterance, to give an account of the knowledge one could acquire from that utterance, it would, at best, be knowledge of certain non-moral truths and of Fred's attitudes, feelings *etc.*.

I hope then that this section has at least given a sketchy account of how, on the present interpretation, our initial platitudes can have some force: either because no adequate explanation of why certain sentences are true could be given, or because such an explanation would lack what I have claimed is its standard importance.

III

Are Moral Requirements Hypothetical Imperatives?*

Editorial Note

The following essay derives from a symposium at the 1978 Joint Session of the Aristotelian Society and the Mind Association. It is a response to a paper read by John McDowell—the other symposiast. McDowell comments that 'There is a neat summary of my paper in Ian McFetridge's first four paragraphs'. For the occasion of this volume, however, he has kindly provided the following account of his essay:

> We should understand 'hypothetical imperatives' (the terminology is not very happy) in terms of considerations which an agent can have fully in view while the question whether they constitute reasons for him to act in a certain way is open, to be settled according to whether or not he has a suitable desire. If such a consideration does rationally influence the agent's will, it does so only conditionally on the presence of the desire.
>
> In 'Morality as a System of Hypothetical Imperatives', Philippa Foot argues that moral considerations are not guaranteed to influence the will of any rational person; the claim that they are is a moralistic fraud. I accept that; my aim is to undermine any suggestion that we are left with no alternative but to regard moral considerations as hypothetical imperatives. There is another possibility, according to which the influence of moral considerations, on the wills that they do influence, is not conditional on the presence of conative or desiderative factors that are extra to having the considerations in view; but not having such a consideration in view—not seeing a situation in the light in which a virtuous person would see it—need not be thought to manifest failure of rationality.
>
> The main philosophical obstacle to accepting such a position is the view that a reason for action must always involve a desire, functioning as extra to any cognitive 'take' on the situation, to supply the motivational energy required for action. Mrs Foot accepts an argument from Thomas Nagel that prudential reasons do not conform to that pattern, and I try to exploit this fact, *ad hominem*, to forestall an objection, at least from an upholder of her position, on those lines.

*I am very grateful to Samuel Guttenplan for help in writing this paper.

> My paper ends with the suggestion that at least some moral considerations yield imperatives that are categorical in a different sense: their dictating of action is not conditional, not only upon the adventitious presence of suitable desires, but also upon the absence of competing reasons that would need to be weighed in the balance with them so as to make sure that they are not outweighed. These considerations (requirements of virtue) do not outweight reasons for acting otherwise, but silence them. I suggest that this conception explains Aristotle's distinction between virtue and continence.

The two essays by McDowell and McFetridge are published, together with other papers from the 1978 Joint Session, in the *Proceedings of the Aristotelian Society, Supplementary Volume*, 52, 1978.

John McDowell suggests that the requirements of morality are categorical, or non-hypothetical, imperatives in two senses. In the first, and central, sense the suggestion is that when a virtuous agent is rationally motivated by what he regards as a moral requirement, the influence on his will of his conception of what, in the circumstances, he takes as imposing the requirement, is not conditional on his possession of any desire. In the second sense, the suggestion is that moral *requirements* (though not *any* moral reasons), if clearly perceived as such, not merely override but silence other considerations. In the presence of such a perception conflicting considerations count for the agent as no reasons at all.

I shall confine myself to discussing some issues raised by McDowell's first suggestion, and shall have to leave untouched many important questions raised, particularly in the final sections, by his striking paper. This first suggestion is opposed to Mrs Foot's view that a man's being rationally swayed by moral considerations is conditional on his possession of suitable desires. She grounds this claim, according to McDowell, on the premiss that an agent can, without irrationality, see no reason to act as morality requires, a premiss with which McDowell agrees. But, McDowell argues, there is a third possibility: that a virtuous agent should act, with reason, on moral considerations simply because his distinctive conceptions of the facts cast, independently of his desires, a favourable light on the actions in question. Since, McDowell argues, it would not be irrational to lack the relevant conceptions, the suggestion occupies a position Mrs Foot's argument might have been thought to rule out.

The distinctive conceptions are thought of as cognitive states, beliefs about how things are. A virtuous agent, then, is not primarily to be characterised as one possessed of certain desires or sentiments, rather as someone with certain distinctive beliefs about the world. Familiarly, such cognitivist accounts of moral psychology have been thought exposed to the objection that a belief is never sufficient, on its own, to constitute a reason for acting: a separate desire is also required. Thus such a view would, absurdly, divorce the notion of a virtuous agent from the idea of someone motivated to act in certain ways. But, McDowell argues, Mrs Foot at least is in no position to urge this general objection, having conceded that prudential reasons are not of this familiar, Humean, type.

For McDowell, if a person acts on a non-hypothetical imperative, in the central sense, an explanation of his action, in terms of his reasons, will proceed merely by ascribing to him a conception of how things are, a belief. Properly understood, this will suffice to reveal the favourable light in which he saw the action. Our ascription to him of a suitable desire is merely consequential on our taking him to have acted for the reason in question. Such a desire, then, can play no rôle in explaining why he saw reason to act as he did. It, no less than the action, is to be made intelligible in the light of the agent's conception of the facts.

I agree with McDowell that there is no good general argument, starting from the nature of belief, or from some independently grounded account of the notion of how things are, against the possibility of such a mode of explaining actions. And clearly Mrs Foot is committed to agreeing with this. To agree, however, that an agent's conception of how things are can serve on its own to explain his seeing reason to act as he did, is not yet to take any view concerning *how* this is possible, or concerning when such explanations are acceptable. Thus to concede, for example, that such explanations are possible in the case of prudential actions may not automatically be to concede the possibility in the case of moral actions. For one's view that it is possible to explain prudential behaviour in this way may rest on a particular model of *how*, there, it is possible: and this model may meet conditions of acceptability which one thought were crucial, but which one saw no reason to think could be met, in general, by explanations of virtuous behaviour which alluded merely to the virtuous agent's conceptions of how things are. I shall explore this suggestion, hoping also to raise some more general issues concerning McDowell's position.

Mrs Foot and McDowell both express, in part, their conception of the rôle of desire in the explanation of prudential behaviour—a rôle duplicated in McDowell's account of virtuous behaviour—by means of a quotation from Nagel's *The Possibility of Altruism.*[1] It is unclear how far either take themselves to be committed to the details of his account of prudential motivation. (In fact, as we shall see, despite appearances, McDowell's own remarks on prudence point to a view distinct from Nagel's.) I shall suggest, though, that Nagel's account does offer a satisfactory view of how an agent's distinctive conception of the world could play a part in explaining why he saw reason, not dependent on his desires, to act in a certain way: but that it serves ill as a model for McDowell's view of virtuous behaviour. Hence if one's commitment to the possibility, in the case of prudential behaviour, was based on acceptance of Nagel's account, one would not be compelled to admit as possible a view of moral behaviour like McDowell's.

McDowell holds that a man's prudential behaviour is to be explained in terms of his distinctive conception of what it is for a fact to concern his own future, a view which he might lack if, say, he thought of the person involved in such a fact as some remote future self. This certainly echoes many remarks of Nagel's, where he suggests that he is going to explain the acceptance of prudential reasons in terms of what it is for an agent to identify future stages of a person as stages of *his* life. But it is an important feature of Nagel's argument that his account of prudential reasons does not in fact relate them to any view the agent has of *his* future, but rather to a view he has of *the* future, and indeed, more generally, of time. Indeed for

[1] Thomas Nagel, *The Possibility of Altruism* (Oxford 1970).

Nagel prudential reasons are reasons relating to any kind of provision for the future and have, in general, no peculiar connexion with the future interests of the agent.[2]

Nagel's concern is to show how, independently of a present desire, an agent can be rationally motivated by the thought that he *will* have reason to promote a certain state of affairs. He finds the solution in a conception he claims we have of time, namely, that all times, past, present and future, are equally real. Fully to possess this conception, Nagel maintains, is to have the belief that the content of any judgment cannot shift with tense. Thus, for example, everything that can be said now about the future, using the future tense, will be statable in the present tense when the future arrives. All that changes is the temporal point of view. This unchanging content can, then, be fully captured in tenseless judgments. This last thought will, Nagel claims, for one who has this conception quite generally, extend to practical judgments, judgments concerning what the agent has reason to do. It follows that an agent's tensed judgment that he *will* have reason to promote a certain state of affairs must, for one fully possessed of this conception, commit him, independently of any present desire, to the tenseless judgment that he has reason to promote that state of affairs. This latter judgment, on this conception, is taken to possess the same content as the judgment, made in the present tense, that he *now* has reason to promote that state of affairs. Since, Nagel claims, to accept such a judgment is, other things being equal, to be motivated to promote that state of affairs, Nagel claims to have shown how, independently of present desires, an agent can be motivated by prudential considerations.

This is only the barest sketch of Nagel's position, omitting much which he would regard as crucial. It will serve, though, to pursue the above suggestion, namely, that conceding that explanations of prudential behaviour could rest merely on an agent's conception of how things are, need not, if the concession involved a commitment to Nagel's account, require one to concede that virtuous behaviour could, in general, be thus explained.

An action is dictated by a non-hypothetical imperative if

[2] *op.cit.*, p. 36.

there is a conception of the facts, possessed by the agent, attribution of which to him serves, on its own, to reveal the favourable light in which he saw the action. It would seem important, then, that if an action is to be taken as dictated by a non-hypothetical imperative, that the relevant conception can be ascribed to the agent and in such a way as to do precisely that. In Nagel's account of prudence this seems to be achieved. The relevant conception of how things are is capable of being ascribed to the agent in a straightforward way—by saying of him that he believes that such-and-such—because it is explicitly stated *what* the relevant conception, the belief, is. And the rôle of ascription of such a conception in revealing why an agent should see reason to act on prudential considerations is of a quite familiar kind. The content of a motivating belief—that the agent now has reason to promote a certain state of affairs—is shown (more or less) to follow from the general conception in question plus an additional premiss, namely, that he *will* have reason to promote that state of affairs. Thus the agent's motivating belief that he has reason to promote that state of affairs is explained in a style familiar from the explanation of beliefs, as being the consequence of other beliefs which he has. Grounds are thus given for the claim, crucial to both Nagel and McDowell, that seeing reason to act in certain ways is a criterion of possession of the relevant conception, properly understood.

Turning to McDowell's view of virtue, and more generally of actions which are non-hypothetically commanded, problems arise concerning the extent to which the relevant conceptions can so much as be ascribed. A first question concerns *who* McDowell thinks of as being able to ascribe such conceptions and, hence, to see the actions in question as being non-hypothetically commanded. The issue may be raised by noting a contrast between a remark he makes during a brief discussion of etiquette (§7) and his treatment of the case of morality in §6. In the case of actions conforming to the requirements of etiquette, he suggests that there need be no absurdity in seeing at least some of these as being explained in terms of distinctive conceptions of circumstances which provide non-hypothetical reasons for action. He goes on to remark that 'one can attribute such conceptions to others without being compelled oneself'.

His remarks about virtuous behaviour suggest a different picture. Here the outsider—one, presumably, quite unmoved by the demands of virtue—is indeed allowed some understanding of virtuous action: but not, here, because he is in a position to ascribe, though himself unswayed, those conceptions of how things are which reveal the virtuous agent's actions as non-hypothetically commanded. Rather the thought is that the outsider can, at best, understand the virtuous agent's seeing reason to act as he does as being conditional on his possession of certain 'natural' desires, an understanding which will be doubly inadequate, in McDowell's view. It will, he claims, at best cover *some* cases of virtuous behaviour, and even there it will not reveal the actions in their true light. My question is: if the relevant kind of understanding is to be denied to a moral outsider, why should it be allowed to the outsider in the case of etiquette?

I shall return to that question later. At the moment, pursuing certain contrasts with Nagel's account of prudence, I wish to raise a more general question about the possibility of ascribing to an agent the kind of conception required to reveal, on its own, the favourable light in which he saw a virtuous action. To do so is to ascribe to him a belief to the effect that the situation has certain features which he takes to require a particular course of action. Now, as McDowell notes (§6), the features of the situation which a virtuous agent takes as requiring the action may be describable in language with which one who sees no reason to act as the virtuous agent does is fully competent, 'by all ordinary tests'. Now presumably part of being thus competent is having the ability to apply the descriptions in question to situations in general conformity with other users of the language, including those swayed by moral considerations. Thus it is perfectly possible that one who sees no reason, in a given situation, to act as a virtuous agent would, may agree on all those descriptions of the situation which the virtuous agent would offer as stating what, in the situation, demanded the action in question. Thus, for example, someone might offer, as his description of what gave him reason to spend so much time with *X*, that *X* was lonely and despairing and needed someone to talk to. Someone else might well accept that description but see it as providing no reason to be in *X*'s company, indeed as providing very good reason for avoiding *X*. Thus remarking of the virtuous agent 'He believed that *X* was lonely and despairing and needed someone to talk to' cannot serve to attribute to him the relevant conception. For the conception was supposedly lacking in the agent who saw no reason to perform the action which virtue might require: and this difference was to explain the difference in their response to the situation. But the foregoing remark may equally be made of the second agent. Suppose then that one imposed the following adequacy condition on claims that an agent's reason for action consisted merely in his conception of how things are, namely, that it be possible actually to ascribe the relevant conception to the agent: one might then be able to concede that, say, prudential reasons were of this sort—for Nagel's account meets this condition—while having doubts concerning whether it was possible that reasons for virtuous behaviour were, in general, of this kind.

This condition will seem less than compelling, though, if we regard, as McDowell does, a virtuous agent's conception of the circumstances as analogous to a perceptual state. For in explanations of actions of a quite uncontroversial, desire-based, kind, we have, in perceptual states, a clear example of an agent's view of how things are being invoked to explain actions, and differences between two agents' views of how things are being invoked to explain differences in action, without its necessarily being possible fully to ascribe the relevant cognitive content or the relevant differences in cognitive content. For example, a man's choice among certain objects, say gramophone recordings or wines, might be acknowledged to result from a combination of certain desires with how he perceptually took the objects to be, even though we, and he, were quite unable explicitly to state what, in the way he took the objects to be, cast a favourable light on his choice. And divergent choices, in the same situation, by different people, might be acknowledged to result, not from their having different desires, but from differences in how they perceptually took the objects to be, again without the relevant details of the differences in their perceptual beliefs being verbally expressible.

I shall suggest, though, what may be a difficulty in taking the virtuous agent's conceptions of situations as being, in *this* way, analogous to perceptual states. We think of perceptual states as cognitive, as capable of representing how things are, while allowing that how, exactly, they represent things to be may exceed our capacity to state. Our ability to think of such states in this way rests on our being able to regard the means by which the objects of perception are brought to consciousness as being, at least in part, of a non-conceptualized kind. (There are familiar difficulties in the philosophy of perception concerning how exactly we are to think of this.) Very crudely, in perception of an object or a situation we can acquire more knowledge than we can say because in perceptual awareness what we are given we are not told. But that need not, it would seem, be the case in our awareness of a situation in which virtue demands a certain action. We may simply be told of the circumstances, in language unfitted to express any conception of the situation distinctive to a virtuous agent and then 'see' what is demanded. What is difficult to understand is how, here, one has acquired knowledge which cannot be fully attributed to one by means of the description of the situation which constituted one's only means of such acquisition. It is not clear, then, that the perceptual analogy can be used to undercut the demand, met by Nagel's account of prudence, that the conceptions which allegedly explain the actions be capable of ascription.

A second important feature of Nagel's account of prudence is that it provides a clear model of *how* ascribing a conception of how things are can, properly understood, reveal certain actions as ones which the agent saw reason to perform, namely by rigorously connecting the conception and the conclusion that the agent has reasons to perform such actions. Grounds are therefore given for the claim that an agent's failure to see reason to perform such actions can be used to deny that he possesses the relevant conception. But there seems no reason to think that such an explicit connection can be generally made out in the case of moral reasons, nor, presumably, does McDowell think that it is necessary. A proper understanding of the conception will, on his view, simply lead us to see that, possessed of that conception, an agent would be motivated in a certain way and, hence, that if he lacks the relevant motivation he cannot possess the conception. Without the kind of detailed connexion offered by Nagel, though, one might claim that this was, in a particular case, a mere stipulation concerning what it was properly to understand the conception. Nagel himself accepts the more stringent requirement[3] which may partly explain something we noted earlier about his views on prudence: that while intuitively he wants to connect susceptibility to prudential motivation with a conception the agent has of his own future, the actual connexion is made with a much more abstract conception of time. For one might suspect that no conception of the agent's future could in fact be connected, in such a manner, with acceptance of prudential reasons. Here, then, might be a second condition one wished to impose on claims that ascription of a conception of how things are might serve, on its own, to explain an agent's action, a condition met by Nagel's account of prudence, which one saw no reason to think could be met, in general, by such claims concerning virtuous behaviour.

I left a question hanging: why, for McDowell, was the outsider in the case of etiquette capable of seeing some actions responsive to the requirements of etiquette as non-hypothetically commanded, while the analogous possibility was denied to the moral outsider? A suggestion might be this. There may be a tension within McDowell's account between two rather different views about the nature of the conceptions which non-hypothetically require certain actions; and two different ways in which these conceptions are not 'available equally to people who are not swayed by them' (§7). On the one hand, the relevant conceptions are thought of as something analogous to perceptual states, and I suggested a possible reason for maintaining this position, namely to account for the failure to be able to represent verbally how, say, a virtuous agent might conceive of a particular situation. Where the conceptions were thought of in this way, then, they might be regarded as unavailable to one who saw no reason to act in the appropriate way in *two* senses. First, the outsider would simply not take things to be as the possessor of the conception would. Secondly, and more strongly, lacking the perceptual capacity yielding those states, which, on the present view, are the only

[3] *op.cit.*, p. 59.

way adequately to represent to oneself how the possessor of the conception takes things to be, the outsider has no access to the content of the relevant conception: he is not even in a position to appreciate, while rejecting, the view that things are as the possessor of the conception takes them to be. He is hence unable to see by what conception the actions in question might be non-hypothetically commanded. At other times, rather, the conceptions are thought of as exemplifying something thought of as a 'world-view' which, despite the perceptual overtones of 'view' would seem to suggest a set of rather general beliefs, more or less articulate or articulable, comparable in these respects, though contrasted with, those yielded by science. A person not holding such a view might then be thought able to have, to varying degrees, access to the content of the conception while not assenting to the claim that things were as the possessor of the conception took them to be. Hence he might be thought of as able to know by what conception the adherents were swayed, while not being so himself. If, then, in thinking of virtue the first picture were predominant, but in the remark following the discussion of etiquette the second, the contrast would be explained. That is, in the first kind of case, of which morality might be an example, the outsider could not appreciate by what conceptions the adherents were non-hypothetically swayed, while in the second kind of case, of which etiquette might be an example, the outsider could have this appreciation, though remaining himself unswayed. If there is anything in this suggestion of a contrast between two ways of thinking of the conceptions in question, the issue would be where, and why, McDowell found the different pictures appropriate. If the suggestion is simply misguided, then I remain puzzled concerning the treatment of the moral outsider, and its contrast with the remark following the discussion of etiquette. In either case, the view of the moral outsider seems too happy a result for morality. For it rules out the possibility that someone might know how the world is taken to be by those committed to morality but simply hold that they were mistaken in thinking that things were like that. One might think that a cognitivist account of morality ought not simply to rule out such a possibility.

To show that the requirements of morality need not be

hypothetical imperatives would not, of course, be yet to show that they could not be. It would not be to show, that is, that a complete explanation of virtuous action, either in general or in the particular case, could not be given in which the motivating capacity of the moral consideration rested solely on a desire of the agent's. McDowell seems to hold that if one thought it possible that the requirements of morality were hypothetical imperatives in the present sense, one would be violating what he regards as Kant's fundamental aim, namely that of denying that '. . . the motivating capacity of moral considerations needs explaining from outside, in terms of desires which are not intrinsically moral'. (§8) But even to espouse that aim need not in itself commit one to the view that one must explain the motivating capacity of moral considerations in McDowell's way, as resting on no desires at all. For it has not yet been shown that the only alternative to that is to explain moral motivation in terms of desires which are, *unarguably*, not intrinsically moral, say by being self-interested: recognizably, Mrs Foot's earlier position. There would still seem to be open the present position of Mrs Foot, namely, that of explaining moral motivation in terms of desires which are regarded as being intrinsically moral, desires such as that for the good of others. Certainly, in her description of such desires, she seems inclined to something like the converse of the mistake attributed by McDowell to Kant. (§8) For she seems to think that if an agent is given reason by his desires to perform virtuous actions then the desires will, primarily, be for ends distinct from the actions themselves. Thus her primary characterisation of the honest man is as one who cares for honesty 'for the sake of the good that honest dealings bring to men'.[4] She thus finds a *prima facie* difficulty concerning cases where no such good is expected. She has been rightly criticized for this attempt to reduce all moral considerations to matters concerning means to ends. Thus, for example, D.Z. Phillips[5] notes that moral considerations may centrally be concerned with the *character* of a man's actions and not simply with the

[4] Philippa Foot, 'Morality as a System of Hypothetical Imperatives', *Philosophical Review* 81, 1972, p. 314.

[5] D.Z. Phillips, 'In Search of the Moral "Must": Mrs Foot's Fugitive Thought,' *Philosophical Quarterly* 27, 1977, pp. 154ff.

end he was pursuing in performing it. But one could hold that moral motivation was grounded in desires—Mrs Foot's fundamental claim—without thinking that such desires were always, or even typically, for certain distinctive moral ends, as opposed, say, to desires that one's actions should have a certain character.

To establish McDowell's position, even granted the Kantian aim, would require that one show that any desires which we could regard as intrinsically moral could *only* be consequentially ascribed, and thus could not serve as the ground for the motivating capacity of moral considerations. I am very unsure about how this would be argued for, or whether McDowell takes himself to have done so. He suggests (§6) that actions motivated by independently intelligible desires (by which, I take it, he means intelligible independently of a distinctive conception of how things are) could not be expected to match exactly those of a virtuous agent. But this seems already to presuppose that we have accepted that a virtuous agent is one possessed of certain distinctive conceptions and not someone possessed of certain desires: plus the thought that these alternative possibilities would diverge in their behavioural outcome. Similarly, when he remarks, in the same section, that behaviour motivated by an independent desire would be, at best, a simulacrum of virtuous behaviour, this may be intended merely as a consequence of the suggested position, not as an argument for it. For it to be the basis for such an argument would require, perhaps, that we had a view of what, in an agent's thought, might constitute the difference between the two ways in which his conception of the situation might weigh with him, a difference such that it was crucial to our notion of a virtuous agent that he had the thoughts associated with a conception's weighing with him non-hypothetically. The problem here would be to see what, for McDowell, such a difference might come to. For he remarks (§7) that for his position it would not matter if someone maintained that *all* reasons for action consisted merely of cognitive states of the agent, that is, that all actions were, in the present sense, non-hypothetically required. If this is not incompatible with McDowell's position, then acting on a categorical imperative cannot manifest itself in, for example, the agent's thought that he 'has to' or 'must' perform the action—a thought rejected by Mrs Foot as perhaps no more than a reflection of our feelings about morality. For clearly we entertain no such thought about our actions in general. Nor, for the same reason, can it manifest itself in the *agent's* thinking that his seeing reason to perform the action was not conditional on his desires.

IV

Recent Work on Wittgenstein*

Perspectives on the Philosophy of Wittgenstein. Edited by Irving Block.
Wittgenstein: Language and World. By John V. Canfield.
Wittgenstein: To Follow a Rule. Edited by Steven H. Holtzmann and Christopher M. Leich.
Wittgenstein and his Times. Edited by Brian McGuinness.
Wittgenstein's Tractatus: An Introduction. By H.O. Mounce.
Ludwig Wittgenstein: Personal Recollections. Edited by Rush Rhees.
Wittgenstein. By Georg Henrik von Wright.**

Wittgenstein famously described his own enquiries as sketches of landscapes made from different directions. The writers in the above volumes survey the landscape of Wittgenstein from a bewildering variety of perspectives, and record their visions in various styles—media, one might almost say. What goals are worth having in thinking about Wittgenstein, and how should they be embodied in writing?—questions not, perhaps, always to be raised explicitly: but many of the present writers show little evidence of having considered them. 'In the course of a scientific investigation we say all kinds of things; we make many utterances whose role in the investigation we do not understand. For it isn't as though everything we say has a conscious purpose; our tongues just keep going'. (*Culture and Value* p. 64.) This captures something I found myself often thinking during my reading for this review.

Von Wright, in his collection of studies, does touch upon some of these issues of *genre*. Let us begin with biographical writings. He remarks that he has never contemplated writing a

* From *The Philosophical Quarterly*, vol. 34, no. 134, 1984, pp. 69–73.

** To avoid clutter, the above works are referred to by the names of their authors or editors.

full-scale biography and continues: '. . . the best pictures to be drawn of Wittgenstein as a man are impressionistic accounts of conversations and episodes'. Taken as a claim about present possibilities, one must agree. But an account of a *life* can illuminate the man: why not in the case of Wittgenstein? The challenge he presents to the art of biography is indeed formidable, but I think it unwarrantedly pessimistic to accept Von Wright's view as a permanent injunction. (As a prediction, it may turn out to be true.) Indeed von Wright's study of the origin of the *Tractatus* partly subverts his own judgment: for (unlike its companion on the *Investigations*) it is as much a chapter of an unwritten biography as an exercise in textual scholarship, and one which illuminates Wittgenstein's relation to his early work. Meanwhile we have, in Rush Rhee's collection, more such 'impressionistic accounts'. Von Wright singles out for high praise Fania Pascal's memoir—and it is a splendid piece. She does not write as a self-effacing epigone. Anger and sharp criticism play a part in her account of the man. Wittgenstein is not diminished by the resulting picture. Parts of other items in this volume read like parodies of their species. Gnomic, banal, or banally recorded remarks remain just that, no matter their topics or provenance. Drury—who contributes notes on his conversations with Wittgenstein—reveals himself as troubled about the value and consequences of publishing such memories. I think he was right to be so: we must consider the uses to which such records of conversations and lectures—as also some of Wittgenstein's own more marginal writings—have been put.

Some have used them to urge us to treat of Wittgenstein not merely as a contributor to philosophy, narrowly conceived, but in relation to broader intellectual and cultural concerns. A number of different projects might be involved here, grounded in different beliefs about the nature and value of his work. One belief might be that Wittgenstein's thinking about, for example, aesthetics or psychoanalysis was of considerable philosophical importance in its own right: a resultant project to substantiate that claim in a particular case. Many writers in this *genre* do little to advance their aim—thinking it enough to intersperse remarks of Wittgenstein's with comments at least superficially in the same style. The results are typically undiscussable. (Rhees's article 'Wittgenstein on Language and Ritual' in McGuinness' collection might serve as an extreme example.) A notable exception, a clear and forthright discussion of its topic, is Cioffi's contribution to Block—'Wittgenstein and the Fire-Festivals'. He seeks to show that Wittgenstein had a damning objection, explicitly to Frazer's treatment of these festivals, implicitly to much work in the human sciences. The objection is that an historical enquiry, such as Frazer undertook, into certain ritual practices is quite irrelevant to the real issues such rituals pose, which concern the nature of the (often deep and sinister) impressions which they make on us. Cioffi notes, of course, that such were not in fact Frazer's questions (and in this, at least, Frazer is typical of anthropologists): and he repeatedly poses the sensible question as to why Frazer should be criticized for failing to answer them. His attempt to find, on Wittgenstein's behalf, a reply struck me as a complete failure. Cioffi partially summarises Wittgenstein's claim thus: '. . . we mistake the nature of the problem involved in accounting for the impressions which perplex, preoccupy or trouble us, . . . thinking that what we want with respect to them are historical reconstructions or causal explanations. . . .' (*ibid.* p. 234). But that contains no reply to the anthropologist's point: which was that he was not perplexed by or preoccupied with our impressions of the rituals, but with the *rituals*. This focus on the impressions made upon us by an object, and the rejection of a causal understanding of them, are central features of the records we have of Wittgenstein's thinking on aesthetics. Paul Ziff's indignant article in the same volume well brings out a parallel irrelevance—to the understanding of a work of art—of the 'puzzles' about our impressions which Wittgenstein raises. I believe that some of Wittgenstein's marginal writings do not deserve the *philosophical* status they have been accorded in certain quarters. Nor do I find their disappointing quality surprising: the most casual survey of the *Nachlass* reveals where his central endeavours lay.

An apparently different ambition would be to deploy such writings as part of an effort to understand Wittgenstein as a cultural phenomenon, reflecting and paralleling work in a wider intellectual milieu than the professionally philosophical. Von Wright is again perceptive on some of the issues here, both in the introduction to his book and his essay in it 'Wittgenstein in Relation to his Times'. This also appears in McGuinness' collection, where the editor himself and J.C. Nyíri make contributions to such a task, discussing respectively Wittgenstein's relation to Freud and to conservative political thought. The relevance of such work to a philosophical understanding of Wittgenstein's thought might seem to raise only particular cases of vexed general issues concerning 'history of philosophy' *vis-à-vis* 'history of ideas'. (Problems enough!) But there is, perhaps, a special difficulty in the case of Wittgenstein. Von Wright poses the question: is there a conceptual (and not merely a psychological) connection between some of his views on the nature of philosophy, language and their roots in the life of a community, and his rejection of much in the spirit of the civilization which surrounded him? Von Wright does not answer his question: nor can I. But pending an answer there is an unclarity concerning what, in proposing a discussion of 'Wittgenstein and his Times', one is proposing.

The position of the *Tractatus* within current philosophy is an odd one, to be contrasted both with that of the writings which form its explicit background (Frege's and the early Russell's) and with its own status in the 20's and 30's. Many now write *about* it, but few *use* it in the course of their own philosophizing. Of course the logical positivists' use of the *Tractatus* rested on gross misreadings: and some have claimed that the role of Frege as a benchmark in contemporary philosophy of language is similarly a product of misunderstanding. It might be held that contemporary 'relevance' is always bought, and wrongly, at the cost of distortion. That judgment might be true: but as philosophers have yet to lose the habit which it condemns it cannot explain why it is not, now, exercised on the *Tractatus*. It is not as if the themes of that book find no contemporary echoes. As Kripke points out (Block, p. 305) there are at least superficially striking parallels with certain doctrines of Davidson and his followers. One might compare also contemporary defences of 'the language of thought' with Wittgenstein's 1919 response to a query of Russell's: 'I don't know what the constituents of a thought are but I know *that* it must have such constituents which correspond to the words of Language'. Of course no-one, perhaps, is now going to swallow the *Tractatus* whole, logical atomism and all: but many who fruitfully use Frege or early Russell show no tenderness towards such things as incomplete entities or sensibilia. Whatever the *explanation* of the current position of the *Tractatus*, the *fact* of it casts something of a pall over much contemporary commentary on it. (Pears, Hacker and Kenny in Block, for example.) The writers are careful, clear, often illuminating on aspects of the text: but the enterprise has a passionless quality. The archaeologists seem to have little enthusiasm for the dig or its discoveries. (A notable exception, also in Block, is Stenius's account and defence of a picture theory of meaning. Dummett too, in the same volume, while sharply rejecting the theory evinces a conviction of the importance of the problems it would have solved.)

It is one of the many virtues of Mounce's modest book on the *Tractatus* that he begins it with a lucid account of the issues in the philosophy of logic which form its problem-background, well conveying a sense of why the work might matter. The book is very much an introduction, directed at students with little knowledge of logic or philosophy. It could not fail to help them in approaching the *Tractatus*. Whether, and why, such a student *ought* to be reading the *Tractatus* is another matter; perhaps as 'background' to the *Investigations*. At a number of points, Mounce makes brief but telling comparisons with the later material, and in a deft final chapter seeks to locate that in the *Investigations* which most centrally contrasts with the *Tractatus*. He finds it in the later work's insistence on the question: how can the meaning of a sign determine its future applications?—a question which is increasingly being seen as lying at the heart of the *Investigations*.

As already noted, von Wright's book contains important contributions to 'pure' scholarship directed upon the later writings: his account and catalogue of the *Nachlass* and his study of the origin and composition of the *Investigations*. The body of such work, and its deployment in interpretative writings, is clearly going to grow. The prospect can seem discouraging to the mere philosopher. Should he feel debarred from commenting on the *Investigations* until he has a detailed mastery of the *Nachlass*, published and unpublished? Two of the more general results of such scholarship (both stressed by one of its doyens, Gordon Baker, in his contribution to Holtzman and Leich) suggest a negative answer. The first is the increased awareness yielded by a study of its composition that the *Investigations* is anything but a haphazard collection of remarks. Its structure, and the final context of individual remarks, have thus a crucial role to play in interpretation. Secondly, we have been led to appreciate the substantial development in Wittgenstein's thought during the 'later period'. The latter fact rules out any simple use of the rest of the *Nachlass* in understanding the *Investigations*: together they encourage the thought that hard thinking, and intelligent reading, directed on the text itself, remain the essential prerequisites of its understanding.

As Baker notes, what does seem dubious in the light of these facts is a procedure long (and still) practised on 'Wittgenstein's later philosophy', which might be caricatured as follows. A certain (alleged) topic of the *Investigations* is proposed for discussion. The writer defends his account of Wittgenstein's position (which, incidentally, he generally endorses) by a judicious selection of passages from a variety of sources in the *Nachlass*, considered apart from their context. (The procedure acquires a further inheritance of guilt when a major role is given, in interpreting central themes of the *Investigations*, to the more marginal writings.) A number of articles in Block exemplify both failings: Canfield's book the former. Central to Canfield's work is the widespread assumption that a key notion of Wittgenstein's later philosophy is a quasi-technical construal of 'criterion'. The aim of the first half of the book is to rebut certain existing reconstructions of this concept, and accounts of its role, and to offer his own. He has a number of sensible points to make *en route*: but the overall project seems misconceived. The widespread assumption just noted would seem to derive largely from the famous passage in the *Blue Book* where an apparently technical contrast between 'criteria' and 'symptoms' is momentarily brought into focus. But writers in this tradition rarely stop to ask: for what purpose did Wittgenstein *here* make this contrast? Is it a purpose which he retained, and which lies behind the uses of the term 'criterion' in the *Investigations*? Is the argumentative force of these uses, in their context, sensitive to differences between the various 'analyses' which have been offered of the notion? A procedure which ransacks the texts for occurrences of 'criterion', seeking to confirm or refute proposed analyses, passes such questions by. Until they have been appropriately answered, I see no reason to accept the presupposition of Canfield's, and others', enterprise.

A popular special case of this presupposition is the view that understanding 'criterion' as a term of art is crucial to the elucidation of 'the private language argument'. Connectedly, it has been widely held that the attack on private languages begins, in the *Investigations*, around §243, its central target being certain ('Cartesian') views on the relationship between sensations and behaviour. Kripke's 'Wittgenstein on Rules and Private Language' explicitly challenges the latter assumption: and his ability to illuminate the topic while ignoring 'the finer exegetical points involved in Wittgenstein's notion of a criterion' casts doubt on the former. As many readers will be aware, Kripke's central claim is that the crucial objections to a private language are to be found in the outcome of the discussions of following a rule, and of using an expression in accordance with its meaning, which dominate §§138–242. Kripke's task, then, is to defend an interpretation of those discussions which will substantiate that claim. He proposes an account which has Wittgenstein raising a sceptical problem about meaning and rule-following, and resolving it only by giving reference to a community an essential role in the assertibility conditions of sentences of the form 'X means so-and-so by "__"'. The important thing to say here is that Kripke's article is by far the most impressive piece of work in the books under discussion. Its exemplary clarity evinces an intellectual passion which repeatedly drove this reader, with an anticipation of pleasure, back to Wittgenstein's text (as relevant a test, surely, of the philosophical expositor as it ought to be of the literary critic). An assessment of Kripke's claims is out of place here: they should and will be given extended discussion. Some may deplore this: may we not be diverted from Wittgenstein's to Kripke's 'private language argument'? Possibly: but divergent accounts of the material can only profit from having to face up to the lucidity and definiteness of Kripke's.

On anyone's view, considerations about meaning and understanding lie at the heart of Wittgenstein's later work. They have also dominated much philosophy of the last fifteen years. The styles could hardly be more different: construction of, and reflection upon, systematic theories of meaning *versus* (apparently) an assemblage of reminders for particular purposes. Do the differences of *ethos* point to conflict in doctrine? Can we deploy the later Wittgenstein against the formal semanticists? Baker (briefly) and Crispin Wright (at greater length) (both in Holtzman and Leich) begin the attempt, basing their difficulties for formal semantics on (vastly different) accounts of Wittgenstein on rules. Peacocke and Evans's essay replies. These symposia do not answer our just-posed questions. (Evans's paper, on semantic structure, is, though, an important contribution to a problem internal to systematic semantics.) Indeed, global confrontations of this kind are not likely to be very fruitful, at least at present. A major difficulty is that there just is no single philosophical position underlying work in formal semantics. Professor X and Dr Y may well agree, say, on the proper 'treatment' of mass terms, but diverge radically on the nature and point of the overall enterprise. Another problem—on the Wittgenstein side—is this. As noted above, there are many apparent points of contact between the problems and doctrines of the *Tractatus* and those of recent philosophy of language. But (as a number of articles in Block reveal) we are still lacking a clear view of what, if anything, the later Wittgenstein would retain from that work. (In some cases—the 'compositionality' of language is a major one—the problem is that of interpreting silence. *Pace* Baker, it need not mean dissent.) How then can we aspire to assess the bearing of his later work on philosophies of which he had no ken? In the battles being waged now by some would-be followers of Wittgenstein, a complex piece of artillery, concerning whose operation the gunners disagree, is being wheeled into action against a scattered and mobile army. Fruitful work here will need to be less ambitious, more detailed, and less partisan. And we should allow ourselves to harbour the suspicion that differences of 'climates of thought . . . of forms of intellectual life' (Baker) are just *that*.

V

Supervenience, Realism, Necessity*

I

Introduction

The central aim of this paper** is to examine just one line of argument. It was presented by Simon Blackburn in 1971 in his paper 'Moral Realism'.[1] (I shall call it Blackburn's argument although he acknowledges obtaining it from Dr. Casimir Lewy.) The argument, though presented over ten years ago, had not, until recently, been assessed in print.[2] This I find surprising. For though I believe the argument largely fails in its objective, it is of the greatest interest, and not merely in relation to its avowed topic—moral realism. I hope my discussion will, like Blackburn's argument itself, cast some light on the three more general topics of my title—realism, supervenience and necessity. Before presenting the argument (rather, one central version of it) let me make some brief and sketchy remarks which may serve to place it in some sort of context, and which I shall draw on towards the end of the paper.

* From *The Philosophical Quarterly* Vol. 35 No. 140 1985, pp. 246–258.

** A revised version of a paper read to the Moral Sciences Club, Cambridge, in March 1983. Earlier versions were read at the University of Birmingham and to my colleagues at Birkbeck. I am grateful to members of these audiences for helpful comments and encouragement, particularly to Chris Hookway, Mark Platts and Martin Davies, and to Leslie Stevenson for helpful suggestions for revisions.

[1] In John Casey (ed.), *Morality and Moral Reasoning* (London, 1971).

[2] See J.C. Klagge, 'An Alleged Difficulty concerning Moral Properties', *Mind* 93 (1984), pp. 70–80. Klagge and I are in agreement concerning the first move to be made against Blackburn's argument—*viz.* the rejection of (L) (see §III of this paper and p. 376 of Klagge's)—but he seems to think this is merely a move the moral *realist* should make. Blackburn, in a compressed reformulation of the argument (see his *Spreading the Word* (Oxford, 1984), pp. 182–187 and, especially, Note 6.1) also holds that the moral realist could reject (L) if the necessity therein is 'metaphysical' necessity. I hold, against both of them, that the rejection of (L), in the only interpretation of it which threatens the moral realist, is implicit in ordinary moral thought (see §§III and IV). Blackburn would seem now (see *op. cit.*, p. 221) to make central the demand for an *explanation* of supervenience which I discuss in §V. It should perhaps here be made explicit that none of the claims of the present paper are meant to tell *against* Blackburn's own non-realist metaphysics of morals.

Suppose two philosophers are engaged in a disagreement about a certain class of statements or judgments—moral judgments perhaps, or mathematical statements. One philosopher—henceforth 'the realist'—holds that when statements of the class at issue are true, they are true in virtue of a fact or state of affairs. His apparent opponent—henceforth the 'non-realist'[3]—while perhaps agreeing that this is so for some *other* classes of statements, denies it for the statements under dispute. These judgments or statements, he says, are not true in virtue of a fact or state of affairs. Does this brief characterisation reveal a genuine, discussable disagreement? One might well think not. Facts, as an ontological category, are widely thought to be disreputable: and the history of theories which attempt to say something significant about truth by deploying the concept of fact or of state of affairs is a dismal one.

Ordinary, as opposed to philosophers', talk of facts looms large when discussion turns to explanation. 'What makes salt soluble in water?'—'The fact that it has such-and-such crystal structure'. Such talk may, or may not, require for its ultimate construal an ontology of facts. But the genuineness of the explanation-seeking question is not impugned by the availability of the ostensibly factless paraphrase: 'Why is salt soluble in water?'—'Because it has such-and-such structure'.

We might then be able to make sense of this realist/non-realist debate by relocating it, in the first instance, as an issue about *explanation* along something like the following lines (which have been extensively explored by, among others, Blackburn himself). The starting point is epistemology, naturalistically conceived (in Quine's sense, though by no means necessarily restricted to stating its claims within the limited set of concepts to which Quine would confine it). The central task would be to outline a conception of the world, and of ourselves within it, in terms of which to explain, in some broadly 'causal' sense, the opinions we form and the judgments in which we evince them. Content might then be given to our realist/non-realist dispute by imposing the following require-

[3] I prefer not to use here the term 'anti-realist', coined by Dummett to introduce one side of what, in my opinion, is a quite different kind of debate, and subsequently used by some other writers to cover an extraordinarily mixed bag of doctrines.

ment of congruence between our naturalized epistemology and our theory of truth. We cannot allow that a statement of a certain class is true in virtue of a fact or state of affairs of a certain kind unless we can find a role, within our naturalized epistemology, for such a fact or state of affairs in explaining (directly or indirectly) the making of such a statement. The non-realist concerning some class of judgments would then seek to show that an illuminating explanation of our practice of making these judgments could be given without invoking (as aspects of reality) facts making these judgments true: the realist to rebut that claim.

Now while all the above might be developed so as to give—to those who accepted its naturalistic framework—a *content* to realist/non-realist disputes, it might do so in such a way as to make them impossible to settle. For, to make just one point, a philosopher's conception of what constitutes an adequate or illuminating explanation is hardly independent of his views of the ultimate furniture of the world. (Consider what Quine will and will not allow into *his* naturalized epistemology.) The notion of explanation may, therefore, provide no fixed point from which to assess the apparently opposed positions; they would then remain merely as alternative pictures. It is here that Blackburn sees a role for an argument which seeks to show that, although the notion of a statement's being true in virtue of a state of affairs may appear vacuous, it has enough content to enable us to see that quasi-formal aspects of truth in a certain area (here, moral truth) would be utterly mysterious if construed realistically. To Blackburn's attempt to refute moral realism by an argument of this style I now turn.

II

The argument

At the heart of Blackburn's argument are two claims about the relation of moral truths (ascribing moral properties to objects) and 'naturalistic' truths (ascribing 'naturalistic properties' to objects).[4] They are:

[4] Some moral realists, and others, might deny our ability to make, or to characterize, the distinction between the 'moral' and the 'naturalistic' here being invoked. I am sympathetic to these worries, but they are not the concern of this paper.

(L) There are moral truths which are not strictly implied by any truth ascribing naturalistic properties to their subjects. *i.e.* with 'M' ranging over moral, 'N' over naturalistic properties:
$(\exists x)(\exists M)[Mx \& \sim(\exists N)(Nx \& \Box(Nx \rightarrow Mx))]$
(S) Moral properties are *supervenient* on naturalistic properties in the sense that it is logically necessary that, if two objects agree in all their naturalistic properties, then they agree in all their moral properties, *i.e.*:
$\Box(\forall x)(\forall y)[(\forall N)(Nx \leftrightarrow Ny) \rightarrow (\forall M)(Mx \leftrightarrow My)]$.

Why then does Blackburn think (L) and (S) together raise a mystery for the moral realist? The argument goes, largely in Blackburn's own words, as follows:[5]

> Imagine a thing A which has a certain set of naturalistic properties and relations. A also has a certain degree of moral worth, say it is very good. This, according to the realist, reports the existence of a state of affairs: A's goodness. Now the existence of this state of affairs is not entailed by A being as it is in all naturalistic respects. This means, since all the propositions involved are entirely contingent, that the existence of this state of affairs is not strictly implied by A being as it is in all naturalistic respects. That is, it is logically possible that A should be as it is in all naturalistic respects, yet this further state of affairs not exist.

But if that's a logical possibility, why isn't it a logical possibility that B should share all A's naturalistic properties and the further state of affairs—B's goodness—not exist?

> If the goodness is, as it were, an *ex gratia* payment to A, one to which it is not, as a matter logic, entitled in virtue of being as it is in all naturalistic respects, then it should be consistent to suppose that although given to A, it was not given to B, which merely shares the naturalistic features which do not entail the goodness.[6]

But, of course, if (S) holds, it is *not* consistent to suppose that.

[5] Only largely, because Blackburn also has another version deploying a concept of supervenience concerning one object at different times which, for reasons of space, I am ignoring. Since I shall not reject either of Blackburn's supervenience claims—far from it—no injustice will be done.

[6] Casey (ed.), *op. cit.*, pp. 110–1.

III

Initial objection

My first objection to this argument is that although (S) is true, (L) is false. In fact, *every* moral truth is strictly implied by some naturalistic truth about its subject. (Even stronger claims about the moral *vis-à-vis* the natural can, I believe, be established.) In trying to show this I shall first treat the necessity operator as a universal quantifier over possible worlds or situations. (I shall consider an objection to this procedure later.) (S) can then be reformulated—using '*w*' as a variable ranging over possible worlds, and reading '*Mxw*' etc. as '*x* is *M* in *w*' etc.—as:

(XYWW) $(\forall w)(\forall x)(\forall y)[(\forall N)(Nxw \leftrightarrow Nyw) \rightarrow (\forall M)(Mxw \leftrightarrow Myw)]$

This tells us, that for any objects *x*, *y*, if in any possible situation they share all their naturalistic properties then in *that* possible situation they share all their moral properties. Put like this, (S) is often said to express intra-world, cross-object supervenience of *M*- on *N*-type properties. But if one starts playing the game of cataloguing different forms of supervenience claims, such ways of referring to them soon become unmanageable. Looking at the matrix of variables, a convenient label for the present formulation of (S) is (XYWW).[7]

Once we have the explicit apparatus of possible worlds variables it is very easy to formulate supervenience claims that involve *cross*-world comparisons. (Such claims *can* be formulated without this apparatus but not nearly so perspicuously.) Fortunately we shall only need, for present purposes, to consider one such: *viz.* the claim that if in a possible world an object is naturalistically just as it is in the actual world then it is in that possible world morally just as it is in the actual world. That is, using 'a' to denote the actual world:

(XXWA) $(\forall x)(\forall w)[(\forall N)(Nxw \leftrightarrow Nxa) \rightarrow (\forall M)(Mxw \leftrightarrow Mxa)]$

Finally, in this style, Blackburn's (L) becomes:

[7] For a brief statement of the merits of the present mode of formulating and labelling (some) forms of supervenience doctrines see the appendix.

$$(L') \quad (\exists x)(\exists M)[Mxa \;\&\; \sim (\exists N)(Nxa \;\&\; (\forall w)(Nxw \rightarrow Mxw))]$$

I shall now argue:
(1) Ordinary moral thought commits us to (XXWA)
(2) Given a plausible assumption about naturalistic properties, (XXWA) is incompatible with (L′). So that,
(3) As ordinary moralists we are committed to rejecting (L′).

(1) It seems to me almost self-evident that ordinary moral thought commits us to (XXWA). But if argument is called for, consider the following passage from Hare:[8]

> If I said 'Smith acted rightly in giving her the money, but he might have given her the money, and in all other respects acted similarly, except that his act was not right', I should invite the comment: 'But how could the rightness of the act disappear like this? If the act, motives, circumstances, &c., were all the same, you would be bound, logically, to judge it right in the hypothetical case as you did in the actual case. The actual action couldn't have been right and the hypothetical action not right, unless there had been *some* other difference between the actions, or their circumstances, or their motives, or something else.'

(2) (L′) is not by itself incompatible with (XXWA). Putting it another way: (XXWA) does not by itself entail that *any* (still less that *every*) moral truth is strictly implied by some proposition ascribing a naturalistic property to its subject, if only (though not in fact only) because (XXWA) (and (S)) is compatible with an object having moral but *no* naturalistic properties. We shall need, then, to show the incompatibility of (L) with (XXWA), some assumption about the possession, by the objects we are here concerned with, of naturalistic properties.

In fact, the assumption we need may be implicit in the use Blackburn makes of (L). (L), when taken in conjunction with (S), might not even appear to raise problems for the moral realist if it merely came to this: that the totality of the object's actual naturalistic properties do not necessitate the moral property *M* in question, on the grounds that the object could, in some other possible world, have all these naturalistic

[8] *Language of Morals* (Oxford, 1952), p. 153.

properties *plus* some more which resulted in the moral property's being, as it were, 'defeated' in that possible world. It seems, rather, that if (L) is to play the rôle it does in Blackburn's argument then we must assume that all the objects with which we have to deal have in the actual world what Jaegwon Kim calls a 'maximal' naturalistic property.[9] Rather than giving his technical definition of this notion we could put the assumption we need in the following intuitive way: every object actually has some naturalistic property (no doubt extremely complex, perhaps an infinite conjunction of properties) which is so determinate in every possible naturalistic respect that no further naturalistic properties can be 'added'. For our purposes, the relevant feature of any such *N*-maximal property, N^* say, is that if x has N^* in the actual world, and also has N^* in some possible world w, then x in w shares *all* its naturalistic properties with x in the actual world. We are assuming, then, that every object with which we are concerned actually has some such property, *i.e.*:

$$\text{(NMA)} \quad (\forall x)(\exists N)[Nxa \;\&\; (\forall w)(Nxw \rightarrow (\forall N')(N'xa \leftrightarrow N'xw))]$$

It is now fairly easy to see that (XXWA) and (NMA) are inconsistent with (L′). Informally the argument goes like this:

(L′) tells us that for some x, and some moral property M which x has, there is no naturalistic property which x actually has which, in every world in which x possesses it, guarantees that x has M therein. This holds, then, even for the *N*-maximal property, N^*, say, which, according to (NMA), x actually has. So there is a possible world, w, say, in which x has N^* but lacks M. But since N^* is *N*-maximal, and x has it both in the actual world and in w, x in w agrees in *all* its naturalistic properties with x in the *actual* world. But (L′) has allowed x to have M in the actual world but lack it in w: contrary to (XXWA). So (retaining (XXWA) and (NMA)) we must reject (L′). Indeed we are committed to saying that every moral truth is strictly implied by at least one naturalistic truth concerning its subject.

I claim to have shown (L′) to be false. But Blackburn did

[9] See his 'Supervenience and Nomological Incommensurables' *American Philosophical Quarterly*. 15 (1978), pp. 149–56.

after all have an argument for it, implicit in the passage quoted, *viz.*

(E) There are some moral truths which are not entailed by any truth ascribing naturalistic properties to their subjects.

(C) Where *P*, *Q* are contingent (as we can assume all the relevant propositions here are) then, if *P* does not entail *Q*, *P* does not strictly imply *Q*. That is, for contingent *P*, *Q*, if *P* does not entail *Q* then it is logically possible that the conjunction of *P* and ~*Q* be true.

In response, I shall claim that there is no reading of 'entails' which both renders (E) a well-attested claim of meta-ethics and also renders (C) (as we are presently interpreting it) true. As Blackburn argues, what repeated arguments against certain versions of ethical naturalism seem to have shown is that for at least some moral truths *Q*, there is no naturalistic truth *P* such that to accept *P* while rejecting *Q* is to make a 'logical error', to be 'illogical as opposed to immoral'.[10] And this claim is very naturally expressed by saying that there is no naturalistic *P* which *entails Q*. For Moore introduced '*P* entails *Q*' just to mean that *Q* is deducible from *P*.

> . . . in the sense in which the conclusion of a syllogism in Barbara follows from the two premisses, taken as one conjunctive proposition; or in which the proposition 'This is coloured' follows from 'This is red'.[11]

So, where *P* entails *Q* in this stipulated but unanalysed sense, one who accepts *P* while denying *Q* has made—in some broad sense of 'logical'— a logical error (perhaps better: some logical or conceptual error). But if it is in this (unanalysed) sense of 'entails' that (E) is plausible, it is highly dubious that (C) holds with the same sense of 'entails' (and with 'strictly implies' being interpreted as we are currently doing).

To take an example from a quite different area. Let *P* be: John drank some water. Let *Q* be: John drank some H_2O. Contemporary essentialists will hold that *P* strictly implies *Q* (in our present interpretation—there is no possible world in which the conjunction of *P* and ~*Q* holds). But clearly no

[10] Blackburn, *ibid.*, pp. 112, 113.

[11] In his *Philosophical Studies* (London, 1960) at p. 291.

'logical' or 'conceptual' error is made by one who accepts *P* while denying *Q*. So *P* does not entail *Q* in the stipulated sense. But it would be a bad move, and a too easy victory over the essentialist, to note that *P*, *Q* are both contingent and to apply principle (C) to conclude that *P* does *not* strictly imply *Q*.

IV

Reply on Blackburn's behalf: the 'wrong modality' response

I suspect the above, especially my last argument, may well have provoked the impatient thought that all this is an elaborate missing of the point. I am invoking, it will be suggested, against a paper written in days of modal innocence, the apparatus of post-Kripkean sophistication (or corruption): and as a result misinterpreting Blackburn. In particular I am interpreting the operator '□' in his key claims as Kripkean metaphysical necessity and, moreover, treating it as a quantifier over possible worlds. Blackburn's good old-fashioned 'it is logically necessary that' (ditto for 'it is logically possible that') was never so intended, it will be claimed. In fact, using a notion to which we have already alluded, the intent of (S) is:

> It would be a logical or conceptual error to hold that two objects were the same in all naturalistic respects but differed morally.

Similarly, the objection goes on, the intent of (L) is simply that there are moral truths *Q* such that for no naturalistic *P* would it be a logical or conceptual error to hold that *P* and ~*Q*. And I have done nothing to show that (L), *thus* interpreted, is false. Moreover, my remarks on (E) show me committed to it. Finally, Blackburn's use of (C) was not—as I represented it—to justify a move from these modal notions to Kripkean metaphysical modality, but simply to avoid objections from those who would not, where *P* was impossible, or *Q* necessary, allow the move from '*P* does not entail *Q*' to '*P* does not strictly imply *Q*'. (They will not accept the 'paradoxes of strict implication' as truths about entailment.)

I don't think this reply salvages Blackburn's argument as an attack on moral realism. That attack requires that certain principles governing moral truth render mysterious—when moral truth is interpreted realistically—the resulting claims about what combinations of moral and natural states of affairs can and cannot exist. But if the modality in (S) and (L) is interpreted along the presently suggested lines then, while I agree that (S) and (L) are both true, they speak (even if one is a moral realist) not about what combinations of moral and natural states of affairs can and cannot exist but merely of what kinds of mistake are and are not made by one who *holds* that certain combinations of moral and naturalistic states of affairs exist. And that raises no particular difficulties for the moral realist.

The point is that if (L) is (in conjunction with (S)) to raise a difficulty for the moral realist, then the modal operator in (L) *must* be interpretable in such a way that the following inference is valid: *from* (a) For no naturalistic property *N* of *x* is it necessary that if *Nx* then *Mx*, *to* (b) For every naturalistic property *N* of *x* it could be that (there is a possible situation in which) *x* has *N* but lacks *M*. For the alleged mystery arises from the claim that the moral state of affairs (as the moral realist will put it), *x*'s being *M*, could have failed to obtain although *x* retained all its naturalistic properties. But the interpretation of 'it is necessary that' mooted in the present section which plausibly renders (L) true does not sustain the above inference. That no logical or conceptual error is involved in holding that *P* does not entail that it could have been that not-*P* (*i.e.* that there is a possible situation in which not-*P*). Just as well, for the present, plausible, version of (L). For the result of applying that inference would lead to something which, I claim to have shown in section III, is simply false.

V

Explaining supervenience

(L) cannot, even if one is a moral realist, be interpreted as a truth about what combinations of moral and naturalistic states of affairs can exist. But (S) certainly can. And in a later passage the focus of Blackburn's attack appears to shift. The claim seems to become not that (L) and (S) taken jointly raise a mystery for the moral realist; but rather—concentrating just on (S)—that the moral realist cannot, while at least one kind of non-realist can, *explain* why (S) holds. Blackburn appears to express the conclusion of *this* line of thought when he writes:

'Supervenience becomes for the realist an opaque, isolated logical fact, for which no explanation can be offered'.[12]

To assess this claim I shall need to say something about how we are to conceive the task—explaining the supervenience of the moral on the naturalistic—at which the moral realist will, allegedly, fail. The first point to note is that supervenience (S) is a modal claim: more specifically, it says of a certain proposition —*viz.* that if two objects coincide in their naturalistic properties then they coincide in their moral properties—that it is necessarily true. The problem, then, of explaining why (S) is true can be seen as a special case of the general problem of explaining why propositions which assert the necessity of other propositions are true. (Which is not to say that all instances of this problem are to be similarly solved.)

Now if the form of realist/non-realist debate I sketched in the opening section is a genuine one, then another case of it would seem to concern such modal judgments. The modal realist will conceive of these judgments as reporting, and being made true by, certain modal states of affairs; and will perhaps construe our epistemically successful modal judgments—our modal knowledge—as arising from a recognition of such modal states of affairs. The modal non-realist (traditionally puzzled by the possibility of such 'recognition') will seek to dispense with such modal facts. Rather, he will aim to explain our making of the modal judgments in question as springing from some aspects of our psychology or our practices, as they relate to a non-modal world containing no 'objective' possibilities or necessities. (Hume on causal modality is of course the paradigm here.)

How one conceives the task of 'explaining' some *particular* modal claim—say our (S)—will clearly depend on whether one's general perspective on necessity is realist or non-realist in the above vaguely delineated sense. Let us first consider it from the point of view of the modal *realist*. For him, in explaining why a given modal judgment is true there is, ultimately, no getting away from modal facts. So, it seems, the most that he can aim to do, in explaining some particular necessity or impossibility,

[12] Blackburn, *ibid.*, p. 111.

is to derive it from one or more other necessities or impossibilities, in such a way as to illuminate it. An example of such a modally realist explanation would be Colin McGinn's attempt[13] to explain the alleged necessity that a person have the parents he actually has as a special case of some more general necessities of 'origin'. But, merely for illustrative purposes, let me suggest[14] a modally realist explanation of another widely believed supervenience claim, *viz.* the supervenience of the psychological on the physical—the view that necessarily, if two creatures share all their physical properties then they share all their psychological properties. This explanation appeals to two further alleged necessities, *viz.*

(1) Necessarily, if two creatures share all their behavioural dispositions then they share all their psychological properties.
(2) Necessarily, if two creatures share all their physical properties then they share all their behavioural dispositions.

The plausibility or otherwise of this 'explanation' is not to the present point. The general point rather is this: if one is a *modal* realist, and seeks to explain the supervenience of *M*-properties on *N*-properties one will need to appeal to some further modally expressed claim about *M*-properties. If one is, in turn, a realist about judgments ascribing *M*-properties then this further claim, deployed in the explanation of the original supervenience doctrine, can be seen as saying something about the 'essential nature' of *M*-facts (facts consisting in the possession of *M*-properties).

We can now return to the moral case and say this: if one is a moral realist, and is also a *modal* realist, then one can only explain the supervenience of the moral on the naturalistic by saying what it is in the essential nature, as it were, of moral facts, that renders (S) true. And, let us assume, as seems quite plausible, that the moral realist cannot do this. Is this an objection to his moral realism? Possibly not. For all that has been said so far, a commitment to an explanation of this sort for (S) would arise not merely from *moral* realism, but from

[13] 'On the Necessity of Origin' *Journal of Philosophy* 73 (1976), pp. 127–35.

[14] For the idea (though deployed rather as an argument for, than as an explanation of, the supervenience of the mental on the physical) see Colin McGinn, *The Character of Mind* (Oxford, 1982), p. 29.

that plus *modal* realism. What we must now ask is: what, in the way of explaining supervenience, can be demanded of a moral realist who is a non-realist about necessity?

The answer, in the abstract, is clear: whatever can in general be demanded of a non-realist explanation of the necessity of some complex judgment (say, of the form 'If *P* then *Q*') compatibly with realism concerning the embedded non-modal propositions (*P*, *Q*, say). But the answer is not very helpful if we as yet lack, as I think we do, a fully worked out account of a global non-realism concerning necessity. So my concluding remarks cannot be as helpful as I should like. Put abstractly the point I should wish to make is this: the non-realist about necessity, in explaining our acceptance of a claim of, say, the form '$\Box(P \rightarrow Q)$', will seek to use facts concerning us, and our practices, as (presumably) they relate to the embedded non-modal judgments *P*, *Q*. And I can see, in principle, no reason why he should not do so, quite compatibly with his being staunchly realist about these non-modal judgments. I suspect that it is only an unacknowledged *modal* realism that leads one to think that the *moral* realist cannot deploy such materials in seeking to explain such supervenience. I wish to suggest this briefly by considering one explanation of supervenience, proffered by Blackburn to the moral realist, and by drawing a possible parallel.

Blackburn supposes, and I shall here agree, that the moral realist can hold that it is an aspect of our thought that we form moral beliefs about things because of their naturalistic properties, and imagines him then attempting to explain supervenience thus:

> it is not possible to hold a belief about one thing because it satisfies some condition, and, at the same time, not hold that belief about another thing which is believed to satisfy the same condition. Therefore, it is not possible to hold a moral belief about a thing, believe a second to be exactly alike in all naturalistic respects, yet at the same time not hold the belief about the thing.

Blackburn comments:

> But this doesn't explain supervenience at all: it merely shows

> the realist putting conditions upon what can be believed to be the truth, not upon what *is* the truth.[15]

I wish to hint at the concealed *modal* realism underlying this last remark by means of the following parallel.

Dr. Edward Craig, in his important paper 'The Problem of Necessary Truth'[16] offers (among other things) an account of our attribution of necessity to certain arithmetical propositions in which a crucial role is played by the claim that we cannot imagine perceiving certain counter-arithmetical situations. Slightly more fully: there are certain combinations of judgments concerning the numbers of objects of certain kinds in certain regions of space which, were they jointly true, would describe a situation counter to our arithmetic. Our view that these combinations of judgments could not possibly be true springs from our inability to imagine situations they would truly describe.

Now this looks like a non-realist account of our appreciation of the necessities and impossibilities in question. (Though that terminology is not, in that paper, Craig's.) And Craig understandably shows no inclination to be a non-realist about the non-modal propositions involved, those stating the number of objects of a certain kind in a given region of space. (In that sense Craig is an '*arithmetical* realist'.) My suggestion now is that if Blackburn's objection to the explanation he proffered to the moral realist is a good one, why should not one equally well object to Craig: that he has merely shown that certain combinations of judgments cannot be *perceived* by us to be true, not that they cannot *be* true? And my further suggestion is that to press such an objection is to appeal, implicitly, to *modal* realism.

Blackburn, I suspect, would himself have no inclination to modal realism. His present line of argument might still be deployed in an *ad hominem* way against a moral realist who embraced modal realism: though even he might brazen it out by remarking that since—on his view of modality—there must be some necessities which are brute, why should not the supervenience of the moral on the naturalistic be one such?

[15] *op. cit.*, p. 115.
[16] In Simon Blackburn (ed.) *Meaning, Reference and Necessity* (Cambridge, 1975).

APPENDIX

Formulating supervenience claims

Claims that a certain type (*M*) of properties supervene on another type (*N*) of properties are most intuitively thought of as 'principles of coincidence', *i.e.* as claims to the effect that if certain objects in certain possible situations (worlds) coincide in all their *N*-type properties then those objects in those situations (worlds) coincide in all their *M*-type properties. Such claims are most perspicuously formulated, as in the body of the text, in a two-sorted (in both orders) second-order language with (i) second-order variables '*N*', '*M*' ranging over *N*- and *M*-type properties respectively, (ii) first-order variables '*x*' '*y*' etc. ranging over the domain of objects which might have the properties in question, and first-order variables '*w*', '*w′*' etc. ranging over possible worlds. We shall also allow ourselves, as in the text, to deploy the world-constant '*a*' to denote the actual world.

The strongest supervenience claim of this sort is clearly this: for any objects *x*, *y*, for any possible worlds *w*, *w′*, if *x* in *w* coincides in all its *N*-type properties with *y* in *w′*, then *x* in *w* coincides in all its *M*-type properties with *y* in *w′*. Using the present mode of formalization, and the system of labelling deployed in the text, this is:

(XYWW′) $(\forall x)(\forall y)(\forall w)(\forall w')([(\forall N)(Nxw \leftrightarrow Nyw') \rightarrow (\forall M)(Mxw \leftrightarrow Myw')]$

Allowing ourselves only the syntactic operations of (i) identifying the object-variables (ii) identifying the world-variables (iii) instantiating a world-variable by 'a' (eschewing such devices as functions from possible worlds to possible worlds) there are only the following seven further weaker principles of coincidence, *viz.*, in the present labelling, (XXWW′), (XYWW), (XYWA), (XXWA), (XYAA), (XXWW), (XXAA). (I ignore trivial variants, *e.g.* (XXAW): the last two of the seven are not, of course, really supervenience claims, being logical truths.) The eight formulations can clearly be mechanically extracted from their labels, as can their logical relations, which are a matter of the most elementary first-order logic. They can be tabulated as follows, the arrows signalling entailment:

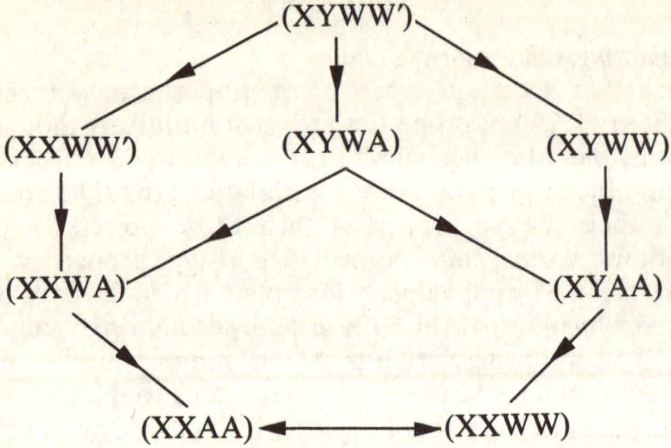

Not everything which has been used to express a supervenience claim in the literature is deductively equivalent to one of the above claims. Thus McGinn, discussing the supervenience of the mental on the physical writes:

> (the thesis of supervenience) . . . seems best captured by means of a condition containing two occurrences of a necessity operator, thus: necessarily, for any mental property instantiated by a creature at a time, there is a physical property the creature instantiates such that, necessarily, if any creature instantiates that physical property, then it instantiates that mental property.[17]

But the cataloguing of the gamut of such 'principles of dependence' (of which we have already met another, *viz.* (L), *i.e.* (L′)) and a discussion of their logical relationships with principles of coincidence is beyond the scope of this appendix.

[17] 'Philosophical Materialism', *Synthese* 44 (1980), p. 197.

VI

The Morality of Deterrence*

1. *Preliminaries*

The title of this session is 'The Morality of Deterrence': but there can be no morality of deterrence as such, or in general. A deters B from doing X if, as a result of A's threatening to do Y if B does X, B refrains from doing X. Whether A was morally justified in so threatening B evidently depends on what he aimed to make B refrain from doing: and on what he threatened to do if B didn't refrain. I shall consider the special case of nuclear deterrence: threats by one state to use nuclear weapons against another state if it does certain things. Indeed, even here I shall consider only a special case. For it is not the nature of the explosive device which raises moral issues. The threat to drop a small nuclear bomb on an enemy submarine located a large distance from any civilian population raises no moral problems not raised by the corresponding threat to drop a so-called conventional bomb. The case I wish to consider is that in which what is threatened is a nuclear onslaught on another power's cities, where it is certain that a consequence will be millions of deaths among the civilian population. The aim of the threat is that of deterring the other power from launching a nuclear first strike against you. It is meant to be part of the content of the threat, and to increase its efficacy, that it is known by the other power that if you carry out your threat millions of the other power's civilians will die. The case is, though special, realistic. Such threats are part of current NATO strategy: Western defence analysts speak of 'mass destruction of Soviet cities' and of 'annihilating an enemy society'. My question is whether the policy of seeking to deter by making such threats is morally justifiable.

* A paper delivered to Birkbeck College students at Cumberland Lodge, Windsor Great Park, in 1987. The paper formed part of a symposium with Roger Scruton. Its purpose was adversarial, and it is possible that Ian McFetridge did not subscribe to all the views advanced in it.

The example is, I just said, realistic. But it is well, if we are to focus clearly on the moral and philosophical issues, *not* to discuss real cases, with real named powers. There the discussion is likely to be befogged by the historical knowledge we presume we have, and our political prejudices. We are not here to discuss whether freedom-loving America is justified in following a strategy of nuclear deterrence against the evil Soviet Empire: nor whether the gallant defenders of socialism may use such threats to deter the capitalist warmongers of the Pentagon. Our question is whether any state would be acting legitimately in using such a threat with the aim of deterring another. To avoid the irrelevant, then, I shall use a fictitious example.

2. *If deterrence fails*

In discussing whether or not it is right to threaten to do something, we should begin by considering whether it would be right, should the need arise, to do the threatened thing. It is not that answering this preliminary question will, by itself, answer our overall question. As we shall see, it might very well be wrong to *do* something which it would be all right to threaten to do. But if doing something is morally O.K., it will rarely be the case that it is wrong to threaten to do it. If a mother does right to smack her child for wandering onto the road, how could it have been wrong to threaten to smack him (with the intention of deterring him from leaving the pavement)? So we must ask if it would be morally acceptable to carry out the kind of nuclear threat we have been considering.

Consider the following imaginary case. The world is dominated by two super-powers, each with its allies, satellites and colonies. They are ideologically in sharp conflict. One state—Eleftheria—supremely values individual freedom: the other—Isotys—values equality. Both try to extend their ideology to other states. Both have had nuclear weapons for some forty years, during which they have followed a policy of seeking to deter a nuclear attack by threatening to respond with a large-scale nuclear counter-attack. The fatal day has arrived. There is an international crisis, and the central committee of the Isotyan ruling party is in emergency session. News arrives that the extremely reliable early warning sytem indicates that an all-out nuclear attack, targeted on Isotyan cities, has just been launched by Eleftheria. In fifteen minutes these cities will be rubble, their millions of inhabitants dead. Time does remain for the Isotyans to launch a full-scale retaliatory attack against the Eleftherian cities, as they have always threatened to do in this eventuality. Would they be morally justified in so doing?

It will be important, in considering this and later questions, to make a broad and crude distinction between two kinds of moral outlook. The first is consequentialist. It holds that the moral assessment of an action, or indeed anything else, depends only on the goodness or badness of the consequences of that action. The paradigm consequentialist position, which is the one I shall consider, is utilitarianism which, at its simplest, says that the goodness or badness of a given outcome is determined by the total amount of individual human happiness or welfare under that outcome. Traditionally opposed to consequentialist views are those the text-books label 'deontological', but this is really too specific to cover the number of different ways one might be a non-consequentialist —which is what I shall call any moral outlook which allows moral appraisals which don't only, or in the extreme case, at all, take consequences into account in morally assessing such things as actions. We shall have an example of such non-utilitarian moral thought in just a moment.

I take it as self-evident that, in almost any circumstances, utilitarianism yields the result that it would be morally *very* wrong for the Isotyan government to carry out their threatened retaliation. Already millions of Isotyans are about to die, millions more to suffer, and this is an enormous loss of human happiness. The killing and suffering of millions of Eleftherians can only add to this disvalue, and there are no counterbalancing goods, utilitarianly speaking. Retaliation will not defend the Isotyans. It would be an act of monstrous wickedness, from this viewpoint, for the Isotyan government to retaliate as they had threatened to do. For the utilitarian, the fact that the Eleftherian government was at least as wicked in launching its first strike is simply irrelevant. To think such a fact *is* relevant is simply to show oneself not to be a utilitarian. Let us try to bring in some non-utilitarian values to see if they yield a different view. Consider the following case. You have been mortally wounded in an unprovoked attack. Your assailant, thinking you dead, turns to leave the scene. You have a gun, and just sufficient strength to fire it and kill him. Are you morally justified in so doing? Of course, in most circumstances the *utilitarian* standpoint will again say 'no'. But we ordinarily deploy a number of non-utilitarian concepts which might be invoked to justify your shooting him. He is guilty of a crime and so deserves punishment. He has grievously harmed you, so you have a right to just retribution. Of course we also typically think that there are good general reasons to forgo individual acts of (capital) punishment or retribution: we set up legal systems to do that. But let us imagine that in this case there is no such system, or it is totally ineffective (making it, of course, more parallel to the international situation). In that case, we might well think that you would be justified in retaliating, even though doing so yields no utilitarianly valuable consequence. You would simply be exercising your right of retaliation.

But even if we accept this, how do we apply it to the international case? There might be two models for how to do so.

a) *Individual model*

A number of individual Eleftherians—most notably the central decision- and policy-makers in the state apparatus—have deliberately unleashed murderous weapons against the Isotyans. They are responsible agents who are guilty of a monstrous crime. Exacting retribution from them is just, even if it does not benefit anyone. Let us grant that. The problem is that while it seems to justify, say, trying and executing the Eleftherian leadership as war criminals, it hardly seems to justify the nuclear retaliation. It is very likely the attack won't even kill the leaders: they will be deep in their well-provisioned shelters. More importantly, it *will* kill millions of innocent civilians. And it is hardly open for the present line to vaunt the value of retribution above that of innocent lives. For the only relevant ground for attaching such a degree of guilt to the act of launching the initial attack would seem to be the loss of innocent life which it entailed.

b) *Neo-Hegelian corporatist model*

On this view, what is waging war against the Isotyans is not a group of individual people—the Eleftherian leaders—but a single super- or corporate person: the Eleftherian state. And the war is also being waged against a person of this category: the state of Isotys. It is the Eleftherian state which is guilty, for it has unprovokedly attacked, indeed is about to destroy the Isotyan state. And it is the latter which has the right to just retribution, which it may enact by retaliating with a massive nuclear strike. The morally relevant description of this act will not be 'killing millions of innocent Eleftherians' but 'wreaking destruction on the guilty Eleftherian state'. Doing that is as justified against such super-persons as individual retribution against individual persons.

Reply: I need not deny the Hegelian ontology. I can accept that much of the conceptual apparatus which applies to individual persons applies to such entities as companies, colleges and states. But I still think that the model cannot be used to bridge the gap between the right of individuals to retaliate and the alleged right of states so to do. I will make two points.

The first is this. Whatever the similarities between individual persons and corporate persons there is still this difference. Corporate persons have parts, or members, who are also (individual) persons. Individual persons do not. This means that moral principles accepted for conduct between individuals cannot be taken over unmodified to the case of conduct between corporate persons, at least not without argument. For the question: how is it appropriate for two persons, which also have parts or members who are persons, to behave towards each other? is not the same question as: how should two individual persons (who do not have persons as parts) behave towards each other. So accepting that individual persons have rights of retaliation, and even accepting that states are corporate persons, does not entail accepting that states have rights of retaliation.

The second point is this. Suppose we did grant that states have rights of retaliation, so that one true description of the act of counter-attacking is 'exercising one's right of retaliation'. Still it cannot be denied that 'killing millions of innocent individuals' is also true of this act. To assess the act we have to assess the relative moral weight of these different descriptions. And why should it be assumed that the now admitted right of the Isotyan state to exact retribution has any chance of outweighing the rights of the millions of Eleftherians to continue living? For after all, they are millions of people, the Isotyan state is only one person, if a big one. But only a Teutonic obsession with size could think that morally relevant. So even if we grant that states, conceived of as persons, have a right of retaliation, it will always be outweighed by the rights of the many individual persons whose death would constitute that retaliation.

I suggest then, that even on a non-utilitarian perspective, it is clear that it would never be morally justified to *carry out* the threat to launch a retaliatory nuclear strike.

3. *Threatening what it would be wrong to do*

Even if we agree with my conclusion that it would always be wrong to carry out such a retaliatory strike, this does not yet settle the question of the rightness or wrongness of a policy of deterrence. For that merely involves the *threat* to carry out such a strike. And it is simply not self-evidently true—and may well be false—that if doing X would always be wrong then threatening that, under certain circumstances, you *would* do X is also wrong. Let us call this principle—that what it's wrong to do it's wrong to threaten to do—the threat principle.

To see that this principle is not self-evidently true, consider again a utilitarian moral theory. This theory may be false, but is not self-evidently so. And if utilitarianism is true, then the threat principle is certainly false. For, on that view, the rightness or wrongness of doing X is determined by the consequences (in the circumstances) of doing X: while the rightness or wrongness of *threatening* to do X is determined by the consequences, in the circumstances, of the quite different action *threatening to do X*. And there are plenty of circumstances in which the consequences of doing X may be very bad, while the consequences of threatening to do X may be very good. Indeed that is precisely the view of most nuclear deterrers. The consequences of launching a nuclear attack are horrendous. The consequences of threatening that, if attacked, one will counterattack, are (it is hoped) very good: *viz* of preventing the launching of such an attack. As long as utilitarianism remains in play as a moral position, appeal to the threat principle as an argument against such deterrence will have no force.

Can we find alternative arguments against such policies of deterrence?

To make progress we must, I think, get a little clearer about what is involved in A's threatening B that he'll do X (this includes the case where X is conditional—doing Y if p). What follows is a bit of conceptual analysis.

i) Must A intend to do X? No. A may be bluffing. Insincere threats are still threats.

ii) Must B believe A will do X? No. A may threaten, and B, rightly or wrongly, not take him at his word.

iii) Must A intend B to believe that he (A) will do X? Yes. If I say to you, later on tonight, that I'll give you bad marks for your ethics essay unless you succumb to my lusts, *making it clear that I'm joking*, I've not threatened you.

iv) Must A intend B to recognize his intention that B believe that A will do X? Yes. You and I have had a row. I leave various weapons I own where you can find them, by chance, as you think. I intend you to believe that I'll kill you. But I've not threatened to kill you: for I didn't intend you to, nor did you, recognize my intention that you believe that I will kill you.

(Cognoscenti will realize we can ask more complicated questions along these lines. Threatening has a Gricean structure.)

v) Must A believe that B doesn't want him to do X? Yes. If the sadist, smacking his lips, says to his masochist friend: if you go on like that, I'll whip you—he's not threatening him, only pretending to. The real threat would be to say: if you go on like that I won't whip you.

In summary: A threatens B with doing X iff

> A acts with the intention that:
> (i) B believes that A will do X
> (ii) B recognizes this intention, and
> (iii) B comes to believe that A will do X in part in virtue of this recognition, where
> (iv) A believes that B does not want A to do X.

The crux of threatening, then, is acting with the intention to bring about a belief. So our question about nuclear deterrence becomes: is one state A morally justified in acting with the intention that another state B believe that A will, if nuclearly attacked, launch a nuclear counterattack?

One's first thought here is that there cannot be a *general* answer to this question. For there are many different ways of acting with that intention, with morally significant differences between them. The most striking difference is that between strategies involving bluff—the deterrer lacks either the capacity or the intention to carry out the threat—and those where the deterrer has both the capacity and the intention to carry out the threat. But my second thought is that there *can* be a general argument against acting with that intention. I shall try to develop it after a few remarks about the morality of the bluffing and of the intending deterrer. By then we shall have identified, I believe, the position which presents the real challenge to the opponent of nuclear deterrence.

To be blunt, the problem with the strategy of bluff is not a moral, but a practical one. It won't work. In these days of spies, moles and surveillance satellites, a state which lacked the weapons, or had not genuinely embodied in her hardware and command structures the intention to retaliate would not convince a potential enemy that it would, if attacked, retaliate. Deterrence, as a matter of fact, requires the intention, if attacked, to retaliate.

At this point many a non-consequentialist will scent victory over the deterrer. For if, as we've argued, it would be evil, even if attacked, to retaliate then surely it must be evil to intend, if attacked, to retaliate. The intention principle—if it would be wrong to do X it is wrong to intend to do X—is, surely, more plausible than the earlier threat principle. Indeed we might try mounting the following argument for the intention principle as central to our moral assessment of agents. The starting point would be the idea that it is relevant to the moral assessment of an agent to consider not merely how he acts in the circumstances he *does* encounter in his life, but how he *would* act in circumstances he could, but as a matter of fact won't, encounter.

Consider now the deterrer. His overall aim is to avoid war:

his method to display to the enemy the intention that if attacked, he will retaliate. If we morally rebuke him for having the evil intention of killing millions of citizens if attacked, he replies that he has that intention becauses he believes that by having it he will prevent a nuclear attack ever being perpetrated. If his policy is successful—as he has good reason to think it will be—he will never have to do anything evil. And his having had that conditional intention will have produced a great good. Let us suppose that his main belief turns out true: he is never attacked and so never has to use the bomb. Call him the successful deterrer.

Consider now the unsuccessful deterrer. He was exactly the same character, intentions etc. as the successful deterrer, but lives in a less fortunate world. He has, for example, a stupid opponent who risks a first strike. True to his intentions, the unlucky deterrer retaliates, thereby performing an action of monstrous evil. The idea of a moment ago then says: the moral assessment of the character and intentions of the lucky and the unlucky deterrer cannot differ. For their character and intentions are the same. Had the successful deterrer been in the unsuccessful deterrer's shoes, he too would have performed an act of monstrous evil. He is merely lucky in not having had to face the situation in which he acted on his (conditional) intentions. But that cannot change the moral assessment of such intentions. The very fact that they could, in unlucky circumstances, issue in extreme evil, shows that even if, luckily, they do not *actually* issue in such evil, they are wicked intentions.

Along such lines, I believe, a powerful argument could be made for the wrongness of intending—even if only conditionally and for the sake of an overall good—to retaliate if attacked. But it is a line of thought that can and will be resisted by the clear-headed consequentialist. For a striking feature of consequentialism is what might be termed its *actualism*. In morally judging an action, an institution, a trait of character, only its *actual* consequences are relevant. It is simply not morally relevant, according to this position, to consider what would have happened if something, which didn't *actually* happen *had* happened. The successful deterrer's policy is justified by its success: the unsuccessful deterrer's strategy is damned by its failure. It is this hard-line consequentialist actualism which provides the greatest difficulty for one trying to show that in general, and in principle, nuclear deterrence is morally unjustified.

Of course, it may well be that, as a matter of fact, given the circumstances, such a policy is, even on utilitarian grounds, unjustified. This would depend on such things as the estimate of the risk of accidental launch: the complicated calculations of strategists and war-gamesters on the success of the policy; and so on. But is there anything *intrinsic* to nuclear deterrence which could show even the hard line utilitarian that it was morally unjustified? I shall briefly try to suggest something.

Lying behind the consequentialist's actualism is the following idea: what is actually the case can have effects, consequences and so be morally relevant: what merely would have been the case if . . . cannot have such consequences. O.K. But people's *beliefs* about what would happen if . . . *are* actual states of affairs in the world and can have very significant consequences. As we saw, the crux of nuclear deterrence is acting with the aim of producing such a counterfactual belief in the opponent: *viz.* the belief that were he to attack, you would massively retaliate. That is, you have to get him to believe you would be prepared, in such circumstances, to do something morally monstrous. And, if you succeed, he will believe that you are prepared so to act. But such a policy is bound, even if it succeeds in its central aim of deterring nuclear attack, to produce endless *other* moral disasters.

Let me instance just two. A deterring power must have an intention which, if acted on, would produce the most appalling consequences: and it must convince the opposing power that it has such an intention. Such a power is unlikely to be, and cannot afford to be seen to be, too morally scrupulous in its conduct of 'small' conventional wars. If it is, and is seen to be, prepared to accept moral limits on the conduct of small wars, how likely is it that it will be, and be believed to be, capable of the massive breach of moral limits which nuclear retaliation would involve. This consequence of deterrence had been sadly noted by the more intelligent Eleftherians and Isotyans. Prior to their nuclear period, they had accepted, both by word and deed, certain rules of war: concerning such matters as legitimate targets, banned weapons and the intervention, without declaration of war, in the internal affairs of other states. As the state of nuclear deterrence went on, these were increasingly abandoned. Both powers were found deploying chemical weapons and mass deportation against the civilian populations of states they had invaded without any declaration of war. They couldn't afford to be seen not to do such things. For if they were not prepared to do those things in opposing the hated enemy ideology, how could they be believed to be prepared to commit the ultimate moral obscenity of nuclear retaliation?

The second consequence of successful deterrence is this. Each side must believe the other is prepared to do something which would be of unparalleled moral depravity. But if they are capable of *that* then, by the principle of the unity of the vices (if you've got one you've got them all) each side is unlikely to estimate the other's moral character in general very highly. In particular, neither side will expect the other to have the virtue of honesty. Hence neither side will expect the other to keep a treaty if it is in his interest to break it. Hence either it will be almost impossible for the two sides to come to sign a treaty; or, if signed, both sides will firmly believe that the other is breaking it, and hence will feel free to break it themselves. Again this is what the Eleftherians and Isotyans found. They did not, in fact, engage in nuclear war. In my earlier example it was found, in the nick of time, that the early warning system was faulty. Deterrence continued and preserved nuclear peace. But the consequences of that peace were literally devastating.

VII

Realism and Anti-Realism in an Historical Context

*Editorial Note**

The following essay derives from a symposium within a conference on *Realism and Reason* held in 1988. It is in part a response to the paper read by the other symposiast (John Haldane) which is entitled 'Mind/World Identity Theory and the Anti-Realist Challenge'.

The latter essay explores something of the relationship between various 'realisms' (ontological, epistemological and semantic) in connection with ideas drawn from the work of Thomas Aquinas. It proposes that commitments to the existence of a mind-independent, 'self-structured' world and to the capacity of thought to engage directly with that world do not of themselves imply a thesis which has been the target of recent semantic anti-realist challenges, *i.e.* that truth is, in principle, (possibly) recognition-transcendent.

The version of Realism discussed in the essay is an unfamiliar one. It maintains *both* that thought and world are independent, and that concepts and what they (re)present are intrinsically connected. Concepts are the structuring principles of thought, just as forms or natures are the structuring principles of the world. The expression 'mind/world identity theory' arises because of the further claim that concepts and forms are the very same entities actualised in two modes of exemplification. This proposal derives from Aquinas' striking thesis that in cognition the thinker becomes, in a certain manner, *identical* with that of which he thinks, *i.e.* to the extent that it is one and the same principle which informs, or determines the nature of his thought (*in esse intentionale*) and its objects (*in esse naturale*).

The two essays by Haldane and McFetridge are to be published, together with other papers deriving from the same conference, in John Haldane and Crispin Wright (eds) *Realism, Reason and Projection*,

* This is the *second* draft of an essay composed out of material drawn from 3 sources: (1) a paper titled: 'Realisms and Anti-Realisms', written largely in 1977 and amended in 1982, and again at some more recent date—a caveat added then reads '. . . Descendants will be either/or more historical/more up-to-date . . .'; (2) a paper titled: 'Realism in an Historical Context', delivered (in reply to mine) at a conference on Realism and Reason held in the University of St Andrews in March 1988; and (3) correspondence (with me) dated 9th June 1987. (J.H.)

Mind Association Occasional Series (Oxford: Oxford University Press, 1991).

(J.H.)

I

John Haldane's essay raises a special case of a general question.[1] To what extent do contemporary discussions of, and attacks on, realism, engage with various historical positions which we might wish to place beneath that heading? Are certain traditional realist positions under attack from contemporary *semantic* anti-realism? No, replies Haldane, for there is a position—that of Aquinas—which embraces distinctively realist theses in ontology and epistemology, but which *need not* be committed to a central target of (at any rate some versions of) such anti-realism: that the truth conditions of sentences can be such as to transcend all possibility of verification. In characterising Aquinas as a realist, despite his alleged rejection of such a notion of truth, Haldane is implicitly rejecting Dummettian claims as to how realism should be formulated. I wish to look at aspects of these claims and at a certain historical thesis which Dummett has enunciated. Part of my aim will be to suggest certain initial difficulties in applying the Dummettian characterization of realism (or anti-realism) to some earlier views one might naturally regard as 'realist' (or anti-realist). So I agree with Haldane's conclusion that there is some question as to whether Dummett's attacks on realism engagc with certain historical positions.

In connection with this I want to explore a number of strands in, or forms of, realism and their inter-connections. For, I shall suggest, there is some unclarity concerning the point or points in realism on which the new anti-realism focuses—an unclarity, therefore, concerning the positive views of contemporary anti-realists. A further aim will be to provide some historical allusions which may then at least partially justify Dummett's claim to be discussing, in a new guise, an ancient dispute in metaphysics.

Dummett has repeatedly urged that disputes about realism with respect to a particular segment of reality should be best

[1] See J. Haldane, 'Mind/World Identity and the Anti-Realist Challenge', forthcoming in *Realism, Reason and Projection*, edited by John Haldane and Crispin Wright (Oxford: Clarendon, 1991).

seen as raising questions about the appropriate notion of truth for sentences which have that segment of reality as their subject-matter. So seen, he further argues, disputes about realism, and about particular realisms, will concern the kind of meaning possessed by sentences in general, or by particular classes of sentences. A central issue, and a number of important sub-issues, in metaphysics will devolve to the theory of meaning.

In the course of developing these views, Dummett and others have made a number of historical remarks. A central one has been that though the approach to the issues is new, the issues themselves are old ones: though the conception of realism came into sharp focus only with Frege, there had been many realists before him. Crispin Wright remarks that 'Dummett's interpretation of realism, and the kind of general anti-realist criticism of it which he presents, are put forward by way of a recommended *Übersicht* on a significant class of disputes in traditional and modern philosophy'.[2] These, however, are large and vague claims. What are the adequacy conditions on recommending an *Übersicht*? How many, and which, debates should be illuminated? In the present context it seems appropriate to begin by raising some rather general questions about how we are to apply Dummett's characterizations of realism to positions formulated independently of his overall characterisation.

Both Dummett's and Wright's remarks suggest that the *Übersicht* is meant to cast light on historically occupied positions earlier than the analytical tradition, that is, prior to Frege. It is notable, though, that when Dummett relates his *Übersicht* to the *details* of positions occupied and arguments deployed prior to, and independently of, his own suggested formulations, these positions he discusses are almost invariably within the analytical tradition. Realist and opposed views of the material world are exemplified in debates, beginning in the 30s, between phenomenalists and their opponents; issues about mental states inspired by the search—largely stimulated by Wittgenstein's *Philosophical Investigations*—to formulate a satisfactory position in the philosophy of mind between (so-called) Cartesianism and behaviourism. Now a feature of these historical debates is that they were already largely conducted within the presup-

[2] C. Wright, *Realism, Meaning and Truth* (Oxford: Blackwell, 1987), p. 9.

position which Dummett claims to be the hall-mark of analytical philosophy and which it owes, in his view, to Frege, *viz*., that the prime task of philosophy is the analysis of thought, and that it is only by the analysis of *language* that we can analyse thought. Characteristic of the debate on phenomenalism were such questions as: Is a sense-datum language possible? Can sentences about material objects be translated into such a language? Of the debate in the philosophy of mind: how do words for mental states acquire a meaning? Do they function differently in first- and third-person ascriptions? Applying the Dummettian *Übersicht* to such positions and debates can therefore be relatively straightforward. It will consist in relating the particular accounts offered of the meaning of the sentences descriptive of the disputed area to the general positions about meaning which Dummett holds to be characteristic of realism and anti-realism.

II

I wish, though, to raise some questions concerning how the *Übersicht* is to be applied to earlier philosophical positions not formulated within the presuppositions of the analytical tradition. We may begin, then, by asking: is realism, as characterised by Dummett, *essentially* a doctrine concerning the correct conception of a theory of meaning for a language, or for particular fragments of a language? Or, alternatively, does it consist of one or more doctrines which though, in Dummett's view, they *should* be debated via questions concerning the nature of a theory of meaning, can at least be stated independently of answers to such questions? Dummett often suggests the former. A fairly recent case is in *The Interpretation of Frege's Philosophy*. He suggests there that 'full-fledged realism' should consist in the 'adoption, for the statements in question . . . of a truth-conditional theory of meaning taking as its base a completely unmodified classical two-valued semantics'[3]—a conception of the theory of meaning which we owe to Frege.

But if realism just *is* that, then it is hard to see how to ask

[3]M. Dummett, *The Interpretation of Frege's Philosophy* (London: Duckworth, 1982).

pointfully if such historical figures as Descartes, Berkeley, or Kant were or were not *realists*, either globally or locally. They may have had views about meaning, but they certainly had no explicit conception, realist or otherwise, of a theory of meaning in the sense here intended, *viz.* a systematic description of what is involved in understanding a language.

Perhaps, then, we ought to take the second option noted above, that is, to conceive of realism as some doctrine or doctrines which, though they *can* be seen to flow from a certain 'realist' conception of theories of meaning, can at least be formulated independently of that conception—of bivalence, say, or the possibility of verification-transcendent truth. The question would then be whether, consistently with their explicit metaphysical or epistemological doctrines, particular earlier philosophers could or could not have adopted these allegedly distinctively realist theses—of whether their positions commit them to realist theses. And it is in fact in these terms that Dummett generally couches his remarks concerning the classification, in terms of his *Übersicht*, of such philosophers as Berkeley or Kant as realists or otherwise. For example, Dummett suggests that when considering Berkeley's final position, with the role assigned to God therein, he ought probably to be classified as a sophisticated realist; though concentrating merely on the phenomenalist-reductionist strand in his thought one might be inclined to view him as an anti-realist about the sensible world. Dummett does not spell out the reasoning underlying these attributions, but in the light of his discussion of phenomenalism elsewhere the point would be that without God, Berkeley is not, but with God he is, entitled to assert the Principle of Bivalence for statements about the sensible world.[4] This application of the Dummettian *Übersicht* requires then that we can detach from a realist conception of a theory of meaning a thesis—here bivalence—which can be taken as distinctive of

[4] In Berkeley's position minus God, any statement about sensible objects must, if true, be true in virtue either of the actual perception, by finite spirits, of appropriate ideas; or, a relatively fitful theme, of the truth of certain subjunctive conditionals concerning what ideas would be perceived, under appropriate conditions, by finite spirits. But, at least on the assumption that such subjunctive conditionals cannot be barely true, this conception of physical reality gives no grounds for the view that for each statement concerning it, there is something in virtue of which it or its negation is true. Consequently, there are no grounds for asserting of each such statement that it is

realism, and ask, concerning an historical philosopher, whether his conception of a certain segment of reality would or would not allow him, or would require him, to embrace that thesis.

A number of critics of Dummett, however, have suggested that what is crucial in his semantic characterization of realism, and in his exposition of what he sees as its serious difficulties, is not bivalence but rather a commitment to a notion of truth under which a statement can be true even if we lack the ability to determine that it is. Again, it seems that if we are to apply such a characterization to pre-Fregean philosophers, we must detach this claim from the further one that such a notion of truth can be used as the central notion of a theory of meaning. This done, it would then seem very natural to characterise Locke, for example, as an arch-realist concerning many aspects of reality. Book IV of the *Essay* abounds with expressions of the thought that contingent, but in many cases irremovable, limitations on our cognitive capacities can debar us from knowing, or even having a conception of, aspects of reality of which, nevertheless, his overall view of reality, in particular his corpuscularianism, compels him to acknowledge the existence. He not only acknowledges that how things are may transcend our ability to determine how things are; he has a picture of the nature of reality, and of our modes of acquiring that knowledge of it, which provides an *explanation* of why reality can outstrip our capacities for knowledge. A clear example is provided by claims about the necessary 'connexions and repugnancies' between the qualities and powers of substances:

---

determinately true or false. Bivalence will fail for such statements. To the extent that Dummett wishes to view the acceptability of bivalence as the hallmark of realism, Berkeley emerges as an anti-realist about the sensible world. The thought would then be that this verdict might change when, in the full picture, God enters. Of course the detailed interpretation of the role of God in Berkeley's philosophy is controversial. But on any view, features of God—be it his perception of, or conception of, an idea-constituted physical realm, or his standing intention to produce appropriate ideas in appropriate circumstances—can be seen as massively extending the range of that in virtue of which statements about the sensible world can be true. The suggestion would be that it would at least be consistent for Berkeley to hold that the features of God in question extended that range sufficiently to render determinately true or false each of the relevant statements concerning the sensible world; that is, on the present conception, to embrace realism with respect to that world.

> Because the active and passive powers of bodies, and their ways of operating, consisting in a texture and motion of parts which we cannot by any means come to discover; it is but in very few cases we can be able to perceive their dependence on, or repugnance to any of those ideas which make our complex one of that sort of things. I have here instanced in the corpuscularian hypotheses, as that which is thought to go furthest in an intelligible explication of those qualities of bodies; and I fear the weakness of human understanding is scarce able to substitute another, which will afford us a fuller and clearer discovery of the necessary connexion and co-existence of the powers which are to be observed united in several sorts of them. This at least is certain, that, whichever hypothesis be clearest and truest . . . our knowledge concerning corporal substances will be very little advanced by any of them, till we are made to see what qualities and powers of bodies have a *necessary* connexion or repugnancy one with another; which in the present state of philosophy I think we know but to a very small degree: and I doubt whether, with those faculties we have, we shall ever be able to carry our general knowledge . . . in this part much further.[5]

It would be natural to think that this position is realism in Dummett's sense concerning necessary connexions and repugnancies between qualities and powers. For it seems precisely to be the claim that these (alleged) aspects of reality can transcend what we can know, even what we could have evidence for. Locke here, unlike Aquinas on Haldane's account, appears to derive from his ontology and epistemology a position vulnerable to attacks from contemporary 'semantic' anti-realism. But one may ask whether in fact Locke's position is so vulnerable. Is Locke here committed to a doctrine about truth which cannot resist the pressure of the kinds of criticisms developed by Dummett and others?

It might seem obvious that he is. Locke's conception of reality, in part derived from contemporary science and his conception of how we can have (what he would call) knowledge, clearly commits him to instances of the following schema:

[5] Locke, *An Essay concerning Human Understanding* edited by A.S. Pringle-Pattison (Oxford: Clarendon 1934) IV, iii, 16.

I It could be that (*p* although we could not know that *p*). Indeed, allowing for the unLockean terminology, he would seem also to be committed to instances of:

II It could be that (*p* although we could have no evidence that *p*).

The particular object-language instances of these schemata do not involve the concept of truth. But to derive from them a commitment to the view that truth can transcend the possibility of verification seems merely to require the acceptability of semantic ascent, licensed by the equivalence, in some sense, of *S* and '*S* is true'. Deploying that, we have Locke committed to many instances of:

III It could be that (*S* is true although we could not know, or have evidence that, *S* is true).

This commitment obviously derives directly from Locke's view of reality and our epistemic relation to it. The question which arises, therefore, is whether the derivability, in this way of instances of III constitutes a commitment to what the Dummettian *Übersicht* would call realism?

There is, I think, at least some reason for doubting that it does. Suppose that III did express something which could be undermined in Dummettian style by considerations concerning what acceptable account can be given of the meaning of the sentences (*S*) involved. This would require that instances of III could be acceptable (true) only under an unacceptable account of the meaning of *S*; but could be seen to be unacceptable (false) when this was replaced by an acceptable account of the meaning of *S*. This can only be so, however, if the applicability or otherwise of the notion of truth involved in III to a sentence *S* depends on what *S* means—that is, on what account of the meaning of *S* is acceptable. It might appear that the claim that this is so is the merest platitude. As Crispin Wright puts it: '. . . truth-values cannot be settled unilaterally, as it were, by the world alone but are a function simultaneously of the meanings of the statements to which they attach'.[6] Whether or not *S* is true in certain circumstances must surely depend on what *S*

[6] C. Wright, *Realism, Meaning and Truth, op.cit.*, p. 5.

means. Hence issues about the applicability of the concept of truth and the properties it can legitimately be taken to possess must be, in part, answerable to questions about what account of the meanings of the sentences to which it applies is acceptable.

However, it is just the apparent platitude elaborated by Wright which should be questioned in the context of assessing the applicability of the Dummettian *Übersicht* to a pre-Fregean philosophical position such as that held by Locke. For to accept it is to prevent semantic ascent from being an innocent way of deriving semantically-expressed theses about the relation of reality to us and our powers of cognition from their object-language correlates. Consider such minimal anti-idealist claims as that the existence of Venus is independent of our existence, that is, that Venus would have existed even if we had not. Does this commit its holder to the semantic claim that the truth of the sentence 'Venus exists' is independent of our existence? If it does, then the notion of truth deployed in it cannot be subject to the platitude that its applicability to a sentence depends on facts about what meaning (and hence that *a* meaning) has been conferred upon it by us. If the notion of truth here did conform to the alleged platitude, what would then be the falsehood, *viz.* that the truth of that sentence was independent of our existence, could not be a consequence of the minimal anti-idealist claim that Venus' existence was likewise independent. It seems here that, if the object-language claim has the semantic one as its consequence, then the notion of truth in the latter must no more involve commitments about what *S* means, or the conditions of *S* meaning what it does, than the object-language sentence *S* itself does.

The question, then, is whether there is any such innocent notion of truth, and the answer is surely that there is, *viz*., that identified by Quine as a device of disquotation, a means of semantic descent. Wishing to assert each of an infinite set of sentences (for example, all the instances of a logical schema) I am debarred from doing it straightforwardly. I need a device for infinite conjunction. Saying 'each of these sentences is true' provides me with such a device. But it would not serve that purpose if, in deploying it, I was undertaking commitments concerning the meaning attached to the instances of the schema, the sentences to which I am applying the notion, commitments not undertaken by the piecemeal assertion of particular instances.

We can suggest now that if Locke, say, is committed to there being verification-transcendent truths—instances of III—simply by his commitment to object-language instances of I and II, then the notion of truth involved in the former should be seen as purely disquotational. It no more involves him in commitments about the kind of meaning possessed by the sentences in question than he is so involved by their unquoted deployment in I and II. In particular, then, he would seem not to be committed to the central target of Dummettian anti-realism: that our grasp of the meanings of sentences is constituted by knowing under what—possibly verification-transcendent—conditions they would be true. If this is so, then mere commitment to III is not enough to constitute realism as characterised in Dummett's *Übersicht*.

III

Related to the question whether Locke's position on necessary connexions and repugnancies between qualities and powers is realist in *Dummett's* special sense, is the issue of the general tenability of Lockean realism, and other historical views which Dummett claims can be placed within the class of philosophical positions against which he has mounted an anti-realist challenge. Here, I wish to distinguish two kinds of philosophical position which deserve the name realism.[7] I shall call them '*subject-matter realism*' and '*realism with respect to representations*'.

Subject-matter realism is expressed in a loose array of thoughts about reality and our place in it. At its most abstract, it consists in the vague thought that how things are in the world is not, in general, dependent on the existence of, or facts about,

[7] Distinguishing versions of realism and idealism is, of course, an old game which Kant, and many others, have played. I shall not try to relate *my* distinctions to those of other writers—particularly not to that of Kant. I increasingly feel that Kant's account of his distinction—between 'empirical' and 'transcendental' realisms and idealisms—is so intertwined with his whole philosophy that subsequent writers' appropriation of his terms rarely embodies more than a loose and unhelpful analogy with his deployment of them.

human beings or other subjects of experience. In particular, how things are in the world is, in general, independent of facts about the cognitive states and capacities of human beings or subjects of experience—independent not merely of the *actual* states of such beings but also of any *possible* states of such beings.

The filling out of such a doctrine at any stage in the history of philosophy will be conditioned by the then current paradigm of a cognitive state and its concomitant notion of how things are in the world—its notion of the 'object' of such a state. Thus, for the bulk of 17th and 18th century epistemology, the model cognitive state was that of *perception* (perceiving *things* rather than perceiving *that*); and the associated notion of how things are was the rather specialised one of an object's existing. In such a framework, subject-matter realism will typically take the form of the thought that the existence of an object is not, in general, dependent on its being the object of any actual (or possible) perceptual state of any human or other conscious subject. Subject-matter anti-realism will accordingly be the denial of that thought. (Clearly weaker and stronger denials are possible.)[8] *Idealism*, if we are going to be strict, is then that special version of anti-realism which emerges in the present framework when, as typically in the 17th and 18th centuries, its ground for denying this version of realism starts from the thought that the only possible objects of perception are entities—*ideas*—the existence of which is dependent on their being objects of perception.

In post-Fregean analytical philosophy, the paradigm cognitive state is, rather, propositional knowledge, knowledge that *p*: and the concomitant notion of how things are in the world is the notion of such and such's being the case.[9] For us, then, subject-matter realism will typically take the form of the thought that something's being the case is not, in general, dependent on any human being's (or other knowing subject's)

[8] In this connection see Haldane's remarks about acceptance or rejection of the strong and weak versions of ontological and epistemological realism as he defines them in his essay: Haldane *op.cit.*, section II.

[9] This notion is sometimes equated with that of the obtaining or existing of a state of affairs. I am inclined to resist any such equation, however, on grounds of suspicion of the ontology of states of affairs.

knowing, or being capable of knowing that it is the case. An adherent of subject-matter realism will thus be prepared to assent to numerous instances of the schema:

(SR) It could be that *p* even though no human being or knowing subject knows, or could know, *p*.

The *global* subject-matter anti-realist will, quite generally, deny this. That is, he will commit himself to accepting all instances of the schema:

(SAR) If *p*, then it could be known (by a human being or subject of experience) that *p*.

Neither realists nor anti-realists of the present kind need be global. They may accept or reject instances of (SR) involving only a limited range of substitutions for '*p*'. Again, the nature of the dispute, be it local or global, can be highly sensitive to the interpretation of the modality 'could be known' in (SR), and to the limitations, if any, to be imposed on the knowing subjects alluded to therein. These matters have been extensively discussed, again most notably by Dummett and Wright. But for the purposes of this paper these issues can largely be ignored; though I shall later make some comments about one form of selective anti-realism—anti-realism with respect to the subject-matter of mathematics.

I wish now to consider one interpretation of the realist schema which appears to put certain instances of it in a very strong position, and hence puts the corresponding *global* anti-realism in a very weak position.

Subject-matter realists are prepared to assert instances of: *it could be that p although no human being or knowing subject could know that p*. Consider the claim as one about the capacities of knowledge possessed by human beings, given how they and the world actually are. Then the resulting version of realism would seem to be, for many substitutions for '*p*', an expression of a number of modal facts which form part of, or are grounded in, our common-sense-cum-scientific view of the world. They are, in Strawson's phrase—'parts of what it is now fashionable to call our general *theory* of the world'.[10]

[10] Strawson, 'Scruton and Wright on Anti-Realism *etc.*' *Proceedings of the Aristotelian Society,* Vol. 77, 1976/7.

We know enough about the natural world, ourselves, and, most importantly, our means of acquiring knowledge of the natural world, to render many instances of the above schema, as currently interpreted, overwhelmingly plausible. We know enough, that is, to know that nothing about the world, or ourselves, guarantees that we must, in general, have the capacity to determine how things are in the world. Thus, to take the vexed example of the past, we know that knowledge of it can be acquired only if the past state of affairs has left sufficient, and sufficiently cognitively transparent, causal descendants which are now, or will become, accessible to us. And we know that such causal descendants are, given how the world is, sadly vulnerable to irrecoverable elimination. We know, therefore, that it is perfectly possible that, for example, the Venerable Bede should have died on such-and-such a day even though things are now such that nothing remains on the basis of which we could determine this. Thus the discovery, which we could well make (perhaps have made) that we shall never gain sufficient information to determine that he did die on such-and-such a day is quite insufficient—as it would not be on the anti-realist conception—to establish that he did *not* die on that day. (And the point can be extended to other cases anti-realists tend to insist on.)

In general, then, we have knowledge of the world and of our own modes of cognitive access to it which enables us to see, in many cases, not merely that the realist possibility of epistemic inaccessibility is an abstract philosophical possibility, but also how and why it is repeatedly realised.

Given the entrenchment of what I am calling subject-matter realism in our view—our theory—of the world and ourselves, it seems to be a *reductio ad absurdum* of any philosophy if it ends up simply denying such cases of (SR). This is not to say that they cannot be denied: but to deny them could not be a merely philosophical enterprise. Rather, they could only be denied by one who was prepared and able to reconstruct our current common-sense-cum-scientific accounts of the world which serve to explain why, and hence justify the claim that, the present version of realism is, in many cases, true.

Returning to Berkeley, in the present perspective he may be seen as a model subject-matter anti-realist, a model rarely followed. The realism Berkeley opposed held that, in general, the existence of an object was not dependent on its being an object of actual or possible perception. Now as was seen above in connection with Locke, one scientific underpinning of that realism, in the 17th century, was an account of the world, and of our perception of it, in which a crucial role was assigned to essentially imperceptible corpuscular constituents of the material world. And Berkeley, quite correctly, saw himself as committed to denying not merely certain 'philosophical' claims of his realist opponents but also the above component of contemporary science.

IV

I have so far hardly related the doctrine I am calling subject-matter anti-realism to the views of contemporary anti-realists. Deliberately so: for as we shall later see, there is considerable unclarity—and not, I think, merely on my part—concerning whether or not their views do reject what I am calling subject-matter realism. But that Dummett does seem disposed to reject it, while misunderstanding its underpinnings, emerges in his response to similar thoughts expressed by Strawson. Reflecting on Dummett's approach to anti-realism, Strawson wrote:

> Certainly the route *into* the areas is comparatively new: the new anti-realism starts from certain views on mathematical truth and mathematical discourse and seeks to generalise them to the extent of advancing counterpart views on discourse concerning the natural world. . . . There is a certain initial air of paradox about this approach; for I suppose that part at least of the appeal of anti-realist views about pure mathematics lay precisely in the *contrast* between the content of that science and the subject-matters of history, geography, natural science and ordinary chat; that it lay precisely in the view that the notion of a realm of facts waiting to be explored, some parts of which might, indeed would, remain undisclosed or be irrecoverably lost sight of, (a matter of speculation or uncertain inference)—that any such notion was quite improperly imported into mathematics from its natural home, *viz*. the natural world.[11]

After quoting this passage in the Preface to his *Truth and*

[11] *ibid.*, pp. 17–18.

Other Enigmas, Dummett seeks to 'dispel this air of paradox' by, in effect, repeating several of the arguments of his 'The Philosophical Basis of Intuitionist Logic', reprinted in the same volume. I can best approach Dummett's response to Strawson, and suggest that it involves a misunderstanding on Dummett's part, by first rehearsing the relevant issues and arguments of that paper.

In the first part of the essay Dummett was concerned with two kinds of issues arising between Platonists and intuitionists in the philosophy of mathematics. The first concerns the status of mathematical *objects*, the intuitionist maintaining that they are 'mental constructions'. The dispute is one concerning realism about the subject-matter of mathematics conducted within a framework like that of 17th and 18th century epistemology. The issue is whether the existence of mathematical objects is or is not dependent on their being the objects of actual or possible human cognitive states. The second issue concerns the nature of mathematical *truth*, and the role it has to play, if any, in an account of our grasp of the meaning of mathematical statements. The Platonist holds that to understand a mathematical statement is to grasp under what conditions it would be true, where it is held that a mathematical statement can be true quite independently of whether or not we could, by means of a proof, determine that it was. The intuitionist holds, rather, that:

> . . . the notion of *truth*, considered as a feature which each mathematical statement either determinately possesses or determinately lacks, independently of our means of recognising its truth-value, cannot be the central notion for a theory of the meanings of mathematical statement.[12]

The Platonist, on this second issue, would appear to be committed to realism with respect to the subject-matter of mathematics, as expressed in the 20th century framework. He would seem to be prepared to assert mathematical instances of: it could be that *p* even though we could not know that *p*. And the intuitionist would appear, on Dummett's account of the

[12] Dummett, 'The Philosophical Basis of Intutitionistic Logic' in *Truth and Other Enigmas* (London: Duckworth, 1978) p. 225.

matter, to reject this for the mathematical case: to hold, that is, that for mathematical *p*: if *p*, then it could be known (*via* a proof) that *p*.

Now at one stage Dummett raises the question whether we can settle the second dispute between the Platonist and the intuitionist *via* settling the first: can we find grounds for accepting one of the opposed views of the *objects* of mathematics, and *thereby* find grounds for the corresponding (as it seems) view of mathematical *truth*? And Dummett argues, to my mind convincingly, that such an attempt would fail on two counts. First, there may be no way of explicating the metaphors involved in the opposed pictures of mathematical objects except *via* their apparent expression in divergent views of mathematical truth. Secondly, and more importantly, there is no valid move from the Platonist view of mathematical objects to the Platonist view of mathematical truth, nor from the intuitionists' view of mathematical objects to their view of mathematical truth. For, he claims, both the following positions are internally consistent: i) mathematical objects are 'mind-independent' but there are no undiscoverable mathematical truths; ii) mathematics treats of 'mental constructions', but there could be truths about these which we are incapable of determining. (One might be encouraged to think that the latter position is consistent by asking the question: was Berkeley, by his view of the status of sensible objects, committed to the view that all questions concerning them were (humanly) decidable?)

Let us return now to Strawson and to Dummett's comments on his suggestion. Strawson, recall, found it paradoxical that we were to be moved to a global anti-realism by considerations first mooted in the philosophy of mathematics; for what, in his view, made mathematical anti-realism at least *prima facie* attractive was some contrast between the subject-matter of mathematics and those areas of thought and discourse which treat of the natural world. And Dummett, in his comments, regards Strawson as having in mind the contrast between the natural world as composed of objects which are 'external' and 'mind-independent'; and mathematics as treating either of no objects at all, or of objects which are not external or mind-independent. Dummett then repeats the arguments from 'The Philosophical Basis of Intuitionistic Logic' that one cannot move from doctrines about the status of certain objects to doctrines about the status, with respect to verifiability, of truths concerning them. In particular, then, realism concerning the subject matters of history, geography etc. cannot be defended simply on the basis that these disciplines deal with 'external' objects.

But it should be evident that Strawson was not appealing simply to that idea. His claim concerning the natural world, which makes realism with respect to it compelling, is that we have sufficient knowledge of the natural world, and our modes of access to it, to see how and why some parts of it, as he puts it, '. . . might, indeed would, remain undisclosed or be irrecoverably lost sight of'. He then suggests that, at the very least, we have difficulties in importing such ideas into our thoughts about mathematics and its subject matter.

Strawson says little concerning *why* we have such difficulties. I shall conclude this section by saying a little about this—about why, if I am right in seeing such ideas as underpinning realism about the natural world, there is such a strong pull in the direction of mathematical anti-realism. I wish to challenge Dummett's thought that such selective anti-realism can spring only from irredeemably metaphorical, and argumentatively inefficacious, views about the difference between mathematical and natural objects.

The rather simple points which I wish to make can be summed up as follows: (1) We have no account of principled mathematical ignorance, no account, that is, of why mathematical instances of (SR) might be true; (2) this is because we are inclined, in various ways, to think Platonistically about mathematics.

Let me first spell out these thoughts in the context of the 'Platonist' position in the philosophy of mathematics. This is the view, mentioned above, concerning the subject-matter of mathematics, which holds that it treats of certain *abstract objects*, objects which are neither mental nor physical, lack spatio-temporal location, are causally inert and (hence) are not possible objects of sensory perception. The attractions, or otherwise, of such a view are not here my concern.[13] I wish

[13] For both, see the extensive treatment in Crispin Wright, *Frege's Conception of Numbers as Objects* (Aberdeen: Aberdeen University Press, 1983).

rather to point out how difficult it is for such a view to explain how or why a mathematical instance of the realist schema (SR) should be true.

Two preliminary points: firstly, many see Platonism in mathematics as conducive to, even as entailing, subject-matter realism concerning mathematics, in the 20th century sense captured in (SR). (As we have seen, though Dummett denies, with plausibility, the entailment.) But they are right to this extent: Platonism does leave room for the abstract possibility of unknowable mathematical truths. It does not entail, in any obvious way, *anti*-realism with respect to the subject-matter of mathematics. For if mathematical propositions owe their truth to how things stand in some mind-independent abstract realm, there is no obvious reason to believe that all such truths must be knowable by us. But, as I claimed above, in the case of propositions about the natural world, we have much more than the mere abstract possibility of unknowable truths. It is this *more* that, I claim, Platonism in mathematics has difficulty in providing.

The second point is this. In contemporary philosophy of mathematics the first (and usually the only) epistemological thought which people have when confronted with the ontological doctrine of Platonism is how difficult, on such a view, it is to account for mathematical *knowledge* (at least in the context of some popular current accounts of knowledge).[14] For example, adherents to causal theories of knowledge ask: how can there be knowledge of truths concerning a causally inert subject-matter? It is commonly held that were ontological Platonism true, we should be doomed to *universal* mathematical ignorance. How then can I claim that Platonism makes it difficult to understand the possibility of principled mathematical ignorance, of undiscovered mathematical truths?

The answer is quite easy. We clearly *do* have mathematical knowledge. If Platonism is not finally to be ruled out of court it is going to have to come up with an epistemology explaining how, compatibly with its ontology, *some* mathematical knowledge is possible. But then, I suggest, it will have difficulties in giving a theory of ignorance in any way analogous to that

[14] For discussion see e.g. Wright *op.cit.* Section *xi*.

which science-cum-commonsense gives us for the natural world. Given a Platonist account of our epistemic 'access' to the abstract realm of mathematics, what account could be forthcoming of how portions of this abstract realm might be, or be rendered, inaccessible to the knowledge-yielding capacity it has discerned? In the case of sensory perception—our fundamental epistemic access to the natural world—we can see at once at least three ways a portion of that world might be epistemologically inaccessible—in virtue of its spatial remoteness, its temporal remoteness, or its size in relation to our perceptual capacities. But none of these can apply literally to a non-spatio-temporal reality. It is hard to see how to begin to develop any plausible analogues for a faculty allegedly giving us access to the abstract.

I have sketched a contrast between the natural world and the subject-matter of mathematics on a Platonist account of the latter. It is worth stressing that, banal though these thoughts have been, they have pointed in the opposite direction to a common thought—namely, that the Platonist, by over-assimilating mathematics to (for example) geography, makes subject-matter realism far too easy. I have left open the question whether, on other views of mathematics, one might 'import' into our thinking about mathematics the ideas Strawson and I see as crucial to subject-matter realism concerning the natural world.

Focusing directly on the epistemology of mathematics, our first thought is likely to be that the prime mode of mathematical knowledge is mathematical proof. (Proving things is, after all, what most mathematicians do most of the time.) We see again how hard it is to introduce analogues of our thoughts about the natural world. We tend to think Platonistically about *proofs*. To say of a mathematical proposition that it is provable is standardly taken to mean that *there is* a proof of it: and the '*there is*' is read Platonistically, that the truth of such a claim is independent of the existence, in the spatio-temporal realm, of a written, spoken or thought token of the proof. We think of such writing, speaking or thinking not as the bringing into existence of the proof but as the discovery of it. Once again, we have no obvious way of spelling out the thought that though there might be (in the present sense) a proof of a mathematical proposition, we might be incapable of knowing the mathematical truth in question because something about us, or the proof, might render us incapable of discovering it. (Of course, on this conception, there are countless proofs that never will, as a matter of fact, get discovered: but such happenstance gives no content to the thought that there are mathematical truths which we are incapable of knowing.)

V

So far we have been discussing what I have labelled subject-matter realism, a doctrine summed up in the idea that how things are may transcend our capacity to know how things are. Such realism embodies a possibly pessimistic doctrine concerning human powers of knowledge as measured against the constituents of reality. My second strand of realism—realism with respect to representations—is rather an optimistic doctrine concerning human powers of representation as measured against the constituents of reality, *viz*. that human beings have the power to represent to themselves how things are in the world. Now this, taken on its own, need not be a doctrine that one would characterise as realism, for it can be founded on the idealist-sounding thought that the very notion of how things are in the world has to be cashed in terms of, and hence in principle could not transcend, how human beings are capable of representing to themselves how things are. But it takes on a realist tinge if we combine it with some version of subject-matter realism. For that, at its most abstract, said that how things are in the world is, in general, independent of our actual or possible cognitive states. The combined doctrines, therefore, entail that we have the capacity to represent to ourselves those aspects of how things are which are independent of, and can transcend, our cognitive powers to determine them. And it is (fleshings out of) this latter doctrine that I wish to label 'realism with respect to representations'.[15]

As with subject-matter realism, the form this doctrine *takes* at any stage in the history of philosophy will depend on the current view of the central form of representation. When, in the classical epistemology of the 17th and 18th centuries, the

[15] In connection with this see section II of Haldane's paper.

essential form of representation consisted of 'ideas', realism with respect to representations consisted in the view that we could represent to ourselves objects the existence of which were independent of their being objects of perceptual awareness (themselves typically conceived as constituted by 'ideas'.) Anti-realism with respect to representations, in this period, is the denial of this. Seen in these terms, two of Berkeley's most famous (or notorious) arguments are, in the first instance, arguments for anti-realism with respect to representations. The first rests on his thought that ideas can be like, hence (on a resemblance theory of representation) can represent, only ideas. The second is the argument which concludes that we cannot so much as conceive—*i.e.* represent to ourselves in the medium of ideas—a tree or other sensible object existing unperceived. For much 20th century philosophy, the prime medium of representation is linguistic. We represent to ourselves ways the world might be by producing sentences which we understand. And we succeed (even if, sometimes, unknowingly) in representing to ourselves how things actually *are* if we produce and understand sentences which are *true*. But since, by the first strand of realism, how things are in the world is, in general, independent of our capacity to determine how things are in the world, realism about representations emerges (in a doctrine familiar to readers of Dummett) as the view that we have the capacity to produce and understand sentences which can be true, independently of our capacity to determine that they are true. The realist with respect to representations, in the present framework, is not prepared to accept that, in general, for any sentence S which we understand, if S is true then we must be able to determine that it is.

I now wish to enquire into the relations between subject-matter realism and realism with respect to representations (in their contemporary forms). Since we have arrived at the present formulation of realism with respect to representations by *incorporating* subject-matter realism, the former trivially entails the latter. (Moreover, the former is a special case of the latter, with the particular subject matter of the truth-value of sentences. So realism with respect to representations is incompatible with *global* subject-matter anti-realism.) The interesting question is the converse: does (global) subject-matter realism entail (global) realism with respect to representations? *Prima facie* the answer would seem to be 'no', for at least two reasons.

Firstly, subject-matter realism concerning (say) the natural world speaks of that world and our ability to know how things stand in it. In particular it says that how things do so stand can transcend our capacity to know. It seems to contain no materials entailing that we have the ability to represent to ourselves in language, those aspects of reality which can thus transcend our cognitive powers. Indeed (given some premisses about knowledge requiring the linguistic representation of what is known) we might argue for subject-matter realism concerning the natural world precisely on the grounds that we have *not* the ability to produce and understand sentences which can be undetectably true. So not merely does anti-realism with respect to representations seem *compatible* with the corresponding subject-matter realism; it might even be a premiss in an argument in favour of the latter viewpoint.

Secondly, if subject-matter realism entailed the corresponding realism with respect to representations, there could be a valid argument, starting from the premiss that if a sentence which we understand is true then we could determine that it is, to the conclusion that we must be able, in general, to determine how things are in the world, *i.e.* how things are in the world cannot transcend our cognitive powers. But such a move—from a claim about the limits of the linguistically representable world to one about the limits of the world—would surely only seem remotely plausible given the further ('idealist') thought, alluded to above, that there could be no more to reality than how we, in sentences, were capable of representing reality to be.[16]

These thoughts concerning the derivability of subject-matter anti-realism from the corresponding anti-realism with respect

[16] An awareness of the quite distinct positions here, but an apparent underplaying of the distinction, emerges in the following passage, where Crispin Wright is defending contemporary anti-realism from the charge of being a species of idealism. 'We do not ordinarily think of those aspects of reality which we are able conclusively to determine as any less *of* the world—or, at least, those of its features to which we can give intelligible expression.' 'Truth Conditions and Criteria' in *Realism, Meaning and Truth* p. 55.

to representations would seem to offer a welcome prospect for those who wish to espouse (as Dummett appears at times to do), in some areas at least,[17] anti-realism with respect to representations. For, as I argued above, to be committed, in such cases, to the corresponding subject-matter anti-realism would involve one in the onerous task of reconstructing or reconstruing[18] those empirical views which, I claimed, underpin such cases of subject-matter realism. If anti-realism with respect to representations did entail the corresponding subject-matter anti-realism, then the former could not remain a self-contained doctrine in the theory of meaning, revisionary, at most, of our logic.

VI

Despite these thoughts, I think a case can be made, not quite for the view that subject-matter realism *entails* realism with respect to representations (and hence that anti-realism with respect to representations would entail subject-matter anti-realism); but for this: one who is prepared to *assert* instances of the schema definitive of subject-matter realism ((SR) above) must (given two further assumptions) be prepared to accept the corresponding instances of realism with respect to representations, and hence must reject *global* anti-realism with respect to representations.

The subject-matter realist is not prepared to hold that, in general,

> (AS) if *p*, then it could be known (by a human being or knowing subject) that *p*.

Suppose, then, that he is actually prepared to assert instances of the denial of this schema, instances of:

> (SR) It could be that *p* even though no human being or knowing subject knows, or could know, that *p*.

Let *S* be a sentence substitution of which for '*p*' in (SR) gives an instance he is prepared to assert. For definiteness let *S* be 'The

[17] For example, in respect of sentences concerning the past, or other minds.

[18] See Crispin Wright 'Strawson on Anti-Realism' *Synthese* 40 (1979) at p. 289f. and in his *Realism, Meaning and Truth* p. 76f. It is interesting to contrast the quite different response of Dummett *Truth and Other Enigmas*, xxiiff.

Venerable Bede died on a Tuesday'. Now if the subject-matter realist believes that by uttering that instance of (SR) he can assert what he takes himself to be asserting, this requires that he believe *inter alia* that:

> A) By uttering 'The Venerable Bede died on a Tuesday', he could assert that the Venerable Bede died on a Tuesday.

Only thus, it would seem, could he think that by uttering 'It could be that the Venerable Bede died on a Tuesday', he could assert that it could be that the Venerable Bede died on a Tuesday.

As was noted earlier it seems to be a general truth about truth that:

> B) By uttering 'S is true' one can assert what one asserts when one assertively utters S.[19]

Putting these thoughts together, someone who is prepared to assert an actual instance of (SR) must believe that he could assert what he intended to assert by means of an instance in which '*p*' is replaced systematically by the relevant instance of '*S* is true'. That is, in the above case, he must be prepared to think he could assert the very same thing by, and hence be prepared to assert:

> It could be that 'The Venerable Bede died on a Tuesday' is true although no human being or knowing subject does or could know that 'The Venerable Bede died on a Tuesday' is true.

He must be prepared, that is, to accept that a sentence which he understands could be true even though it could not be known to be true. That is to say, he must accept at least one case of realism with respect to representations and *ipso facto* deny global anti-realism with respect to representations.

Contraposing, then: someone who accepts global anti-realism with respect to representations (i.e. who holds that, for

[19] See e.g. John McDowell in G. Evans and J. McDowell (eds) *Truth and Meaning* at p. 46; W.V.O. Quine, *Philosophy of Logic* p. 12. There are indeed arguments, of the 'translation' sort, modelled on Church's objections to Carnap's account of assertion, which have been deployed against this thought. Despite these, it is hard to believe that there is not a notion of asserting (hypothesizing etc.) the same thing, in which, at least for one who understands *S* (and this is implicit throughout the above discussion), he can use '*S* is true' to assert etc. what he asserts etc. by means of *S*.

any sentence which we can understand, if it is true it could be known to be true) seems debarred from accepting any instance of the above schema which is definitive of subject-matter realism. But then, it seems, he is committed to denying those commonsense-cum-scientific views which (we argued) render many such instances overwhelmingly plausible. By this argument, then, global anti-realism with respect to representations seems committed to being massively revisionary of everyday thought and of science.

VII

Before I say what I think the anti-realist with respect to representations ought to say about all this, I wish to raise a preliminary question: is Dummett, when he presents arguments for what *he* calls anti-realism, within the context of the theory of meaning, espousing what *I* am calling anti-realism with respect to representations? Is he, that is, denying that a sentence could be true independently of our ability to determine that it is? Now it may be said that this is precisely what Dummett *is* denying (laying aside what I view as irrelevant entanglements with bivalence). For he typically states realism, expressed as a doctrine in the theory of meaning, in the following terms. In 'The Reality of the Past' realism is the view that:

> We have . . . succeeded in ascribing to our statements a meaning of such a kind that their truth or falsity is, in general, independent of whether we know, or have any means of knowing, what truth-value they have.[20]

Again:

> The fundamental tenet of realism is that any sentence on which a fully specific sense has been conferred has a determinate truth-value independent of our actual capacity to decide what that truth-value is.[21]

It would seem, therefore, that the anti-realism which is opposed to this would be precisely the doctrine that, in general, the truth-value of a statement is *not* independent of our capacity

[20] At *Truth and Other Enigmas* p. 358.
[21] *Frege: The Philosophy of Language* (London: Duckworth, 1973) p. 466.

to determine that truth-value. Hence, for all sentences *S* which we understand, if *S* is true then we can determine that *S* is true. And this just is the version of anti-realism with respect to representations which, in Section VI, I argued led to a highly implausible version of subject-matter realism.

In fact matters are more complicated than this. If one searched the relevant texts for a statement of the doctrine which Dummett conceives the anti-realist as holding, in opposition to the realism he has defined, it is not—at least not always—the view that if *S* is true then we are capable of determining that it is. Rather one finds such things as the following:

> In the case of a sentence for which we have no effective means of deciding its truth-value, the state of affairs which has, in general, to obtain for it to be true is, by hypothesis one which we are not capable of recognizing as obtaining whenever it obtains. Hence a knowledge of what it is for that sentence to be true is a knowledge which cannot be fully manifested by a disposition to accept the sentence as established whenever we are capable of recognizing it as true: it is knowledge which cannot, in fact, be fully manifested by actual linguistic practice; and therefore it is a knowledge which could not have been acquired by acquiring a mastery of that practice. Rather, when we are concerned with sentences of this kind, we should regard an understanding of them as consisting in an ability to do just what we actually learn to do when we learn to use them, that is, in certain circumstances to recognize them as having been verified and in others as having been falsified. The truth- and falsity-conditions for any sentence should instead be taken as ones which we are capable of recognizing effectively whenever they obtain: it is in just this that the difference resides between the realist conception of truth and falsity and the alternative conception of verification and falsification.[22]

Or, more briefly,

> . . . we could not possibly have come to understand what it would be for the statement to be true independently of that which we have learned to treat as establishing its truth. . .[23]

[22] *Op.cit.*, p. 467.
[23] *Truth and Other Enigmas*, p. 362.

Let us concentrate for the moment on the second quotation. It could be seen as ambiguous. Or rather, I shall force an ambiguity on it. It could be seen as saying: we could not possibly have come to understand the conception that a statement might be true independently of what we learned to treat as establishing its truth. That is, we cannot understand the idea that a statement might be true in a situation in which it could not be known to be true. This would be to say that we simply cannot understand the position which I have called realism with respect to representation, which would presumably entail that something had gone wrong if we attempted to embrace that position.

This, of course, is not the point Dummett intends to make. He does not think he cannot understand the position he seeks to oppose.[24] Rather, Dummett's characterisation of anti-realism is supposed to have the following force: concerning any particular statement, we cannot have come to understand what it would be for that statement to be true in a situation in which we could not establish its truth. And *this* doctrine is not, as it stands by itself, incompatible with our realism with respect to representations—that, simply said, there can be statements which are true even though we could not know them to be true. The present Dummettian formulation of anti-realism, in conjunction with that, merely entails that, for such sentences, we cannot understand what it would be for them to be true. And in the preceding passage we saw Dummett arguing in precisely this way. That is, from the premiss that there are sentences the truth of which *can* transcend our powers of verification to the conclusion that we cannot, for such sentences, represent a speaker's knowledge of their meaning as an understanding of the conditions under which they would be true. Thus construed, Dummett's views in the theory of meaning—his denial of a truth-conditional theory of meaning and his replacement of it by one centering on verification and falsification—far from denying what I am calling realism with respect to representations, rest squarely upon that doctrine.

[24] We might compare here, though, a familiar complaint about Kant's transcendental idealism: that, on his own principles, he ought not to have been able to give content to the transcendental realism by contrast with which his own position was, in part, defined.

Though I think this position—acceptance of realism with respect to representations as a ground for rejecting a truth-conditional conception of meaning—is, at points, Dummett's —it is not, I think, consistently so. It is not too difficult, even in advance of consulting his writings, to see why this might be so. The present position combines the thought that while there are sentences of our language the truth conditions of which transcend our abilities to determine whether or not they obtain, we cannot have acquired, nor can we manifest, any knowledge of what such truth conditions are. We know that the sentences have verification-transcendent truth conditions while not knowing what these might be. And this seems an unhappy thought.[25]

Presumably to avoid this unhappiness, we find Dummett, at other points, espousing anti-realism with respect to representations (and thereby depriving himself of his central argument against truth-conditional theories of meaning). In one place he writes as follows:

> The actual fact of our linguistic practice is that the only notions of truth and falsity which we have for such sentence are ones which do not entitle us to regard the sentence as determinately true or false independently of our knowledge. The truth of such a sentence can consist only in the occurrence of the sort of situation in which we have learned to recognize it as true or false . . .[26]

Hence if a sentence is true we could recognize it to be true. And the whole tenor of his writings makes it clear that the anti-realism with respect to representations he espouses is of a very strong form: he is talking of capacities for recognition which we actually possess and can manifest in our actual use of

[25] Some evidence of this unease may be found in Wright's paper quoted above. Thus in one paragraph he begins by writing of sentences of which our '*standard conception* (my emphasis) of the truth conditions of the sentence is such that if actualized, they would not, or need not, be recognizably so.' 'Truth Conditions and Criteria', in *Realism, Meaning and Truth* (p. 53). (And later he speaks of '. . . sentences whose truth conditions we *picture to ourselves (ditto)* as (possibly) verification-transcendent. *ibid.* p. 54) But he goes on to say, of such sentences that '. . . in cases like these there is not, or need not be anything in which this alleged knowledge (of truth conditions) can consist'. So we can have a 'conception' or a 'picture' of these verification-transcendent truth conditions, but no 'knowledge'.

[26] *Frege op.cit.*, p. 468.

sentences in the position in the world in which we find ourselves. How then can he avoid the collapse, by the argument of VII, into an extreme, and absurd, version of subject-matter anti-realism?

VIII

I shall conclude by making a suggestion as to how Dummett might avoid this collapse—a suggestion which does render Dummett's anti-realist views in the theory of meaning in a sense consistent with subject-matter realism, though at the cost of rendering anti-realism in the theory of meaning an extremely bizarre doctrine.

As I remarked above, Dummett's anti-realism in the theory of meaning appears, in the first instance, to be based squarely upon what I called realism with respect to representations. Dummett's view was not the denial of that but was rather the doctrine that to understand a sentence is not, in general, to know under what conditions it would be *true*; or, still more vaguely put, that the meaning of a sentence is not, in general, given by its truth conditions.

These slogans are vague. I think we can best get some grip on what they come to by outlining a conception of the role of a theory of sense for a language developed by McDowell.[27] The conception might be crudely and briefly stated along the following lines. A theory of sense for some language *L* must entail, for each indicative sentence of *L*, a theorem which can, initially, be represented schematically as follows: *S* . . . *p* where '*p*' is to be replaced by a sentence of the meta-language. The most basic requirement on the sentence replacing '*p*' is that it can serve to specify the content of the propositional acts performed by speakers of *L* by means of utterances of *S* (and sentences related syntactically to *S*). That is, given information that the speaker, in uttering *S* (or an appropriately related non-indicative sentence), is asserting (commanding, asking or whatever), then we must be able to use the sentence replacing '*p*' in the theorem for *S* correctly to complete the description of his act as, say, asserting that *p* (asking whether *p*, and so on).

[27] See his 'Truth Conditions, Bivalence and Verificationism', in Evans and McDowell (eds.) *op.cit.* especially pp. 42–47.

The kinds of theory of sense Dummett considers all conceive of the '. . . .' in the schematic form of such theorems as being filled to yield something syntactically of the sort: *S* is *C* iff *p*. The theorems can then be described, in a convenient shorthand, as stating the *C*-conditions of the (indicative) sentences of *L*. And we can, if we like, say that, on a given view of this kind, a speaker's understanding of a sentence *S* is constituted by his knowledge of the conditions under which *S* would be *C*.

Dummett's most general requirement on such a representation of speaker's knowledge is that it be capable of being fully manifested in his use of sentences. And he takes this to require that, where '*C*' is the proposed filling in theorems of the above style, for any *S*:

If *S* is *C* then we can know it to be *C*.
If *S* is not *C* then we can know it not to be *C*.

And his initial objection to truth-conditional theories of meaning, based precisely on realism with respect to representations is that where '*C*' is read as 'is true', these conditions are not met. Sentences can be *unknowably* true and false.

But, as we saw at the end of section VII, Dummett does not consistently maintain this position. He seems also inclined to take the line of *rejecting* realism with respect to representations: that is, of holding that the above two requirements *are* met if '*C*' is read as 'true'. There is then no objection to representing speakers' semantic knowledge as knowledge of the truth conditions of sentences, provided it is conceded, in accordance with *anti*-realism with respect to representations, that truth cannot out-run our powers of recognizing truth.[28] How then, can Dummett avoid being committed to the very strong version of (global) subject-matter anti-realism noted at the end of VII? We can spell out, in the present framework, the argument of V, which tries to extract the commitment from anti-realism with respect to representations, as follows. If the

[28] In writing later than any here considered, Dummett takes precisely this line, criticizing his own earlier formulations. See *Truth and Other Enigmas* p. *xxii*. But in still later writings he seems to revert to the old way of putting it, which the Preface to *Truth and Other Enigmas* had rightly criticized. See *e.g. The Interpretation of Frege's Philosophy* pp. 434–5. Earlier on p. 434 *ibid.* he also moves, between sentences, from formulations concerning subject-matter realism, to formulations concerning realism with respect to representations.

sentence replacing '*p*' correctly gives the *C*-conditions of some sentence *S*; and if correctly giving the *C*-conditions of any sentence entails its being usable to give the content of acts of uttering it; and if (by the Dummettian requirement on '*C*') it cannot be the case that *C* (or not-*C*) without our being able to know that *C* (or not-*C*), then it must be that, (where '*p*' is replaced by the sentence *S* in question):

> if *p*, then we can know that *p*
> if not-*p*, then we can know that not-*p*.

To avoid global subject-matter anti-realism, there must be some substitutions for '*p*' for which these two latter claims fail. This then can *only be* because some substitutions fail to give the *C*-conditions of any sentence of the language in question. But it is presumed that giving the *C*-conditions of a sentence *S* is what is required to be usable to give the propositional content of utterances of *S*. There must be, therefore, some sentences '*p*' of the meta-language (which can, of course, be the object-language *L*)—*viz.* those which yield true instances of the schema for subject-matter realism (SR)—which cannot be used to give the propositional content of any assertoric act performed by a sentence *S* of object-language *L*. For such a substitution for '*p*' it must be the case that we can never truly report the content of an act performed by uttering a sentence *S* as: asserting that *p*. And this holds even when the sentence replacing '*p*' is *S* itself.

Let us now return to the original version in section VI of the argument which claimed that acceptance (as common sense and science compel) of particular instances of subject-matter realism compelled acceptance of realism with respect to representations. A key premiss was the thought that by uttering the sentence the speaker did succeed in asserting that *p*, where *S* is, and '*p*' is replaced by, the very sentence substitution of which in the realist schema gave a truth attested by common sense and science. (The example used was: by uttering 'The Venerable Bede died on a Tuesday' one could assert that the Venerable Bede died on a Tuesday; where, in turn, in accord with subject-matter realism, that he did so die could unknowably be the case.) And it is this key premiss which the present version of anti-realism in the theory of meaning must deny, if it is not to collapse into global subject-matter anti-realism.

But if, in assertively uttering 'The Venerable Bede died on a Tuesday' we are not asserting that the Venerable Bede died on a Tuesday, then what *are* we asserting? I think that if the present formal preservation of subject-matter realism is to be possible, the answer must be: nothing. For, on the present view, a sentence '*S*' can be used to give the content of an assertive use of 'The Venerable Bede died on a Tuesday' only if *S* has *C*-conditions which cannot obtain undetectably. But as the Venerable Bede could have died, undetectably, on a Tuesday, *no* sentence the *C*-conditions of which meet this Dummettian requirement can have the same content as, *i.e.* serve to report the assertoric act performed by the utterance of 'The Venerable Bede died on a Tuesday'.

The position, then, is that the anti-realist with respect to representations can formally preserve subject-matter realism in this sense: he can utter, without contradicting anything he holds in the theory of meaning, instances of the realist schema (SR). But he can give no account of what, in uttering such instances, he is asserting. On this position we preserve our realist view of the world at the cost of depriving ourselves of any natural account of what, in uttering those sentences which purport to express that view, we are doing.

VIII

Logical Necessity: Some Issues*

1. *Demarcating the Topic*

Even when I had hoped to write a paper on modal realism, I had intended to focus on the issue of realism concerning only one modal notion—so-called 'logical necessity'. But in exploring certain crucial preliminaries, I found a number of questions arising, some only tangential to my initial concern with modal realism. This paper addresses some of these issues.

'Modal', as it occurs in such contexts as 'modal realism' is, by origin, a grammarians' term. It applies to certain verbs, to a (possibly improper) subclass of auxiliary verbs. Paradigmatic modal verbs of English are 'can', 'may', 'must', 'ought' and other tenses of these. Modal realism, at its broadest, would be some general claim about the nature of these verbs, or of statements containing them. But it is unlikely that any *single* philosophical thesis would be plausible across such a range—there are just too many modal verbs. Moreover, each such verb would seem to be capable of a variety of uses. Consider the present tense of 'may'. It can be used to express *permission*—'You may have some more ice cream'. It can also be used to express an apparently distinct notion of *possibility*—'She may be in the kitchen'. This simple example brings out another feature of modal verbs: many are connected with one or more notions which can be expressed by nouns—*possibility*—adjectives—*possible*—or adverbs—*possibly*: which notions, and statements involving them can, in turn, be termed modal. We have already seen that there is apparently a many-one relation between such notions and particular constructions involving modal verbs. Things become yet more complicated when we recall that the modal notions which have most concerned philosophers—necessity and possibility—have frequently been divided by

* This paper exists in several versions, of which this seems to be the most complete. In places where the style was obscure I have made minor adjustments. (RS)

them into a number of subnotions—epistemic possibility, logical necessity, physical necessity. Again it is unclear, if such distinctions can be made out, that a single philosophical view would apply to *all* of the notions of necessity or possibility. I wished to narrow my focus to 'logical' necessity. But what is 'logical' necessity?

One place where it is philosophically traditional to invoke *a* notion of necessity is in giving an account of what it is for an argument to be deductively valid. Thus Aristotle famously wrote:

> A deduction is discourse in which, certain things being stated, something other than what is stated follows of necessity from their being so.[2]

Deductive validity is the central topic of logic. So if, as Aristotle and others have thought, to think of an argument as deductively valid requires us to deploy *a* notion of necessity, then that notion, if any, will deserve the label 'logical' necessity. There will be a legitimate notion of 'logical' necessity only if there is a notion of necessity which attaches to the claim, concerning a deductively valid argument, that if the premisses are true then so is the conclusion.

Let us, for the moment, allow the Aristotelian assumption that a notion of necessity *is* involved here. (We shall consider scepticism on this point later.) There is still a problem in demarcating our subject-matter. For how do we tell if a given claim to the effect that something is necessarily the case involves the *same* notion of necessity as that involved in the assessment of an argument as deductively valid? How, that is, given that one has ascertained that *a* notion of necessity is being deployed in some claim, does one determine whether or not it is *the* notion of 'logical' necessity?

On certain traditional assumptions there would be a fairly easy way of telling if a given use of a notion of necessity was a use of the notion of 'logical' necessity. The most crucial assumption here is that logical necessity is the *strongest* notion of necessity. That if it is logically necessary that *p*, then it is necessary that *p* in any other use of the notion of necessity there

[2] Aristotle, *Prior Analytics*, 24^b 18–19.

may be (physically, practically *etc.*). But that the converse need not be the case. Something could be *e.g.* physically necessary without being logically necessary. Equivalently, then, logical possibility is the weakest kind of possibility. If something is practically, physically (*etc.*) possible then it is logically possible. But the converse is not the case.

Even on traditional assumptions this last claim is not quite right. For there is *a* notion of possibility—mere time- and person-relative epistemic possibility—which can be asserted even when logical possibility cannot. I mean the notion expressed by that use of 'It may be that *p*' which just comes to, 'For all I know, not-*p*'. Clearly there are undecided mathematical propositions p such that I will assent to, in this sense, 'It may be that *p*' without committing myself to the logical possibility that *p*: for *p* may be false, and if it is then, on traditional assumptions, it is logically necessarily false. We need then to assume that we can detect, and rule out as irrelevant to the ensuing test, the occurrence of the merely epistemic notion of possibility.

Here then is the test. Consider someone who has revealed his possession of the notions of logical necessity and possibility by deploying them in the assessment of arguments as deductively valid and invalid. He now makes a claim of the form 'Necessarily, *p*'. Our question is: is the person committing himself to the claim that *p* is logically necessary? We ask if there is any sense in which, despite his ascription of necessity to *p*, he holds that it is possible that not-*p*. If there is, and if we can rule out the merely epistemic reading, then the original claim that necessarily *p* was *not* a claim of 'logical' necessity. It could not be the strongest necessity as it did not rule out *some* kind of non-epistemic possibility of the negation. Conversely, if the person will accept no non-epistemic sense in which it is possible that not-*p*, his original claim did involve the *strongest* necessity *i.e.* (on the traditional assumption) 'logical' necessity.

The test will work given the traditional assumption. But why should we accept the traditional assumption? Even if (*pro tem*) we agree with Aristotle in accepting that *a* notion of necessity is involved in ascriptions of deductive validity, why must that be the strongest notion of necessity? There might be views which held there were at least two notions of necessity, only one of which was involved in ascriptions of validity, and which were incommensurable in strength: some propositions possess the 'logical' notion of necessity but lack the other one, while others possess this latter notion of necessity but are not logically necessary. Dorothy Edgington has developed a view of precisely this structure.[3] (We shall look at the details and an example in a moment.)

I wish to defend the traditional assumption and also bring in certain materials to which we shall return; or rather, at the moment, I wish to defend a hypothetical version of the traditional assumption. *If* the claim that an argument is deductively valid involves a notion of necessity then it involves the strongest notion of necessity. More fully: I understand the antecedent to be the view that for an argument '*p*, so *q*' to be valid is for it to be necessary, in some sense, *i.e. logically* necessary that if *p* then *q*. The consequent then claims that if it is logically necessary that if *p* then *q*, then there is no other sense of 'necessary' in which it is *not* necessary that if *p* then *q*, *i.e.* no sense of 'possible' in which it is possible that *p* and not-*q*.

The argument rests on two assumptions: first, that it is a distinctive and important feature of deductive validity (one in which it contrasts with inductive strength) that adding extra premisses to a valid argument cannot destroy its validity. In particular, then, if the argument '*p* so *q*' is valid then so is the argument '*p*, *r* so *q*' *for any r*. The second assumption is that there is this connection between deducing *q* from *p* and asserting a conditional: that on the basis of a deduction of *q* from *p* one is entitled to assert the conditional, *indicative or subjunctive*, if *p* then *q*.

Suppose then that '*p* so *q*' is valid, *i.e.*, by the hypothesis of the above claim, it is logically necessary that if *p* then *q*. But suppose that the consequent of that claim is false. Suppose that it is possible that *p* and not-*q* in another sense of 'possible'. But if that *is* a possibility, we ought to be able to describe the circumstances in which it would be realised: let them be described by *r*. Consider now the argument '*p* and *r* so *q*'. By the first assumption if '*p* so *q*' is valid, so is '*p* and *r* so *q*'. But then, by the second assumption, we should be entitled to assert:

[3] Dorothy Edgington, 'Epistemic and Metaphysical Possibilities', unpublished.

if *p* and *r* were the case then *q* would be the case. But how can this be assertible? For *r* was chosen to describe possible circumstances in which *p* and not-*q*. I think we should conclude that we cannot allow, where there is such an *r*, that an argument is valid. Logical necessity, if there is such a thing, is the highest grade of necessity.

Let us deploy this abstract argument against the views, and an example, of Edgington's. Her position is that logical necessity—the notion relevant to assessing validity—is an epistemic notion: epistemic necessity which, she claims, is the old notion of the *a priori*.[4] Like Kripke she thinks that this notion is two-way independent of another modal notion—metaphysical necessity. She thinks, therefore that an argument can be valid—it is knowable *a priori* that if the premisses are true then so is the conclusion—although it is metaphysically possible that the premisses should be true and the conclusion false. Her position is thus of the above structure.

The example is Kripke's: on the basis of his observations and calculations, the astronomer Leverrier concludes that certain planetary perturbations must be caused by a hitherto undiscovered planet which he dubs 'Neptune'. Following Kripke and Evans Edgington claims, and I agree, that he knows *a priori* that if Neptune exists it is a planet causing such and such perturbations. Thus, on her account, the argument: 'Neptune exists, so Neptune causes such and such perturbations' is deductively valid. But there is certainly a 'timeless' metaphysical possibility that the premiss should have been true and the conclusion false: suppose Neptune had been knocked off course a million years ago. What then, of the argument: 'Neptune exists and was knocked off course a million years ago, so Neptune is the cause of these perturbations'. If the original argument is valid so is this one (by the first assumption). But if it is we ought (by the second assumption) to be entitled to assert: if Neptune had existed and been knocked off its course a million years ago then it would have been the cause of these perturbations. But of course we are not entitled to assert that: had the antecedent been true the consequent would have been false.

[4] *ibid.*

The following objection might be presented. Take a *p* and *q* such that I think the argument '*p*, so *q*' is valid. Then by my own first assumption, I must also regard '*p* and not-*q* so *q*' as valid. But by the second I ought to be entitled to assert: if *p* and not-*q* were the case then *q* would be the case. But isn't that just as unassertible as the kind of counterfactual with which I belaid the opposition?

No. For I here regard the antecedent as impossible in the fullest sense. The assertibility of this odd counterfactual can thus be seen as a special case of the vacuous truth of counterfactuals with fully impossible antecedents. The vacuity is brought out by the fact that, supposing I embrace Double-Negation-Elimination, my second assumption will commit me to the opposite counterfactual: if *p* and not-*q* were the case then not-*q* would be the case. Those taking the opposed position, holding that *p* and *r* (and hence *p* and not-*q*) represented a possibility, did not wish to be committed to the view that, were *p* and *r* true, anything whatsoever would be the case. But that is what they would be committed to if they retained the idea that '*p* so *q*' was valid despite the possibility that *p* and not-*q*.

The moral of this section is this: if validity involves a notion of necessity, and obeys the two assumptions above, then the necessity involved must be the *strongest* necessity.

2. *The point of modal notions: a difficulty for modal realism?*

'The world is everything that is the case', as Wittgenstein famously said. As theoretical speculators, we might hope (as an ideal) to grasp the world by coming to know everything that is the case. But what rôle in this enterprise is played by our modal beliefs—our beliefs expressible by modal constructions? What is the point of having such beliefs and the means to express them? Central to modal realism is the view that having modal beliefs has exactly the same kind of point as having non-modal beliefs about, say, cabbages or kings. Just as someone lacking beliefs about cabbages or kings would lack beliefs about everything that is the case, so too would one who lacked modal concepts and beliefs deploying them. For the modal realist holds that part of the totality of what is the case, the totality of facts, are such things as that certain events could have happened, others could not have happened, that certain propositions are necessarily true, others impossible, that if such and such had happened then so and so would have been the case. The modal realist holds that reality contains such modal facts, and these facts are *irreducible*: no modal fact is equivalent to any set of non-modal facts. On this view, then, we need modal concepts and beliefs in order to stand a chance of encompassing, in our thought, the totality of what is the case. Any system of thought lacking the modal concepts would be condemned to overlooking an aspect of reality.

Modal realists differ considerably among themselves as to the nature of the modal reality of which our modal thoughts treat. We need only, for present purposes, distinguish two broad kinds which I shall label objectual and non-objectual modal realism. The objectual modal realist holds that an account of that in virtue of which modal beliefs are true ineliminably involves certain distinctive modal *objects*—typically labelled 'possible worlds'. (What makes objects 'modal'? Answer—the modal expressions are interpreted as various kinds of quantifiers over them. And of course such treatment appears to have been illuminating, in logic and elsewhere. A full discussion would need to speak to that fact as an argument for modal realism.) The 'extreme' example is, of course, David Lewis. As well as this world and all its occupants—from electrons to galaxies—there is a vast number of other possible worlds each with its own occupants, in some cases very like those of our world, in other cases unimaginably different. Our various modal operators are to be interpreted as various kinds of quantifiers over such worlds. Our modal judgments, when true, are true in virtue of how things stand in this domain of possible worlds. The aim of modal thought is accordingly to represent how things are in this realm.

The non-objectual modal realist rejects this ontic interpretation of modal notions. For him there *is* only this world and its inhabitants. Modal judgments, on this view, are made true by how things stand with respect to this world and its inhabitants, though not by how things *actually* stand with respect to them but rather, as one might put it, by how they *modally* stand. On this view the world and its inhabitants possess certain irreducibly modal properties—being necessarily φ, being possibly φ, being such that if *p* were the case then *q* would be the case. The aim of modal thought, on this realist view, is to get right the modal properties of the world and its inhabitants.

Familiar objections to either form of modal realism are either (a) *ontological*—one just refuses to believe that there are such possible worlds, or are such modal properties; or (b) *epistemological*—how can any way of knowing with which we are familiar entitle us to claim knowledge about the properties of other possible worlds, or the modal properties of this one? I wish, for present purposes, to by-pass such objections. Let us grant the modal realist his metaphysics and some appropriate epistemology. On his view, then, there will be a body of truths—the modal truths—which the would-be omniscient enquirer has reason to aim to believe; and achieving that aim is not beyond our powers. But it is unclear why someone with less theoretical, more practical, interests should, on the present realist account, have much interest in having modal beliefs. If I get things wrong about how people, possums and planets actually behave, I may come a cropper: but how am I helped if, as well as knowing how things actually behave, I know how they *must* behave? And how am I hindered if I remain ignorant of how they might have behaved, or would have behaved if. . . ? It is apparently unclear why, if modal judgments aim to record either facts about other possible worlds or the *modal* properties of this-worldly objects, I, as a practical person, should be interested in them. 'What might have been is an abstraction,/Remaining a perpetual possibility/Only in a world of speculation.' But we do not live in such a world of speculation. The suggestion, then, is that modal realism, by itself at any rate, is impotent to explain the point or interest which modal judgments might have for us.

It may help us to see what force this line of thought has if we consider a statement of it by Simon Blackburn and a recent objection to it. Blackburn is apparently focusing on the objectual ('possible worlds') version of modal realism and writes as follows:

> . . . the position that we are [in making modal judgments] simply describing different aspects of reality needs a supplementation which it finds hard to give. If the possible worlds

> . . . represent a new realm of fact, why should we be interested in it? Talking of possibilities would be as optional to us, interested in the actual world, as talk of neighbouring countries would be to us, if we are interested in the here and now. . . . Why should it interest me if in such spheres [of possible worlds] something holds, or in some it does not, or if in ones quite similar to the actual world things do or do not hold, if I want to discover and use truths about the way things actually are?[5]

Bob Hale, in his interesting critical notice of Blackburn's book,[6] compared this argument with a notorious argument of Kripke's against David Lewis, and claimed that Blackburn's suffered from the same effect. On Hale's view, the realist has no problem about explaining our interest in modal judgments.

Let us first recall Kripke's anti-Lewis argument and its alleged defect. Lewis, as we mentioned above, believes that modal claims are made true by how things stand in this and other possible worlds.[7] Famously, too, he holds that no (concrete) object exists in more than one world. Thus, for Lewis, claims about what could have happened to an object (in this world) are not made true by how things stand with *it* at some other possible world, for it does not exist at any other world. Rather such claims are made true by what holds of a counterpart of it—some maximally resembling object—at some other possible world. Kripke objected:

> According to the counterpart theorist, if we say 'Humphrey might have won the election' then we are not talking about something that might have happened to *Humphrey* but to someone else, a 'counterpart'. Probably, however, Humphrey could not care less whether someone *else*, no matter how much resembling him, would have been victorious in another possible world.[8]

Why does Hale see Blackburn's and Kripke's arguments as coming from the same box? I suppose the idea is that both Blackburn and Kripke are objecting to accounts of what is

[5] S.W. Blackburn, *Spreading the Word*, Groundings in the Philosophy of Language (Oxford, Clarendon Press, 1984), pp. 214–5.

[6] Bob Hale, 'The Compleat Projectivist', *Philosophical Quarterly* 36 (1986).

[7] David Lewis, 'Counterpart Theory and Quantified Modal Logic', *Journal of Philosophy* 65 (1968), pp. 113–26.

[8] Saul Kripke, *Naming and Necessity* (Oxford, Blackwell, 1980), p. 45n.

involved in the truth of certain modal judgments on the grounds that on these accounts we, or Humphrey, could not sensibly *care* whether or not these judgments were true.

What, allegedly, goes wrong with Kripke's argument? The standard response, to which Hale alludes with approval, is due to Allen Hazen. It has two steps: first, Kripke simply mis-states the truth-conditions which the counterpart theorist assigns. He represents the counterpart theorist explaining the modal predication of H in 'H might have won' by means of a modal predication of some counterpart of H—'Some counterpart of H would have been victorious in another possible world'. Maybe H—if he understands this mixture of modal and counterpart-theory talk—has no reason to be interested in whether some counterpart has that modal property. But that is not what the theory offered as an account of what is involved in the thought that H might have won. Rather—and this is the second step—the theory's account of this modal claim is that there is a world in which a counterpart of H wins. And H has every reason to be interested in *that*—for that is what the theory holds (and for all that has been said, correctly holds) 'Humphrey might have won' comes to.

How does this line of thought apply to Blackburn? Clearly no analogue of Hazen's first move can be relevant: there is no particular modal realist truth-condition which Blackburn simply gets wrong. And indeed Hale merely applies an intended analogue of the second part of the above argument:

> There is no problem about why we should be interested in the truth-value of propositions such as 'That uninsulated wire may be live'. . . . These are modal truths and falsehoods about the actual world. No-one in his right mind will argue, if it turns out that the wire wasn't live, that we had no good reason to treat it so gingerly. What makes such modal propositions true or false, on a possible worlds account, is how things are in other possible worlds. If there is a world . . . in which this wire . . . is live, then it is true in the actual world that that wire might be live. Since that is so, we have every reason in the world (in the actual world!) to be interested in whether there is some such possible world.[9]

[9] Hale, *op.cit.*

Hale's response is worth discussing because it well brings out how hard it is for some (good) philosophers to understand the explanatory and naturalistic approach of a writer like Blackburn (an approach I fully share). Let us return briefly to Kripke. Kripke starts from two presuppositions: (i) that modal propositions have truth-conditions and (ii) we can rationally care about whether or not these truth-conditions obtain. His aim was to show that counterpart theory got those truth-conditions wrong. And he merely used the presumption that *e.g.* H cared whether or not he might have won to try to show that counterpart theory was mistaken. For, he argues, H wouldn't care whether or not the truth-conditions the counterpart theorist allegedly assigned did obtain. In this argument, though, talk of caring was quite incidental: for Kripke's purpose he could as well have considered what Humphrey was believing, wondering, doubting *etc.* when he believed, wondered or doubted that or whether he might have won.

Blackburn's perspective is quite different. First, he is agnostic as to whether modal judgments *have* truth conditions in any substantive sense: whether in making them we are describing *any* further aspects of reality. And although he discusses modal realism in its possible worlds account, the point he is making is supposed to tell against any realist account of our modal judgments. Secondly, and more importantly, while in a sense it is a datum that we care about modal judgments—we constantly make them, have serious standards by which to appraise them—this is not a datum which he is prepared to allow the realist, or indeed anyone else, to take over without explanation. That is, Blackburn seeks an account of what we are up to in making modal judgments which will *explain* why we are seriously interested in making them. And it is this which he finds lacking in a realist account which says first (and maybe last) that the point of modal judgments is to get the facts right. Hale protests that since, on possible world semantics, (many) claims about possible worlds are equivalent to modal claims about the actual world which (of course!) we are interested in: we have reason to be interested in claims about other possible worlds. But the objection is that the account gives no *explanation* of why we are interested in ordinary modal claims. In particular the semantic account of these judgments in terms of possible worlds offers no such explanation. On the contrary, we are appealing to our intuitive, and unexplained, interest in these judgments to explain why we might be interested in the obtaining of the truth-conditions which the theory assigns.

I suggest, therefore, that Blackburn is right: that a realist account of modal claims, by itself, provides no philosophically illuminating account of the point or interest to us of such claims. Such realism at least requires supplementation at this point. But the thought arises that if appealing to a realist semantics for modal judgments does nothing towards explaining their point, then the idea that modal judgments reflect a realm of modal fact may, ultimately, prove quite irrelevant to a philosophical account of our use of such judgments. Nothing in the rest of this paper will begin to argue for that. But that speculative thought might be seen as hovering in the background in the two ensuing sections, in which I return to the particular modal notion partially delineated in the first section—'logical' necessity.

3. *Dispensing with Necessity: Quine and a Response*

In §1 I argued for a hypothetical doctrine: *if* there is a concept of necessity which attaches (perhaps *inter alia*) to the claim, concerning a deductively valid argument, that if the premisses are true then so is the conclusion, then that necessity—'logical necessity'—is the strongest species of necessity. The denial of the antecedent is, in the literature, widely attributed to Quine, who is reputed to have directed arguments against the acceptability of a notion of logical necessity. But it is actually quite hard to find out where or what these arguments are supposed to be.

Certainly Quine has been a persistent critic of modal logic—the logic of possibility—but his animadversions in this area do not pretend to be a case against the very notion of logical necessity. Again Quine would claim, probably rightly, that the class of logical truths needed in serious science—those of first-order logic—can be *demarcated* without appeal to modal notions. But again this would not show, nor would Quine think it did, that no notion of necessity *did* attach to these truths. I suppose when people speak about Quinean scepticism about necessity, we are intended to think of the arguments of 'Two Dogmas of Empiricism'. That paper famously argues against various attempts to define an analytic/synthetic distinction: and its final sections might be thought to cast doubt on certain *epistemic* properties—unrevisability, perhaps even *a prioricity*—which the laws of logic have been thought to have. But nothing seems to be said directly against the view that the propositions of logic are necessary truths. Perhaps Quine, or maybe those who report him, simply assume that the necessity many attribute to the truths of logic stands or falls with claims about analyticity or unrevisability which Quine *has* attacked. I wish to reject this claim, and to argue that the belief that principles of logic are in the highest degree necessary is a meaningful, contentful and essential thought which survives any possibly successful Quinean attack on traditionally associated epistemic claims about logic. In this section, though, I discuss an attempted rescue of necessity from Quinean scepticism and argue that it fails, largely as a result of too close an association between the modal and the epistemic.

Crispin Wright is one of those who have represented Quine as sceptical about logical necessity, his scepticism being grounded, Wright suggests, in the arguments at the end of 'Two Dogmas'. Accordingly Wright, as one wishing to retain the notion of logical necessity, though giving a highly non-realist account of it, has, in a number of places, tried to rebut, or rather restrict the range of, the considerations offered in those few famous pages. I wish briefly to consider Wright's most recent assault on this target in order to show that, however forceful his argument, it does not establish what Wright here and elsewhere takes it to establish.

Quine, at the end of that paper, outlines a holistic theory of knowledge. Our beliefs face the tribunal of experience as a whole. Recalcitrant experience may require revisions of our overall theory but cannot dictate any particular one. Revisions are to be made in the light of various pragmatic criteria such as those of overall simplicity and minimum mutilation. This last maxim will make some, very general, beliefs highly, but not completely, immune to revision. In particular, then, Quine holds that it could prove that the most rational adjustment of the overall theory in the light of certain recalcitrant experiences would be to modify the logic we have hitherto employed.

Wright's counterargument[10] seeks to show that at least *one* class of statements *cannot* owe their acceptability to these forms of holistic appraisal *viz.* those involved in the claim that a certain course of experience is recalcitrant with respect to a certain body of theory and its associated logic. What kinds of statement are these, and why does Wright hold they must be exempted from the Quinean picture?

As a first sketch of the Quinean picture we can represent things as follows. Let θ be some theory and L the logic deployed in it. We are to suppose we derive from θ by means of L a conditional $I \rightarrow P$, the antecedent describing certain initial conditions and the consequent the resulting prediction. Experience E will be recalcitrant if it inclines one to assent to 'I and not P' (though it cannot compel one to do so). Judgments of recalcitrance, at a first shot, appear to rest on such claims as that $I \rightarrow P$ is derivable from θ by means of L. Call this claim W:

$$W\text{: } \theta \vdash_L (I \rightarrow P)$$

So the judgment that E is recalcitrant rests on W. But then Quine, if he is to apply his account globally, must hold that *one* option, confronted by E, is to deny that E *is* recalcitrant *via* denying W. But how are we to assess this, relative to alternative courses of revision? *One* crucial test is the extent to which the various alternatives are confronted with recalcitrant experience. But how do we assess *that* if the claim that a course of experience is recalcitrant with respect to this or that alternative is itself an hypothesis to be assessed by seeing how well it does in comparison with alternatives? The account clearly leads to a regress: no determinate guidance on how to operate the theory has been given.

This is a powerful argument. And the initial conclusion drawn by Wright seems well-taken. He puts it:

> If we are supremely certain of the truth of at least some such statements [as *W*] the source of this certainty cannot be accounted for by Quine's generalised holistic model. The very coherence of the model requires an account of a different sort.

[10] C. Wright, 'Inventing Logical Necessity', in *Language, Mind and Logic*, ed. Jeremy Butterfield (Cambridge, CUP, 1986).

> The right account is, I believe, the obvious one: such statements, or at least an important sub-class of them, admit of totally convincing *proof*. We must, I suggest, take seriously the idea of proof, as a theoretically uncontaminated source of rational belief.[11]

Well and good. What is surprising is the immediately ensuing section, which opens:

> I wish to carry forward two things from the preceding. First, I shall take it that we do possess some sort of concept of logical necessity. Second, the correct account of the basis for the majority of judgments of logical necessity which we are prepared to make must make reference to the utterly convincing, self-contained character of suitable proofs.[12]

And in Wright's book on Wittgenstein he describes an ancestor of the present argument as:

> .... a quasi-transcendental argument to the effect that the practice of predictive theorizing *requires* that there is such a thing as necessity.[13]

What is surprising is that nothing in the anti-Quinean argument showed any need for the statements established by these 'proofs' to be regarded as *necessarily* true: merely true, and conclusively established in a way neither requiring nor vulnerable to holistic appraisal. But this feature seems not to add up to a notion of necessity.

There is an explanation, in terms of Wright's own positive views on necessity, for his quick move from a demonstration that certain statements must have such *epistemic* features to the claim that they are necessary truths. Wright wishes to espouse a non-realist, indeed non-cognitive account of logical necessity. Crucial to his account is the idea that the acceptance of a statement as necessary always involves an element of decision. But a decision to do what? Well, to use the statement in a way characteristic of the use of statements we regard as necessary truths. But what is that characteristic way? It is here that Wright makes crucial use of epistemic notions. For he extracts

[11] *ibid.* p. 194.
[12] *ibid.* p. 195.
[13] C. Wright, *Wittgenstein's Philosophy of Mathematics* (London, Duckworth, 1980), p. 415.

from Wittgenstein, and wishes tentatively to accept, the idea that what *is* characteristic of such use is the decision not to accept any description of the world that would conflict with the statement we have accepted as necessary (more accurately: with a 'suitably related' contingent statement). But this idea seems doubly mistaken. (Wright is, of course, aware of these difficulties.) On the one hand, such use seems at best characteristic of those statements we regard as necessarily true and concerning which we are also indefeasibly certain of their truth. But it is perfectly possible to accept, but only tentatively, statements we regard as (if true) necessarily true. On the other hand, this account seems not to distinguish between accepting as necessarily true, and accepting, dogmatically, as true. And there certainly seems to be such a distinction.

I conclude then, that Wright's powerful argument against Quine's epistemology does not amount to a quasi-transcendental argument for the necessity of necessity; and that its failure is traceable to an inadequacy in Wright's account of what it is to regard a statement as logically necessary.

4. *What is involved in the belief that a statement is logically necessary etc.*

Can we give a better account than Wright's of what is involved in the belief that a statement is logically necessary, or that a mode of inference is logically necessarily truth-preserving? And can we give a better 'quasi-transcendental' argument for the conclusion that we *need* such beliefs? I think I can begin to offer a rather simple-minded suggestion.

I take as my clue the following remarks of Mill and David Lewis. Mill wrote (in discussing *causal* necessity):

> That which is necessary, that which *must* be, means that which will be, whatever supposition we make with regard to other things.[14]

And Lewis writes:

> . . . . a co-tenable premiss is not only true, but also necessary to some extent.[15]

[14] J.S. Mill, *A System of Logic* (London, Longmans, 1956), Book III chapter IV sec. 6, p. 222.

[15] D.K. Lewis, *Counterfactuals* (Oxford, Blackwell, 1973) p. 70.

Let me try to spell out these remarks, and especially to explain the technical term 'co-tenable' in Lewis's observation.

When we begin logic, we are all told to distinguish assessing an argument as *valid*, and assessing its premisses as *true*. These, we are told, are independent activities. In particular, then, the acceptability in an argument of some mode of inference, is supposed to be quite independent of whether or not the overall premisses of the argument represent beliefs we have or mere suppositions we are making, as we put it, for the 'sake of argument'. Deductive inferences, then, are supposed to remain valid when they are applied to mere suppositions, and indeed regardless of what suppositions they are applied to, or are made in the course of the argument.

The second point to note is that, on anyone's view, there ought to be a close connection between reasoning from a supposition and asserting a conditional *i.e.* between the processes of thought in (i) *Suppose* John had come to the party; *then* Mary would have been upset; in that case *etc* . . . and (ii) *if* John had come to the party then Mary would have been upset; in that case *etc* . . . I suggest then that we might illuminate some aspects of the role of deductive principles, and more generally logically necessary truths, in reasoning from suppositions by drawing on the theory of conditionals, in particular the theory of subjunctive conditionals; not though, for reasons outlined in §2, but for more traditional reasons.

The central idea of Goodman's classic discussion of counterfactuals[16] was this. 'If that match had been scratched, it would have lighted' is true if there are suitable truths from which, in conjunction with the antecedent, the consequent can be inferred by means of a logical, or more typically natural, law. Goodman famously found two problems with this schematic account. One (which will not be our concern) was how to demarcate the class of natural laws. The second, and for us more important, concerned how to demarcate the set of 'suitable' truths from which, with the antecedent, the consequent was to be inferred. We cannot allow as auxiliary premisses the totality of truths; for typically this will include the negation of

[16]Nelson Goodman, 'The Problem of Counterfactual Conditionals', *Journal of Philosophy* 44 (1947), pp. 113–28.

the antecedent which, with classical logic, would yield any consequent. Goodman concluded that the auxiliary assumptions had to be *co-tenable* with the antecedent: where that means, it is not the case that if the antecedent were true they would be false. Unfortunately, as Goodman pointed out, we have now used the counterfactual construction we were trying to analyse. But this will not be a difficulty if we change priorities and try rather to understand reasoning from a supposition.

Let us consider the following case. An experimental scientist firmly believes a theory T_1. But a colleague has put forward an incompatible theory T_2 which it is his duty to test. He therefore has to work out what, on the supposition that T_2 is true, he might expect observationally. But it is an important point, due to Duhem, that purely logical reasoning from a single scientific hypothesis will not typically yield any observational consequences. The scientist will need to assume, explicitly or implicitly, a whole battery of auxiliary propositions: some theories, some laws, some hypotheses concerning the make-up of his apparatus. By what principle can he decide *which* auxiliary suppositions he can make? The crucial point is the one made by Goodman: not everything he believes firmly about the world can be retained when he is reasoning from the supposition that T_2 is true. In particular he cannot sensibly retain T_1—precisely because it is not co-tenable, in the above sense, with T_2: he believes that were T_2 true T_1 would not be. And this relates to the *interest* one might have in seeing what would be the case were T_2 true, *viz.* to see if T_2 is observationally confirmed *possibly at the expense of* T_1. A procedure which allowed you, while working out the consequences of T_2, to retain T_1 as an auxiliary hypothesis would undermine that interest. For we know *a priori* that such a combination will have endless unacceptable consequences.

This example illustrates another point. In reasoning from particular suppositions, about matches, jumping off buildings *etc.* we typically retain, implicitly or explicitly, as auxiliary premisses those propositions which we regard as laws of nature. Laws of nature, we might say, have a wide range of co-tenability. But the example illustrates that they do not have a universal range of co-tenability. There are some suppositions, *e.g.* conflicting hypotheses, with respect to which even deeply entrenched laws are *not* co-tenable.

The quotations from Mill and Lewis, then, can be seen as expressing the idea that the range of co-tenability of a proposition or a principle offers something like a measure of its necessity. I claimed in §1 that logical necessity, if there is such a thing, is the strongest form of necessity. I therefore wish to suggest that we treat as the manifestation of the belief that a mode of inference is logically necessarily truth-preserving, the preparedness to employ that mode of inference in reasoning from any set of suppositions whatsoever. Such a preparedness evinces the belief that, no matter what else was the case, the inferences would preserve truth. And the suggestion is that it is just this preparedness which is built into the idea that the validity of an argument is quite independent of questions about the truth of its premisses. A central point of interest in having such beliefs about logical necessity is to allow us to deploy principles of inference across the whole range of suppositions we might make.

But could we abandon the idea that the validity of an inference was totally independent of the nature of the overall suppositions of the argument in which it occurred? Could we think that while a number of modes of inference could be deployed under a wide range of suppositions, none could be deployed under the universal range of suppositions? To think that would, on the present suggestion, be to reject the idea that any mode of inference is *logically necessarily* truth-preserving. So my question is: could we abandon a belief in logical necessity? I wish to suggest not.

To abandon the belief in logical necessity would be to believe that for every acceptable mode of inference *M* there is at least one proposition *r* (it might be a very long disjunction) such that it is illegitimate to employ *M* in an argument which makes the supposition that *r*. Two cases now arise depending on whether or not it is known under which suppositions *r* the mode of inference *M* is illegitimate. Let us take the first supposition: that *r* is known. But then I claim that the position is self-refuting. For the following mode of inference will be one which can be deployed under all suppositions: *viz. M* when applied to whatever kind of premisses it originally was applied to, conjoined with not-*r*. (Or as one might put it: *M* can be applied, under the supposition that not-*r*. Can this be undermined if we add the further supposition that *r*?)

More interestingly suppose you believe only that there is such an *r*, but you do not know any particular one. Then, I claim, your rules are unusable. For, to know that your rule *M* can be applied under the supposition *p* you have to know if the rule is co-tenable with *p*; *i.e.* you have to know whether, if *p* were the case, *M* would not be truth-preserving. But how can you find that out? You would need to start some reasoning from the supposition that *p*. But which rules could you here apply? Not *M*: for its status under the supposition that *p* is *sub judice.* But no other. For the same problem will break out again, on the view that no rule is co-tenable with the universal range of suppositions.

I conclude then, that on the present view of what it is to regard a rule of inference as logically necessarily truth-preserving, we are constrained to believe that there are such rules. For if we abandoned that belief, we would be unable to reason from suppositions at all.

IX

Descartes on Modality

I

Descartes' discussions of modality are rather brief and scattered. The topic does not constitute for him an explicit central theme in the way that it does for Leibniz or Kant; or in the way that the depreciation of the senses or the distinction between mind and body do for Descartes himself. Many of his most direct pronouncements on the topic occur in expositions of his notorious doctrine that the eternal truths were freely created by God. And most of these occur, not in works published in his lifetime, but in his letters.

This 'creation' doctrine has been the focus of a considerable literature. Frankfurt[1] provides an admirable list of some interpretative problems which it raises, many of which have been explicitly addressed by him and other commentators. By 'explicitly' I here mean: the writers have been aware of, and argued against, answers other than their own to these interpretative questions. A (vague) issue in this area, which has rarely been discussed explicitly (in this sense) might be put thus: does Descartes hold that the necessity we attach to the eternal truths has its source in the nature of our minds? Most commentators have rather firm opinions on something like this question, but show little awareness of the need to defend their answer against opposed accounts. Among the aims of this paper is to clarify the question; to bring out the variety of answers which have been offered to it; and to trace this variety to important, but ignored, tensions in Descartes' thought.

This and other issues about Descartes' view of modality have an importance not merely for Cartesian scholarship, but for the philosophy of modality itself and its history. It is a commonplace of the historiography of philosophy that much of the 'problematic' of subsequent philosophy was set by

[1] 'Descartes on the Creation of the Eternal Truths' *Phil.Rev.*, 86, 1977 at p. 37.

Descartes. His method of doubt, his view of the mind, and his conception of 'ideas' are widely held to have set the terms for later discussion of central philosophical problems, most notably of 'our knowledge of the external world' and of the relation of mind to body. Even anti-Cartesians hold that his philosophy encapsulates certain compelling and abiding aspects of these problems. I wish to argue that his discussions of modality—brief and scattered though they be, and eccentric though some of them have been found—do the same in that problem-area. Here too, his deep and subtle thought reveals a sensitivity to a persistent set of issues.

This fact—which I hope to establish—should not be surprising. The metaphysics and epistemology of Descartes' *Meditations* were designed to lay the foundations of Cartesian science. And despite much in Descartes' philosophy which really is, or was imagined by him to be, anti-Aristotelian, he held that at least the basic laws of such science should have a feature central to Aristotle's account of scientific knowledge: that what they state could not be otherwise.[2] Descartes' conception of science—essentially Aristotelian in at least this respect—could not but make questions about necessity, rarely though they may surface in his writings, central to his philosophical enterprise.

II

I shall first introduce some of the themes of the present paper

[2] One might compare, among many texts, *Posterior Analytics* 71^{b}9:—

> We think we understand a thing *simpliciter* . . . whenever we think we are aware both that the explanation because of which the object is is its explanation, and that it is not possible for this to be otherwise.

with Descartes' remarks:—

> . . . . I would think I knew nothing in Physics if I could only say how things could be, without proving that they could not be otherwise. (Letter to Mersenne, 11 March 1640.)

> Further, I showed what the laws of nature were, and without basing my arguments on any principle other than the infinite perfections of God, I tried to demonstrate all those laws about which we could have any doubt, and to show that, even if God created many worlds, there could not be any in which they failed to be observed. (*Discourse on Method* Part Five. AT VI 43)

> . . . . and I confess that no reasons satisfy me even inphysics unless they involve that necessity which you call logical or analytic, provided you except these things which can be known by experience only. . . . (Letter to More, 5 February 1649. PL 243)

via a chronological approach to certain key texts. I shall suggest a rather simple hypothesis about the development of Descartes' thought which is at least strongly supported by these texts. The difficulties for this hypothesis, and most questions about my stance *vis-à-vis* other commentators, will be temporarily suppressed.

Descartes' *Rules for the Direction of the Mind* contains the earliest of his views on modality which are available to us. The date of the writing of the *Rules* seems not to be known with certainty. The crucial point is:—

> Amongst the large number of historians of philosophy who have discussed the date of this work, not one of any weight places the date of composition later than 1629.[3]

Let us begin with Descartes' account of 'intuition' and 'deduction'. Descartes explains *intuition* thus:

(1) By 'intuition' I do not mean the fluctuating testimony of the senses or the deceptive judgement of the imagination as it botches things together, but the conception of a clear and attentive mind, which is so easy and distinct that there can be no room for doubt about what we are understanding. Alternatively, and this comes to the same thing, intuition is the indubitable conception of a clear and attentive mind which proceeds solely from the light of reason *(op.cit.* Rule 3. C I 14, H&R I 7, AT X 368).

Further on he writes:

(2) . . . . two things are requisite for mental intuition: first, the proposition intuited must be clear and distinct; second, the whole proposition must be understood all at once, and not bit by bit (*op.cit.* Rule 11. C I 37 H&R I 33 AT X 407).

And after the first passage he gives some examples of what can be known in this way:

(3) Thus everyone can mentally intuit that he exists, that he is thinking, that a triangle is bounded by just three lines, and a sphere by a single surface, and the like (*op.cit*. Rule 3. C I 14 AT X 368).

We have here at least two elements: first an alleged

[3] L.J. Beck *The Method of Descartes: A Study of the Regulae* (Oxford, 1952) p. 10.

psychological phenomenon; that there are certain propositions which we cannot doubt to be true when they are attended to appropriately: secondly, an apparent explanation of what it is about these propositions and our grasp of them which produces this assurance; that the proposition is 'clear and distinct' and grasped 'in its totality'.

Intuition, then, involves a single act of a kind of mental 'vision' and it is in this respect that it contrasts with another mode of knowing, *viz. deduction*. This Descartes explains as 'the inference of something as following necessarily from some other propositions which are known with certainty' (AT X 369). Descartes is thinking of cases where someone comes to know something as the result of a series of inferential moves, taking him through intermediate propositions, starting from 'true and known principles'. He insists it is by intuition at each stage that we know that the proposition there inferred does follow necessarily from one or more earlier propositions.

(4) The self-evidence and certainty of intuition is required not only for apprehending single propositions, but also for any train of reasoning whatever. Take, for example, the inference that 2 plus 2 equals 3 plus 1: not only must we intuitively perceive that 2 plus 2 make 4, and that 3 plus 1 make 4, but also that the original proposition follows necessarily from the other two (AT X 369).

Nevertheless, although intuition is thus involved in deduction, they are to be distinguished

(5) . . . . on the grounds that we are aware of a movement or a sort of sequence in the latter but not in the former, and also because immediate self-evidence is not required for deduction, as it is for intuition; deduction in a sense gets its certainty from memory (AT X 370).

Intuition, from the examples above, appears sometimes to yield knowledge of contingent truths. I mentally intuit that I exist: although I might not have existed. But I also know by intuition that $2 + 2 = 4$, which Descartes thinks is necessarily true. Moreover intuition itself yields knowledge *of* necessity, most centrally in our perception that certain propositions are necessary consequences of others. How, according to Descartes, can intuition yield such knowledge of necessity?

In the *Rules*, Descartes appears to sketch a theory of the

source of necessity which connects it very closely with his account of how we recognize it. In Rule 12 he is considering what 'things' are appropriate objects of knowledge. The notion of 'thing' here is very broad, including properties ('natures') and propositions. (Descartes has an elaborate dichotomy into 'simple' and 'composite' things, which need not enter here.)[4] He writes

(6) .... the conjunction between these (simple) things is either necessary or contingent. The conjunction is necessary when one of them is somehow implied (albeit confusedly) in the concept of the other so that we cannot conceive either of them distinctly if we judge them to be separate from each other. It is in this way that shape is conjoined with extension, motion with duration or time, etc., because we cannot conceive of a shape which is completely lacking in extension, or a motion wholly lacking in duration. Similarly, if I say that 4 and 3 make 7, the composition is a necessary one, for we do not have a distinct conception of the number 7 unless in a confused sort of way we include 3 and 4 in it (AT X 421).

Descartes appears to be giving an account of the source of at least some necessities which would seem to make our knowledge of them unproblematic. Suppose we ask the author of the *Rules*: what *makes* it necessary that whatever has shape has extension? The answer appears to be something about *us*. We cannot conceive of a shape which is lacking extension. And that Descartes cannot so conceive would apparently be something of which, like other first-person psychological facts (*e.g.* that he is thinking) he could have 'intuitive' knowledge. Knowledge of necessity would seem to be a kind of self-knowledge. (Note how this picture explains the grouping together of such psychological knowledge with knowledge of logical relations.) At a date no later than 1629, then, Descartes appears to have held that the fact that certain 'things' are necessarily connected depends on facts about our powers of conception.

On 15 April 1630, Descartes wrote to Mersenne concerning a treatise on Physics he was writing. He announced that in it he would

[4] But see Leonard Miller 'Descartes, Mathematics and God' *Phil.Rev.* 66 (1957) Reprinted in A. Sesonke and N. Fleming (eds.) *Meta-Meditations* (Belmont, California 1965), an extremely perspicacious article.

(7) . . . . discuss a number of metaphysical topics and especially the following. The mathematical truths which you call eternal have been laid down by God and depend on Him entirely no less than the rest of his creatures. Indeed to say that these truths are independent of God is to talk of Him as if He were Jupiter or Saturn and to subject Him to the Styx and the Fates. Please do not hesitate to assert and proclaim that it is God who has laid down these laws in nature just as a king lays down laws in his kingdom. . . . (Letter to Mersenne, 15 April 1630. PL 11–12).

The exposition and defence of the newly-announced doctrine of the 'creation', by God, of the eternal truths continues in subsequent letters to Mersenne. For example:—

(8) As for the eternal truths, I say once more that they are true and possible only because God knows them as true or possible. They are not known as true by God in any way which would imply that they are true independently of Him. . . . In God willing and knowing are a single thing in such a way that by the very fact of willing something he knows it and it is only for this reason that such a thing is true. So we must not say that if God did not exist nonetheless these truths would be true; for the existence of God is the first and most eternal of all possible truths and the one from which all others derive . . . since God is a cause whose power surpasses the bounds of human understanding, and since the necessity of these truths does not exceed our knowledge, they must be something less than, and subject to, the incomprehensible power of God. (To Mersenne 27 May 1630 PL 13–14).

The truth and necessity of such propositions are now seen, not as deriving from features of our mind, but from the incomprehensible power of God, who has decreed that certain truths should be eternally, immutably and necessarily true. The simple hypothesis about the development of Descartes' thought is just that there was a move away from the idea that the necessity attaching to certain truths derives from facts about what we can and cannot conceive; that this change is connected with his espousal of the 'creation' doctrine; and that it had profound consequences for some of the most central aspects of his mature philosophy.

It is certainly easy to find texts in Descartes' post-1630 writings which seem explicitly to deny that the necessity of, say, the truths of mathematics, is dependent on features of the mind. Thus in a famous passage in *Meditations* V, writing of those 'natures, essences or forms' which are the subject-matter of the eternal truths he says:

(9) When, for example, I imagine a triangle, even if perhaps no such figure exists, or has ever existed, anywhere outside my thought, there is still a determinate nature, or essence, or form of the triangle which is immutable and eternal, and not invented by me or dependent on my mind. This is clear from the fact that various properties can be demonstrated of the triangle, for example that its three angles equal two right angles, and that its greatest side subtends its greatest angle, and the like; since these properties are ones which I now clearly recognize whether I want or not, even if I never thought of them at all when I previously imagined the triangle, it follows that they cannot have been invented by me. (*Meditations* V, AT VII 64)

The connection with the topic of necessity (implicit in talk of essence) is made clear a little later:

(10) But from the fact that I cannot think of God except as existing, it follows that existence is inseparable from God, and hence that he really exists. *It is not that my thought makes it so, or imposes any necessity on any thing* (my emphasis); on the contrary, it is the necessity of the thing itself, namely the existence of God, which determines my thinking in this respect. (*Meditations* V, AT VII 66–7)

And this theme is, in Descartes' thought, explicitly connected with the 'creation' doctrine. The authors of the *Objections* VI had asked:

(11) And how . . . could (God) have made it untrue from eternity that twice four makes eight, or that a triangle has three angles? Either these truths depend solely on the intellect that is thinking them, or on existing things, or else they are independent, since it seems that God could not have brought it about that any of these essences or truths were not as they were from eternity. (*Objections* VI AT VII 418)

Descartes, in replying, concludes by saying that:

(12) . . . . we should not suppose that eternal truths 'depend on the human intellect or on other existing things'; they depend on God alone, who, as the supreme legislator, has ordained them from eternity. (*Sixth Replies* AT VII 294)

The central change in Descartes' philosophy which, I believe, is connected with the apparent change of view about the source of the necessity of the eternal truths, concerns the extent of 'what can be called into doubt'.

Rule Two of the *Regulae* states that 'We should attend only to those objects of which our minds seem capable of having certain and indubitable cognition'. The text then goes on to argue that, 'of all the sciences so far discovered, arithmetic and geometry alone are . . . free from any taint of falsity or uncertainty'. 'Where these sciences are concerned it scarcely seems humanly possible to err, except through inadvertence.' (*Rule 2* AT X 365)

Descartes, early in the *Meditations*, notoriously argues that doubt *can* be cast on our knowledge of the truths of arithmetic and geometry by the following consideration: that for all he knows (at this stage of the *Meditations*) there may be a powerful and malicious demon who is deceiving him in his most firmly held beliefs even about such 'simple' things. Relatedly, in *Meditations* III he writes:

(13) . . . . whenever my preconceived belief in the supreme power of God comes to mind, I cannot but admit that it would be easy for him, if he so desired, to bring it about that I go wrong even in those matters which I think I see utterly clearly with my mind's eye. (*Meditations* III, AT VII 36)

But if Descartes' view in the *Meditations* was (as it appeared, sketchily, to be in the *Rules*) that the necessary truth of such propositions had its source in what he could, or could not, conceive, then it is unclear how a malicious demon, or a supremely powerful God, could so deceive him. He would have to be deceived concerning what he could or could not conceive. But such matters—which concern the contents of his mind—are the sorts of things which Descartes believes are invulnerable even to the 'metaphysical' doubt raised by the thought of an all-powerful God. That doubt, applied to the propositions of mathematics, concerns the question whether there is a deceiving God who could bring it about that something in which Descartes sees a 'manifest contradiction' should nevertheless be the case. If such a doubt is to be possible, then what makes it (necessarily) true that, say, 3 and 4 make 7 cannot be that he sees a manifest contradiction in the supposition that 3 and 4 *not* make 7. And the 'creation' doctrine does appear to deny that these truths are necessary in virtue of such facts about his mind. They are necessary because of the will of God, who has freely brought it about that certain truths hold immutably and necessarily. The 'creation' doctrine appears to open, in Descartes' thought, a gap between that *on the basis of which he asserts that* certain propositions are necessarily true, and that *in virtue of which* they are necessarily true. This gap leaves room for the metaphysical doubt.

Note that it is only this negative aspect of the 'creation' doctrine—the apparent denial of 'mind-dependence'—which for the moment I am suggesting is a *sine qua non* of the metaphysical doubt. As Margaret Wilson points out, all this doubt requires of the power of a deceiving God is that he can make me '*think* that the eternal truths are other than they are'.[5] It does not require, what the 'creation' doctrine seems positively to state, that God could have made the eternal truths other than they are. What this positive aspect of the 'creation' doctrine comes to is an issue to which we now turn.

III

A central question in the interpretation of the 'creation' doctrine concerns what its essential modal content is. Two broad views may be distinguished. The 'no necessity' account claims that the doctrine involves the view that 'really' or 'ultimately' there are no necessary truths. A prominent defender is Frankfurt.[6] Opposed to this is the 'iterated modality' interpretation ably defended by Curley.[7] This holds that, for Descartes, the eternal truths are indeed necessarily true, but they are not necessarily necessary.

Many passages support the idea that, for Descartes, the eternal truths are not (really) necessarily true. Descartes often expresses the doctrine in such terms as:

[5] *Descartes* (London 1978) p. 34.
[6] *op. cit.*
[7] 'Descartes on the Creation of the Eternal Truths' *Phil.Rev.* 93 (1984).

(14) . . . . it was free and indifferent for God to make it not to be true that the three angles of a triangle were equal to two right angles. . . . (To Mesland, 2 May 1644)

(15) . . . . I do not think that we should ever say of anything that it cannot be brought about by God. For since everything involved in truth and goodness depends on His omnipotence, I would not dare to say that God cannot make a mountain without a valley, or that one and two should not be three. (To Arnauld, 29 July 1648)

If Descartes held anything to be necessarily true it would be such propositions as that one and two is three, or that if there is a mountain then there is a valley. He seems to be saying, even of these, that God could have made them not to be true. But if God could have made them not to be true they could have been not true. So, it seems, Descartes is committed to the view that they are not really necessarily true.

The qualification 'really' is doing some work here. For Descartes repeatedly stresses, in the vicinity of such passages, that he cannot comprehend how such propositions could not be true.

(16) I merely say that He has given me such a mind that I cannot conceive a mountain without a valley, or an aggregate of one and two which is not three, and that such things involve a contradiction in my conception. (*ibid.*)

Such facts about what he cannot conceive will make certain propositions appear to be necessarily true. But, on the present interpretation, reflection on the power of God reveals that this is *mere* appearance. Really such propositions could have been false.

Nevertheless, many of the very texts which support the above interpretation, and others, contain passages which clearly conflict with it. After all, Descartes' doctrine is that God 'created the eternal truths'. And Descartes repeatedly expresses this idea by saying that what God has done is, precisely, to make some truths eternal, immutable and necessary.

(17) . . . . it is because he willed that the three angles of a triangle should necessarily equal two right angles that this is true and cannot be otherwise. (*Sixth Replies* AT VII 431)

(18) .... so I do not think that the essences of things and the mathematical truths which we can know concerning them are independent of God. Nevertheless I do think that they are immutable and eternal, since the will and decree of God willed and decreed that they should be so. (*Fifth Replies* AT VII 380)

The idea that God has (really) made some things necessary, by making their negations impossible, is found in passages which also strongly suggest the 'iterated modality' interpretation of the doctrine. In the first letter quoted, Descartes responds to Mesland's difficulty in understanding the 'creation' doctrine as follows:

(19) It is easy to dispel this difficulty by considering that the power of God cannot have any limits, and that our mind is finite and so created as to be able to conceive as possible things which God has willed to be in fact possible, but not to be able to conceive as possible things which God could have made possible but which he has in fact wished to make impossible.

Let us consider some proposition *p*, which God has wished to make impossible. Since it is an omnipotent God who has so wished, it *is* impossible that *p*. But God could have made it possible that *p*. So it is possible that *p* have been possible. On this view, some things, though impossible, could have been possible. Assuming the standard connexion between necessity and possibility, the implication for necessary truth is as follows. Consider some necessary truth, *p*. Since it is necessary that *p*, it is impossible that *not-p*. But it was possible that *not-p* be possible. That is, it is not necessary that *not-p* be impossible. That is, it is not necessary that *p* be necessary. This text thus appears to say that there *are* necessary truths, but they are not *necessarily* necessary. This is just the position ascribed to Descartes by the 'iterated modality' interpretation.

A little later in the letter to Mesland, Descartes seems almost to state this explicitly. He writes:

(20) .... even if God has willed that some truths should be necessary, this does not mean that he willed them necessarily; for it is one thing to will that they be necessary, and quite another to will them necessarily, or to be necessitated to will them.

Even here, though, Descartes' words do not express unequivocally merely the iterated modality interpretation. To do that, the final clause should have run '. . . and quite another to will them necessarily to be necessary, or to be necessitated to will them to be necessary'.

More generally put: to express unequivocally the iterated modality view, Descartes should *not* (i) give God power to make not to be true such unmodalized propositions as that one and two make three, but *should* (ii) give God power to make not true such modalized propositions as that it is necessary that one and two make three, or that it is impossible that there be a mountain without a valley. We have already seen (in the first two passages quoted in this section) that Descartes *does* do (i). And it is only very occasionally that he explicitly does (ii). One of these rare occasions is in the immediately preceding sentence of the letter to Mesland:

(21) God cannot have been determined to make it true that contradictories *cannot* (my emphasis) be true together, and therefore he could have done the opposite.

This does seem to ascribe to God: *not* the power to make contradictories true together; but merely the power to make false the modalized proposition that contradictories *cannot* be true together.

So far, I suggest, we have simply found the texts ambiguous as between the view that (really) there are no necessary truths, and the conflicting view that there are, but they are not necessarily necessary. I shall postpone consideration of how this ambiguity should be diagnosed until we look at a further tension in Descartes' thought in this area, one which has been reflected, but rarely assessed, in the very diverse opinions of commentators.

IV

In section II I suggested that in his mature philosophy Descartes rejected an idea which seemed to be present in the *Rules*, namely that the necessity attaching to certain truths, or to certain connections between 'simple things', was a matter of what he could or could not conceive. We saw a number of texts which deny this explicitly. And I argued that denying this was a prerequisite of the metaphysical doubt.

More generally, the central thrust of Descartes' mature philosophy is to stress that the (necessary) truths he seeks to establish in his metaphysics, the foundation of his mathematized physics, concern 'what is there *anyway*'—in a phrase of Bernard Williams[8]—where this implies that the truths he is concerned with are not dependent on how things are merely for our consciousness, or from the human point of view. He puts the point most explicitly, applied particularly to truths about God, in the *Second Replies*:

(22) As everyone knows, there are two quite distinct ways of speaking of God. The first is appropriate for ordinary understanding and does contain some truth, albeit truth which is relative to human beings; and it is this way of speaking that is generally employed in Holy Scripture. The second way of speaking comes closer to expressing the naked truth—truth which is not relative to human beings; it is this way of speaking which everyone ought to use when philosophizing, and that I had a special obligation to use in my *Meditations*, since my supposition there was that no other human beings were yet known to me, and moreover I was considering myself not as consisting of mind and body but solely as a mind. (AT VII 142–3)

In general, Descartes distinguishes what concerns 'mere consciousness' and what concerns 'the truth about the world',[9] and holds that '. . . our mind is not the measure of reality or of truth'.[10] And we have already seen (in section II (9) and (10)) Descartes expressing the view that, specifically, the necessity involved in statements of essence is not imposed by his thought. Overall, then, it seems not to be Descartes' intention to see the necessity we attach to the eternal truths as dependent on what he can or cannot conceive or, more generally, on features of the human mind.

Nevertheless, a number of commentators ascribe to the

[8] *Descartes: The Project of Pure Enquiry* Harmondsworth, 1978, p. 64.

[9] 'I did distinguish between what belongs to me, or to my nature, and what belongs only to my consciousness of myself; but it cannot be deduced from this that my metaphysics reaches no conclusions about anything outside consciousness. . . . It is easy for the reader to tell when I was discussing mere consciousness, and when I was discussing the truth about the world.' (To Hyperaspistes, August 1641. PL 112)

[10] To More, 5 February 1649. PL 242.

mature Descartes versions of this (vague) idea: not merely as a strand within a possibly inconsistent body of thought, but as his central position on the relationship between modality and the human mind. I shall quote some such views. Margaret Wilson writes that

> It is clear enough . . . that Descartes did regard the 'necessity' we perceive in mathematical propositions as *in some sense and degree a function of the constitution of our minds* (my emphasis) —themselves finite 'creatures'.[11]

She suggests that Descartes should be congratulated for anticipating later views.

> From Hume and Kant onward it has been widely held that alleged perceptions of 'necessity' cannot be taken for granted, and that we must in some sense or other have recourse to the structure and workings of our own minds to give an account of these 'perceptions'.[12]

Frankfurt sketches something rather similar.

> The propositions we find to be necessary . . . need not be truths at all. The inconceivability of their falsity . . . is not inherent in them. It is properly to be understood only as relative to the character of our minds. We cannot escape this character, of course, but we *can* realize that God might have made it different from what it is. . . . The necessities human reason discovers by analysis and demonstration are just necessities of its own contingent nature. In coming to know them, it does not

[11] *op.cit.*, p. 125. The clash I am describing between two kinds of interpretation of Descartes shows up as a tension within Wilson's treatment. For in her later discussion of the passage about essences or natures in *Meditations* V she says that:

> . . . . Descartes presumably means to hold that geometrical essences strictly depend only on the will and understanding of God, and not at all on any finite minds that may think of them. (*op.cit.* p. 171)

This seems absolutely right as a treatment of this passage (contrast Ishiguro's remark in 'The Status of Necessity and Impossibility in Descartes' in A. Rorty (ed.) *Essays on Descartes' Meditations* (Univ. of California Press, 1986), at p. 461 where she says that 'These (eternal) truths concern the immutable forms of the *internal objects of our imaginings and thinkings* . . .' (my emphasis).) What Wilson does not note is that since talk of the essence of a triangle is talk of what holds necessarily of triangles, the view she is ascribing to Descartes here seems to be at odds with her account, based on her expositions of the 'creation' doctrine, of his view of the 'necessity we perceive in mathematical propositions'.

[12] *ibid.*

necessarily discover the nature of the world as it is in itself, or as it appears to God.[13]

Hidé Ishiguro, in a paper I find rather unclear,[14] at least sometimes seems to be saying things along the same very broad lines:

> The reason why when we add two and three we cannot but get the sum of five is because eternal truths, according to Descartes, have their seat in the mind. . . . They do not, it is true, depend on how particular individual minds are made. . . . In fact, what Descartes means by eternal truths having their seat in the mind seems closer to Kant's view on the *a priori* than it does to epistemic views like that of Hume. What is at issue is the universal validity of these eternal truths in our mental constitution. . . .[15]
>
> It is not only the necessity of 2 + 2 = 4 and other arithmetical truths that depend on God's creation of our mind. The very concepts of natural number and of addition or multiplication depend on God's having made our minds in the way he did.[16]

(Despite the apparent broad consensus on the present matter, it should be noted that these three writers differ considerably concerning the issue of section III—the modal content of the 'creation' doctrine.)

Noting the comparison both Wilson and Ishiguro make between Descartes and Kant, we might contrast these views with the remarks of Guéroult in his monumental *Descartes selon l'ordre des raisons*:[17]

> Far from supposing that a methodological idealism can suffice, Descartes has never admitted that the human mind can define and posit the reality of things by virtue of its own proper necessities. . . . In this way he differs completely from Kant. . . .[18]

A final witness to the present issue, and one of the few to note the real tension in Descartes' thought, is Leonard Miller.[19] He

[13] *op.cit.* p. 45.
[14] *op.cit.*
[15] *ibid.* p. 463.
[16] *ibid.* p. 465.
[17] tr. Roger Ariew, Minneapolis, 1984.
[18] Vol. I, p. 15; cf. *ibid.*, p. 264–5.
[19] *op.cit.*

well sees the aspects of Descartes' writings which seem to have influenced Wilson *et al.* but notes that the kind of position they ascribe to him is not really, or fully, his.

> If Descartes had asserted throughout his work that the necessity of the truth of the so-called 'eternal' verities may arise not from the nature of the simples themselves but from the nature of the created mind that apprehends them, his position would be more consistent, for this view, unlike the one which maintains that the necessity is something objective revealed to us, is consistent with both his theory of simples and his theology. Despite these by no means trivial considerations, however, he really cannot bring himself to accept this view, for it strikes at the very heart of his rationalism. He cannot discount the conviction that the necessity of certain relations is revealed clearly and distinctly by the light of reason.[20]

Before trying to make more precise what might be at issue between, on the one hand, Wilson, Frankfurt and Ishiguro, and, on the other, Guéroult and Miller (and I take these writers merely as exemplary of the interpretative positions I wish to discuss), it will be well to have before us some of the texts which appear to express the kind of position the former group wish to ascribe to Descartes. I think they may usefully be divided into three groups.

(i) *Possible for God/Impossible for us?*

Often, when Descartes is expounding the 'creation' doctrine, he expresses the idea that the possibilities which that doctrine seems to leave open to God (I here prescind from the issue of section III—*viz*. of the modal expression of such possibilities) go beyond what *He* can conceive. Thus in section 6 of the letter to Arnauld of 29 July 1648, he writes:

(23) I would not dare to say that God cannot make a mountain without a valley, or that one and two should not be three. I merely say that He has given me such a mind that I cannot conceive a mountain without a valley, or an aggregate of one and two which is not three, and that such things involve a contradiction in my conception. (PL 236–7)

Very similarly, he writes to More (5 February 1649):

[20] A. Sesonke and N. Fleming (eds.) *op.cit.* pp. 46–7.

(24) For my part, I know that my intellect is finite and God's power is infinite, and so I set no bounds to it; I consider only what I can conceive and what I cannot conceive, and I take great pains that my judgment should accord with my understanding. And so I boldly assert that God can do everything which I conceive to be possible, but I am not so bold as to deny that He can do whatever conflicts with my understanding—I merely say that it involves a contradiction. (PL 240–241)

Another statement of the idea that what the 'creation' doctrine leaves 'open' for God is not comprehensible by us is:

(25) . . . . there is no need to ask how God could have brought it about from eternity that it was not true that twice four make eight and so on; for I admit that this is unintelligible to us. (*Sixth Replies* AT VII 436)[21]

The suggestion of these passages might then be that when we ascribe necessity (rightly or wrongly—an issue of section III) to certain truths we do so on the basis of the fact that their negations are 'impossible for us': our understanding cannot comprehend how there can be alternatives to these truths. So, it might be held, when Descartes asserts that certain truths are necessary, the *content* of this assertion, in his view, is no more than this: that *he* cannot comprehend any alternative to these truths, or that their negations involve a contradiction in *his* conception—the kind of position ascribed to him by Wilson *et al.*

(ii) *Eternal truths as imprinted*

Another strand in Descartes' thought (one stressed particularly by Ishiguro) which connects the eternal truths with aspects of our intellect is the idea that they are 'inborn', 'innate', 'have their seat in' our minds. (A form of the doctrine of 'innate speculative principles' famously attacked by Locke.) The thought seems important in Descartes' epistemology. It embodies an attempted explanation of why, at least when one has (by means of the Cartesian propaedeutic) freed the mind from 'prejudices', one can 'clearly and distinctly' perceive the eternal truths to be true. (See *Principles* I, 50.) The idea is

[21] For further expressions of the same idea see: To Mersenne, 15 April 1630, PL 12; 6 May 1630, PL 14; 27 May 1630, PL 15: to Mesland 2 May 1644, PL 151.

sometimes expressed as part of the exposition of the 'creation' doctrine. Thus, during its very first statement, Descartes writes:

(26) Please do not hesitate to assert and proclaim everywhere that it is God who has laid down these laws in nature just as a king lays down laws in his kingdom. There is no single one that we cannot understand if our mind turns to consider them. They are all inborn in our minds just as a king would imprint his laws on the hearts of all his subjects if he had enough power to do so. (To Mersenne 15 April 1630. PL p. 11)

The idea of God's implanting such truths recurs in the *Discourse*:

(27) What is more, I have noticed certain laws which God has so established in nature, and of which he has implanted such notions in our minds, that after adequate reflection we cannot doubt that they are exactly observed in everything which exists or occurs in the world. (DM V AT VI 41)

But apparently similar ideas also occur where the idea of God's implanting them in our minds seems not to be in play. *Principles* I, 49 tells us that:

(28) . . . when we recognize that it is impossible for anything to come from nothing, the proposition *Nothing comes from nothing* is regarded not as a really existing thing, or even as a mode of a thing, but as an eternal truth which resides within our mind. Such truths are termed common notions or axioms. . . . It would not be easy to draw up a list of all of them; but nonetheless we cannot fail to know them when the occasion for thinking of them arises, provided that we are not blinded by preconceived opinions.

(iii) *The Rules doctrine in Descartes' mature work*

The passages which seem most puzzling for the simple hypothesis of section II are those in which Descartes, without invoking the 'creation' doctrine, appears to state explicitly the view we located in the *Rules* and argued was abandoned in his mature thought, that necessity (and, correlatively, possibility) depends on facts about what we can and cannot conceive.

A striking example in the *Second Replies* seems to assert of possibility precisely what *Meditations* V (passages (9) and (10)) denied of necessity. Mersenne, anticipating Leibniz' famous objection, claimed that Descartes' ontological argument required the premiss that the nature or essence of God is possible or not self-contradictory. In an important passage, Descartes, after criticizing Mersenne's formulation of the objection, writes:

(29) . . . . you should have denied the major premiss and said instead 'What we clearly understand to belong to the nature of a thing cannot for that reason be affirmed of that thing unless its nature is possible, or non-contradictory'. But please notice how weak this qualification is. If by 'possible' you mean what everyone commonly means, namely 'whatever does not conflict with our human concepts', then it is manifest that the nature of God, as I have described it, is possible in this sense, since I supposed it to contain only what, according to our clear and distinct conceptions, must belong to it; and hence it cannot conflict with our concepts. Alternatively, you may well be imagining some other kind of possibility which relates to the object itself; but unless this matches the first sort of possibility it can never be known by the human intellect, and so it does not so much support a denial of God's nature and existence as serve to undermine every other item of knowledge. For as far as our concepts are concerned there is no impossibility in the nature of God; on the contrary, all the attributes which we include in the concept of the divine nature are so interconnected that it seems to us to be self-contradictory that any one of them should not belong to God. Hence, if we deny that the nature of God is possible, we may just as well deny that the angles of a triangle are equal to two right angles, or that he who is actually thinking exists; and if we do this it will be even more appropriate to deny that anything we acquire by means of the senses is true. The upshot will be that all human knowledge will be destroyed, though for no good reason. (AT VII 150–1)

And later in the same *Replies* he writes that:

(30) All self-contradictoriness or impossibility resides solely in our thought, when we make the mistake of joining together mutually inconsistent ideas; it cannot occur in anything which is outside the intellect.

V

I argued in section III that Descartes' texts are ambiguous as between two interpretations of the modal content of the 'creation' doctrine. Sometimes he appears to be asserting the 'no necessity' view, that really there are no necessary truths. That is, for all *p*, not *Lp*. (Equivalently, for all *p*, *Mp*.) At others, he seems to allow that there are necessary truths, but to hold that they are not necessarily necessary—the 'iterated modality' interpretation. (For all *p*, not *LLp*. Equivalently, for all *p*, *MMp*.)[22] In this section I wish to make some suggestions about what, in the structure of problems about modality, and in Descartes' position, may explain this ambiguity. I shall suggest that Descartes' views, in certain respects, exemplify certain persistent difficulties in this area.

Descartes, like many other philosophers, offers an answer to the seemingly legitimate question: why are certain truths necessary? Thus Michael Dummett posed the question about the 'source' of necessity:

> The philosophical problem of necessity is twofold: what is its source, and how do we recognize it? God can ordain that something shall hold good of the actual world; but how can even God ordain that something is to hold good in all possible worlds? We know what it is to set about finding out if something *is* true; but what account can we give of the process of discovering whether it *must* be true?[23]

Descartes' official answer is unequivocal: they are necessary because God has willed that they be. Two preliminary points need to be made about how he takes the question and the answer. The first is that what is asked for and offered is definitely not what would now be thought of as an analysis or explication of the concept of necessity or of modal notions in general. Unanalysed modal notions are deployed in the answer:

[22] Weaker versions of both interpretations have been proposed. The issue concerns whether, on either view of the modal content of the 'creation' doctrine, certain propositions—notably those which themselves express God's omnipotence—lie outside its scope. I shall not discuss this issue, important though it is in a full account of Descartes' thought in this area: it lies somewhat apart from the questions I wish to canvass. Some of the problems are discussed in Frankfurt *op.cit.* section VII, and Curley *op.cit.* section VII. See also Jean-Luc Marion *Sur la Théologie blanche de Descartes* (Paris, 1981) pp. 297ff.

[23] *Truth and Other Enigmas* (Duckworth, London 1978) p. 169.

(31) . . . . it is because he willed that the three angles of a triangle should necessarily equal two right angles that this is true and cannot be otherwise. (*Sixth Replies* AT VII 431) (But contrast *Rule 6 e.)*

Rather, secondly, Descartes sees his answer as 'causal', in one sense of that (Aristotelian) term:

(32) There is no need to ask what category of causality is applicable to the dependence of this goodness upon God, or to the dependence on him of other truths. For since the various kinds of cause were enumerated by thinkers who did not, perhaps, attend to this kind of causality, it is hardly surprising that they gave no name to it. But in fact they did give it a name, for it can be called efficient causality, in the sense that a king may be called the efficient cause of a law, although the law itself is not a thing which has physical existence, but is merely what they call a 'moral entity'. (*Second Replies* AT VII 436)

Now although there are very interesting questions concerning the theological and philosophical *grounds* Descartes had for holding what most have thought to be a bizarre doctrine,[24] I shall mainly explore the possible *consequences* of his answer to the above question. I shall claim that they exemplify a pattern common to a wide range of such answers, many of which have been thought far from bizarre by contemporary philosophers, and that some of these consequences can explain the ambiguities in his position.

Suppose a philosopher asks why those truths which are (apparently) necessary are necessary, and seeks a quite general answer. That is, he seeks an answer which can be applied to each and every necessary truth, a principle q which generates, for every relevant instance, a theorem of the form Lp because q. Suppose, further, the philosopher is moved to ask, concerning the instances of q: is it necessary or contingent? Then, I claim, there will be strong pressure for him to say that it is contingent. For suppose q is itself a necessary truth. Then, if the original question about the necessity of p was legitimate, it seems we can legitimately ask: why is it necessary that q (why is this instance of q necessary)? And it is unclear that he can answer

[24] See e.g. Frankfurt *op.cit.* section III, Curley *op.cit.* section III and the very extensive treatment in Marion *op.cit.*.

that question compatibly with his claim to have found a *global* explanation of the necessity of necessary truths. Clearly it is not a good answer to say: it is necessary that *q* because *q*. It seems he will have to find some other proposition *r*, (which might be a different instance of *q*) such that it is necessary that *q* because *r*. But then either *r* is in turn necessary—and the question then breaks out again; or *r* is itself contingent, and it is this contingency which is the ultimate explanation of the necessity of the truths concerning which the question first arose. It seems then that a general and ultimate answer to the question will have to be expressed in some proposition which is contingent.[25]

I see no reason to think Descartes was moved to explain the necessity of the eternal truths as deriving from contingencies by anything like the above line of thought. But his own particular answer to the initial question produces the same overall result. These truths are necessary because God (freely) willed that they be so. And Descartes evidently holds, as many do, that if *X* has (freely) willed that so-and-so, then it is not necessary that *X* will that so-and-so: *X* could have done otherwise. So, although for reasons other than those sketched in the previous paragraph, Descartes is committed to claims of the form: *Lp* because *q* where it is *contingent* that *q*.

But if *p* is necessarily true because *q*, where *q* is contingent, doesn't that entail that it is not really necessary that *p*? Isn't there 'a strong pressure to feel that the original necessity has not been explained or identified, so much as undermined'?[26] The pressure is, though, resistible. Why might it be thought that there is a difficulty in accepting both:

Lp because *q*

and

$\sim Lq$?

[25] For a similar argument see Simon Blackburn 'Morals and Modals' in Graham Macdonald and Crispin Wright (eds.) *Facts, Science and Morality* (Oxford, 1986) at pp. 120–121. Blackburn believes the problem arises only for a 'truth-conditional' account of modal claims. Of this I am unsure. I do think that he oversimplifies the effect of adopting the view that what explains the necessity of necessary truths is itself a contingent matter. See below.

[26] *ibid.* p. 121.

Perhaps the following principle seems plausible. That if *p* because *q*, and it is not necessary that *q*, then it is not necessary that *p*. This principle might be rejected, at least in certain bizarre circumstances.[27] But even if accepted, all it entails, in the present case is that that p is necessary is not itself necessary. That is, the most that seems to be required by the doctrine that the necessity of certain truths is to be explained by a contingency—be it linguistic conventions, forms of life, or God's will—is that one deny the S4 principle *viz.* that if *Lp* then *LLp*. This may be thought objection enough to any position, such as Descartes', which has this feature.[28] But my aim here is not to assess Descartes', or similar, views, but to understand them. The present point is simply that one feature of Descartes' thought—that what explains the necessity of necessary truths is itself something which is contingent—does not *require* him to say that these truths are not (really) necessary. Merely—what the 'iterated modality' interpretation ascribes to him—that they are not necessarily necessary.

I argued, though, that this was by no means Descartes' unambiguously stated position. I think I can begin to explain why. One strand in the explanation is just that it is not (and is still not—I forbear giving examples) always clear to a writer when he is making a claim about those propositions which (he holds) are necessary truths: and when he is making a corresponding claim about those propositions which ascribe necessity to the former propositions. That is, in the case where the issue is that of 'explaining' necessity, there is often a tendency to confuse a doctrine which explains the *truth* of those propositions which are necessarily true, with the corresponding explanation of their *necessity* (equivalently, of the truth of those propositions which ascribe necessity). Where 'q' is what

[27] Cases of some kind of overdetermination. Suppose that had *q* not been the case, then *r* would have been the case: and that had *r* been the case then *p* would (still) have been the case, and would have been the case because *r*. Then if, in the appropriate sense, it is necessary that either *q* or *r*, there seems no reason to think that the contingency of *q* will 'feed back' to the contingency of that which (as it happens) it explains, namely, *p*.

[28] But see Crispin Wright's 'In defence of the Conventional Wisdom' section III, in Ian Hacking (ed.) *Exercises in Analysis* (Cambridge, 1985) for some difficulties about arguing *for* the S4 principle against an opponent who adopts a position of the present structure.

is offered as an explanation, the difference is between things of the form of:

(1) If *Lp*, *p* because *q*.

and the corresponding claim of the form of:

(2) If *Lp*, *Lp* because *q*.

If it is contingent that *q*, I suggested, doctrines of the form of (2) may require that propositions of the form '*Lp*' also be contingent (the denial of the S4 principle). It would only be the corresponding doctrine of the form of (1) which might entail that for no *p* is it the case that *Lp*. However, even if it were the intention of a philosopher to accept only something of the form of (2), he might find himself, through confusing (2) with (1), committed to the much more radical apparent consequence of (1), in the case where it is contingent that *q*, *viz.* that (really) there are no necessary truths. That Descartes was inclined not to distinguish clearly between things of the forms of (1) and of (2) is, I believe, exhibited in the excerpt from the letter to Mesland quoted on p. 165.

The tendency to confuse a case of (2) with the corresponding exemplar of (1) will be more than a mere slip if there is in fact no way a writer can prevent his philosophical motivation for his version of (2) from providing as good a motivation for the corresponding instance of (1). And this is surely Descartes' position, and the second strand of my explanation of the ambiguity in his position.

He holds that to deny that the necessity of the eternal truths stems from God's free will is to derogate from His omnipotence. He therefore accepts:

(2D) If *Lp*, then *Lp* because God willed that *Lp*.

But this motivation for (2D) would surely provide, for Descartes, the same objection to a position which did embrace (2D)—the *necessity* of these truths depends on God's will—but denied that their *truth* was thus dependent. Such a position would, for Descartes, equally show an improper appreciation of God's omnipotence. It is therefore difficult to see how Descartes, whatever his intentions and however clearly he had distinguished the two doctrines, could have held back from:

(1D) If Lp, p because God willed that p.

And this may explain why, apparently inconsistently with his repeated insistence that there *are* necessary truths, he does not, in the texts, hold back from (1D).

This point—that Descartes' motivation for (2D) (which at most entails the 'iterated modality' view) carries over to (1D) (which seems to entail the 'no necessity' view)—emerges ironically in Curley's very illuminating defence of the 'iterated modality' interpretation.[29] Curley gives very good reasons for saying that the 'no necessity' position is not straightforwardly Descartes', and could not be consistently with major features of his philosophy.[30] He then attributes to Descartes two principles which it is plausible to say underlie his views in this area.

The first concerns a connection between volition and contingency. It is that for any agent a, if a wills that p then it is possible that a not will that p.

(i) $(a)(p)(\text{if } Wap \text{ then } M\sim Wap)$.

The second is an expression of God's omnipotence *viz.* that a proposition is true if and only if God wills that it be true.

(ii) $(p)(p \text{ if and only if } Wgp)$

where 'Wgp' reads 'God wills that p'. Curley then shows that (i) and (ii) entail that for all p, even if it is necessary that p then it is not *necessarily* necessary that p. Equivalently,

I $(p)MMp$

—the position his 'iterated modality' interpretation ascribes to Descartes.

The problem, for Curley's interpretation, is that the very same pattern of argument shows that (i) and (ii) entail:

II for all p, Mp

the 'no necessity' view which Curley wishes to reject as an interpretation of Descartes.

[29] *op. cit.*
[30] *op. cit.* section II.

Proof: Let p_1 be *any* truth, necessary or otherwise, *i.e.* assume:

(iii) p_1.

An instance of (ii), from left to right is

(iv) if p_1 then Wgp_1.

An instance of (i) is

(v) if Wgp_1 then $M \sim Wgp_1$.

Detaching the consequents of (iv) and (v) yields

(vi) $M \sim Wgp_1$.

That is, it is possible that God not will that p_1. But since, by (iv), p_1 only if God wills that p_1, this entails

(vii) $M \sim p_1$.

Since p_1 was a randomly selected truth, we can generalize to

(viii) (p)(if p then $M \sim p$)

which is equivalent to the modal formula which Curley rejected as an interpretation of Descartes' doctrine *viz.*

II $(p)Mp$.

So if, as Curley suggests, Descartes accepted (i) and (ii) he would be committed not merely to the 'iterated modality' view, but to the 'no necessity' position, contrary to Curley's own interpretation.

VI

In section III I argued that Descartes' texts could be seen as containing two conflicting statements of the modal content of the 'creation' doctrine. One asserts that there are necessary truths, though they are not necessarily necessary. The other that, really, there are no necessary truths. In section V I suggested one diagnosis of this fact. A different, though not conflicting, diagnosis might be to hypothesise that the notion of necessity (and, correlatively, of possibility) is ambiguous in Descartes. In one sense, 'necessary$_1$', certain propositions are necessarily$_1$ true (though not necessarily necessary$_1$). In another sense, 'necessary$_2$', no truths are necessarily$_2$ true. A structurally similar hypothesis would also resolve the vague issue of section IV. Necessity in one sense would be, in another sense would not be, 'a function of the structure of our mind'. Can such a hypothesised ambiguity help elucidate Descartes' texts and his problem-situation? Up to a point I believe that it can: this section explores certain aspects of this hypothesis.

We have already seen one text which explicitly speaks of two senses or kinds of possibility (29). But I wish, temporarily, to prescind from that and also from the issue of the modal content of the 'creation' doctrine. I shall first look in detail at a passage which is unequivocal with respect to *that* question: it decisively asserts the 'iterated modality' position.[31] I shall argue that this reveals a deep, but understandable, conflict in Descartes' thought, one which relates to and helps clarify the issue of section IV—the 'mind-dependence' or otherwise of modality.

It is important first to say more about that aspect of the human mind to which, if any, Descartes relates modal notions *viz.* its powers of conceiving. To do this we must pay some attention to Descartes' psychological vocabulary.

Descartes makes an important distinction between two cognitive verbs—*intelligere* ('know/understand') and *comprehendere* ('grasp'). A typical exposition runs:

> It does not matter that I do not grasp the infinite, or that there are countless additional attributes of God which I cannot in any way grasp, and perhaps cannot even reach in my thought; for it is in the nature of the infinite not to be grasped by a finite being like myself. It is enough that I understand the infinite, and that I judge that all the attributes which I clearly perceive and know to imply some perfection—and perhaps countless others of which I am ignorant—are present in God either formally or eminently. (*Meditations* III AT VII 46)

The distinction is made, in French, in the letter to Mersenne of 15 April 1630:

> The greatness of God . . . is something which we cannot comprehend (*comprendre*) though we can know (*connaître*) it. (PL 11)

[31] From the letter to Mesland 2 May 1644 already quoted at (18), (20), (21).

And it appears that the distinction can be made between these two acts or states even when their object is not the infinite:

> For the idea of the infinite, if it is to be a true idea, cannot be grasped at all, since the impossibility of being grasped is contained in the formal definition. Nevertheless, it is evident that the idea which we have of the infinite does not merely represent one part of it, but really does represent the infinite in its entirety. The manner of representation, however, is the manner appropriate to a human idea; and undoubtedly God, or some other intelligent nature more perfect than a human mind, could have a much more perfect, i.e. more accurate and distinct idea. Similarly, we do not doubt that a novice at geometry has an idea of a whole triangle when he understands that it is a figure bounded by three lines, even though geometers are capable of knowing and recognizing in this idea more properties belonging to the same triangle, of which the novice is ignorant. Just as it suffices for the possession of an idea of the whole triangle to understand that it is a figure contained within three lines, so it suffices for possession of a true and complete idea of the infinite in its entirety if we understand that it is a thing which is bounded by no limits. (*Fifth Replies* AT VII 368)

It would seem that, for Descartes, although the novice knows or understands what a triangle is, he does not fully grasp or comprehend it (in the way a geometer might). Grasping or comprehending something, then, involves much more than what suffices for knowing or comprehending it. The former is, somehow, a much richer cognitive activity.

As remarked above, the crucial Cartesian psychological notion which, if any, is connected with modal notions is that of conceiving ('*concipere*'). It is an important point in this area[32] that, for Descartes, conceiving lies, in terms of richness or adequacy, on the side of grasping ('*comprehendere*') rather than that of merely knowing ('*intelligere*'). In the letter to Mersenne of 27 May 1630 he writes:

> . . . . I know that God is the author of everything and that these (eternal) truths are something and consequently that he is their author. I say that I know this (*je le sais*), not that I can conceive

[32] Stressed by Jean-Marie Beyssade, 'La Création des vérités éternalles', *Studia Cartesiana* 2, (1981) pp. 86–105; an article which I have found helpful on the topic.

> (*conçois*) it or comprehend (*comprends*) it; because it is possible to know that God is infinite and all-powerful although our soul, being finite, cannot comprehend or conceive Him. In the same way we can touch a mountain with our hands but we cannot put our arms around it as we could put them around a tree or something else not too large for them. To comprehend something is to embrace it in one's thought; to know something it is sufficient to touch it with one's thought. (PL 14–15)

In the *Conversation with Burman* the distinction recurs, along with a little more about what is involved in conceiving something:

> Now here one must carefully distinguish between *understanding, conception* and *imagination*—a distinction of great value. Take for example the perfections of God. We do not *imagine* these, or *conceive* of them, but we understand them: the way in which God understands all things in a single mental act, or the way in which his decrees are identical with himself, are things we *understand*, but we do not *conceive of*, since we cannot, so to speak, represent themselves to ourselves. (B 21)

What is this 'conceiving'? Cottingham's comments on the passage are helpful. I shall quote extensively.

> It seems to me likely that what Descartes had in mind is something like our idea of 'grasping' an idea or concept. Take the idea of a million pigs. This is a notion which I can clearly understand—I am perfectly aware of what is meant. On the other hand, I cannot imagine or picture such a vast number of pigs except in a very vague and confused way; such are the limitations of the human brain. What I can do, however, is to try to *grasp*, or 'get my mind round' the bafflingly large number, so that my conception of what is involved is rather more vivid than the pure and simple understanding of what is meant. One way of going about this might be to think of ten groups of one hundred pigs; then think of this number put together in a field; then think of a thousand such fields. . . . To *conceive of X*, then, is to have what may be called a dynamic working knowledge of what X involves.[33]

[33] *Descartes' Conversation with Burman* translated with introduction and commentary by John Cottingham, Oxford, 1976. p. 76. Cottingham sees confirmation for this way of regarding *conceptio* in the passage from the letter to Mersenne we have just quoted.

It does seem absolutely right that if there is to be a notion of conceiving such that there is some connection (as we shall see Descartes wants to make) between an ability to conceive of something, and that thing's possibility, and an inability to conceive of something and that thing's impossibility, then conceiving of something should be a more exiguous task than merely that of 'understanding'. Not all possibilities, and not all impossibilities, are *immediately obvious* ones. We have to be able to set out on the task of trying to 'conceive of *X*', or 'conceive of *p*'s being the case' and *discover* that we fail. To set out on the task we must understand the phrase '*X*' or the sentence '*p*'. Phrases or sentences which describe impossibilities cannot all be mere gibberish to us, or wear the inconceivability of what they describe on their face. But for that very reason our mere ability to 'understand' cannot be a sufficient condition of possibility. There has to be something like the gap Descartes annotates in his distinction between understanding and conceiving.

With this grasp (or understanding!) of Descartes' notion of conception, let us turn to the passage from the letter to Mesland of 2 May 1644. I shall argue that this reveals an internal contradiction in Descartes' position; one which is independent of his haverings on the modal content of the 'creation' doctrine; and which can best be removed by postulating two notions or kinds of possibility. The passage runs (I have numbered phrases for later reference):

> . . . . the power of God cannot have any limits, and (that) (i) our mind is finite and so created to be able to conceive as possible things which God has wished to be in fact possible, but (ii) not to be able to conceive as possible things which God could have made possible, but which he has in fact wished to make impossible. The first consideration shows us that (iii) God cannot have been determined to make it true that contradictories cannot be true together, and therefore that (iv) he could have done the opposite. The second consideration shows us that even if this be true, (v) we should not try to comprehend it since our nature is incapable of doing so.

Let us introduce some abbreviations:

'*Cp*' for 'We can conceive of *p*'s being the case'

'*Gp*' for 'God has wished that (and hence made it the case that) *p*'
'*Mp*' for 'It is possible that *p*'

(i) above tells us that if God has wished that it be possible that *p* then we can conceive of *p*'s being possible.

(A) For all *p*, if *GMp* then *CMp*[34]

(ii) contains two claims. The first is that if God has wished to make something impossible than we cannot conceive of it as possible. In our notation:

(B) For all *p* if *G*~*Mp* then ~*CMp*.

The second is that there *are* things which God has wished to make impossible but which he *could have* made (hence could have wished to make) possible. This 'could have' is a notion of possibility. Let us assume (for the purpose of *reductio*) that his can be seen as the same notion of possibility we have already. That is that the present claim is:

(C) For some *p*, *G*~*Mp* and *MGMp*.

From other texts we know that Descartes holds God to be the source of all truth. That is, if anything is true, then God has wished it and made it, to be true.

(D) For all *p*, if *p* then *Gp*.[35]

This also makes him the source of all possibility. That is, as a special case of D we have:

(D_M) For all *p*, if *Mp* then *GMp*.

(A) and (D_M) yield that if something is possible, we can conceive of its being possible. That is:

(E) For all *p*, if *Mp* then *CMp*.

We are now in a position to discover a contradiction in Descartes' position. Let p_1 be some instance of (C). That is:

[34] A worry: does *CMp* differ from *Cp*? If so, does it affect the ensuing argument?
[35] One half of the statement of His omnipotence which Curley (*op.cit.*) ascribes to Descartes. See (ii) on p. 179 above.

(1) $G{\sim}Mp_1$ and $MGMp_1$

The first conjunct, with B yields:

(2) ${\sim}CMp_1$

The second, with E yields:

(3) $CMGMp_1$

We can now proceed in two ways. The first is to continue our exposition of the text of the letter. What is this opposite that (iv) says God could have done? The previous phrase implies that God made it true that contradictories cannot be true together (though he was not *determined* so to do). Now our p_1 above, which God made impossible, can be the conjunction of a pair of contradictories. What (iv) tells us that God did was to make it that p_1 couldn't be true *i.e.* $G{\sim}Mp_1$ (the first conjunct of (1)). He could have done the opposite, that is, made it the case that p_1 *could* be true. Supposing, as before, that this 'could have' is the same '*M*' this is: $MGMp_1$ (the second conjunct of (1)). But we are now told that this is something we cannot comprehend (= cannot conceive). That is:

(4) ${\sim}CMGMp_1$

directly contradicting (3).

We can reach (4), and hence the contradiction, in another way (perhaps thereby bringing out how deeply rooted in Descartes' thought (4) is). In Descartes' strong sense of 'conceive', the following principle seems hard to resist. If we can conceive of the possibility of A's making it the case that *p* (and hence, the case that it is possible that *p*), then we can conceive of the possibility of *p*'s being the case.[36] That is:

(F) For all *p*, if *CM*(*A* brings it about that *p*) then *CMp*.

So, for the special case where *A* is God, and *p* is Mp_1:

(5) If $CMGMp_1$ then $CMMp_1$.

[36] Think of it in terms of Cottingham's gloss. If we can have a dynamic working knowledge of what the possibility of *A*'s making it the case that *p* involves, then we can have a dynamic working knowledge of what the possibility of *p*'s being the case involves. This seems very plausible.

But we already have (see (2) above) that we *cannot* conceive of the possibility of p_1's being the case ($\sim CMp_1$). So, once more allowing for the fact that in this instance we are dealing with the possibility of its being possible that p_1, *i.e.*, MMp_1, we again arrive, by contraposition of a correspondingly adapted version of (2) *i.e.*, $\sim CMMp_1$, at:

(4) $\sim CMGMp_1$

which is in direct contradiction to (3).

How is Descartes to avoid this contradiction? He certainly needs, for purposes we shall shortly explore, *a* notion of possibility (possibility_1) for which (A) and (B) hold. For what (A) and (B) are needed to guarantee—in the context of the view that God is the creator of possibility and impossibility[37]—is that if something is possible_1 we can conceive of it(s possibility), and that if something is impossible_1 then we cannot conceive of it(s possibility). That is we need (A) and (B), governing possibility_1, in order to have an assurance that:

(E) For all p, if M_1p then CM_1p, and

(G) For all p, if $\sim M_1p$ then $\sim CM_1p$.

If there was *no* notion of possibility for which these held then there would be no notion of possibility to which what we can/cannot conceive would be a reliable guide. And we would have no other.[38]

What the contradiction shows is that the 'could have', the first 'possible' in the second conjunct of (C), ($MGMp$), *cannot* be subject to (E). The possibility involved in the thought that God *could have* made possible_1 certain things which he has in fact made impossible_1 has to be a different notion of possibility—possibility_2—for which (E) fails. That is it is not the case that if it is possible_2 that p then we can conceive of p's being the case. The correct formulation of (C) is thus:

(C*) For some p, $G{\sim}M_1p$ and M_2GM_1p.

(The failure of (E) for possibility_2 requires in turn that for this

[37] That is of doctrines, special cases of (D): (D_M) If Mp then GMp. ($\text{D}_{\sim\text{M}}$) If $\sim Mp$ then $G{\sim}Mp$.

[38] See, *inter alia* passage (29), to which we shall shortly return.

sense of possibility (D_M) and (A) do not both hold. That is, he must either say that possibilities$_2$ are *not* created by God:[39] or hold that it is not true that we can conceive of everything God has made possible. But I shall not pursue the issue of which line Descartes should, and perhaps did, adopt.)

The crucial feature of possibility$_1$ is that something is possible$_1$ if we can conceive of it(s possibility). That is:

(H) For all p, M_1p iff CMp.

The crucial feature of possibility$_2$ is that there can be, indeed are, things which are possible$_2$ though they are not conceivable by us. These possibilities$_2$ derive from, indeed express, the infinite power of God. Hence:

(J) For some p, M_2p and not-Cp.

Let us see how far postulating these two senses of 'possible' or kinds of possibility will explain the ambiguities and tensions in Descartes' thought. First we should consider the 'modal content' of the creation doctrine. Corresponding to the two notions of possibility there will be two notions of necessity. It will be necessary$_1$ that p iff it is impossible$_1$ that $\sim p$ iff we cannot conceive of $\sim p$'s being the case. Many truths are, for Descartes, necessarily$_1$ true—all those the negations of which 'involve a contradiction in his conception'. The passages which appear to assert that no truths are necessarily true are asserting that no truths are necessarily$_2$ true. To assert that L_2p would be to assert that $\sim M_2 \sim p$. But Descartes cannot assert any such thing. The fact that he cannot conceive of $\sim p$'s being the case does not suffice to assert that it is impossible$_2$ that $\sim p$. More strongly his understanding (not his grasp) of God's power leads him to assert that God's power 'can have no limits'. That is:

> For all p, it is possible$_2$ that Gp. That is, for no p is it necessary$_2$ that p.

We have thus given a vindication of the 'no necessity' view: there are no necessary$_2$ truths; and a vindication of part of the 'iterated modality' view: some truths *are* necessary$_1$. But is it the case, as the rest of the 'iterated modality' interpretation claims,

[39] A version of the restriction of the 'creation' doctrine which some have ascribed to Descartes.

that they are not *necessarily* necessary$_1$? That is are they possibly not necessary$_1$? It would seem that in at least one of the senses of 'possible' they are possibly not necessary. God could have given Descartes a mind such that he could conceive of things of which, as he is, he cannot conceive. If, as we must suppose, God had still been benevolent, the connection between possibility and conceivability asserted by (H) and (J) above would still hold. So, had God made these things conceivable he would also have made them possible$_1$. So, under that dispensation, some things which are actually necessary$_1$ would not have been necessary$_1$.

In which sense of 'necessary' will it not be necessary that it is necessary$_1$ that, say, $2+2=4$? Equivalently: in which sense of 'possible' will it be possible that it is not necessary$_1$ that *e.g.* $2+2=4$? It must at least be the weaker of the two senses of 'possible'. That is, Descartes must at least say that it is possible$_2$ that it is not necessary$_1$ that $2+2=4$. This possibility, like other expressions of God's power, need not be conceivable by Descartes.

But should Descartes hold also that it is not necessary$_1$ that it is necessary$_1$ that $2+2=4$? That is, should he hold that it is possible$_1$ that it is not necessary$_1$ that e.g. $2+2=4$? I shall argue that he should not. That is, he is committed to the view that, using the first notion of necessity, necessary truths are necessarily necessary. Suppose he did hold that it is possible$_1$ that it not be necessary that $2+2=4$. That is, suppose he holds that

(1) $M_1{\sim}L_1\ (2+2=4)$.

Then by (H) he is committed to the view that he can conceive of its not being necessary that $2+2=4$. That is to:

(2) $C{\sim}L_1\ (2+2=4)$ i.e. $CM{\sim}(2+2=4)$.

But this is precisely the kind of thing the letter to Mesland denies that he *can* conceive of:

> . . . . our mind is finite and so created . . . not to be able to conceive as possible things which God could have made possible, but which he has in fact wished to make impossible.

That is Descartes cannot accept (2). He is committed to:

(3) $\sim C \sim L_1 (2+2=4)$

Hence by (H) to:

(4) $\sim M_1 \sim L_1 (2+2=4)$ That is to $L_1 L_1 (2+2=4)$

We can argue this in a different way. Given God's benevolence, the only circumstances in which it would not be necessary$_1$ that 2+2=4, that is possible$_1$ that 2+2 not be 4, would be circumstances in which God had made him able to conceive (what he cannot actually do) of 2+2's not being 4. So to be able to conceive of the possibility$_1$ of 2+2's not being 4 (which is required for that possibility$_1$ to be itself a possibility$_1$) he would have to be able to conceive of his conceiving of 2+2's not being 4. That is (1) above entails:

(5) $CC{\sim}(2+2=4)$

But, on Descartes' sensibly strong reading of 'conceive', I think (5) is false. For, on that reading, I think we should accept:

(6) if CCp then Cp

If I have a dynamic working knowledge of what is involved in having a dynamic working knowledge of what *p*'s being the case involves then I surely need to have a dynamic working knowledge of what *p*'s being the case involves. Where '*p*' is 'not-(2+2=4)' I have no such dynamic working knowledge. I may, that is, 'understand' the notion of being able to conceive of 2+2's not being 4: but I cannot 'grasp' it.

Summing up the consequences for this structure for the modal content of the 'creation' doctrine, we have:

I For all p, $\sim L_2 p$.
II For some p, $L_1 p$.
III For all p, not $L_2 L_1 p$ (a special case of I)
IV For all p, if $L_1 p$ then $L_1 L_1 p$.

An immediate objection to what we have so far is that this apparatus would also allow Descartes to give a sense to the claim that it is *not* possible that God bring it about that 2+2 not be 4. Since Descartes cannot conceive of 2+2's not being 4, then, (by (F) above) he cannot conceive of God's bringing it about that 2+2 not be 4. That is, it is impossible$_1$. But Descartes never says, in any sense, that such things are impossible for God. The point is well made. But two things reduce its force against the present line of thought. The first is that the hypothesis is not that Descartes explicitly had in mind that he was deploying two notions of possibility. (I am not saying that *he* might have gone through his works inserting subscripts.) So it need not have occurred to him that he had a notion of possibility in which some things were impossible for God. More importantly: Descartes would not be much interested in assertions of 'impossibility$_1$' *about God.* For such assertions would be trivial consequences of the general fact that God's nature and power go beyond our conceiving. They would not reveal anything distinctive about God.

In the passage from the letter to Mesland, and in most others expressing the 'creation' doctrine, Descartes shows no consciousness of two notions of possibility.[40] I hypothesised these two notions in order to provide a way out from an unnoticed contradiction in his position. But we have already quoted a passage (29) in which *Descartes* speaks of two notions of possibility. One means 'whatever does not conflict with our human concepts' the other is a 'kind of possibility which relates to the object itself'. A nice theory would be that the hypothesised and the stated ambiguity coincide. That is: that our possible$_1$ is Descartes' 'whatever does not conflict with our human concepts' and that our possible$_2$ is his 'kind of possibility which relates to the object itself'. This theory would seem also to resolve the vague issue of section IV. Possibilities$_1$ (and necessities$_1$)—defined in terms of 'our human concepts'—would be a 'function of our minds'. Possibilities$_2$ (there are, we argued, no necessities$_2$ for Descartes) would not: they would 'relate to the object itself'.

This nice theory will not work. Let us first note that the hypothesised ambiguity resolves the discovered contradiction only if 'possibility$_1$' and 'possibility$_2$' differ, not merely in intension, but also in extension: in particular, only if there are

[40] A clear indication of this is that he shows no consciousness of the fact that he deploys a notion of possibility—our 'possible$_1$' in which it is *not* possible$_1$ that it is not necessary$_1$ that *e.g.* 2+2=4. Equivalently, that in this sense of 'possible' there are things which it is not possible$_1$ that God should bring about. There is only one text which hints at this *viz.* the letter to More of 5 February 1649. See PL p. 241. I cannot here explore the interesting questions that this passage raises.

things which are possible$_2$ but not possible$_1$. (We found no reason to deny that whatever is possible$_1$ is possible$_2$.) But Descartes, in the passage from the *Second Replies*, says that unless the second possibility there mentioned ('which relates to the object itself') *matches* the first ('whatever does not conflict with our human concepts') then:

> it can never be known by the human intellect, and so it does not so much support a denial of God's nature and existence as serve to undermine every other item of knowledge. For as far as our concepts are concerned there is no impossibility in the nature of God; on the contrary, all the attributes which we include in the concept of the divine nature are so interconnected that it seems to us to be self-contradictory that any one of them should not belong to God. Hence, if we deny that the nature of God is possible, we may just as well deny that the angles of a triangle are equal to two right angles, or that he who is actually thinking exists; and if we do this it will be even more appropriate to deny that anything we acquire by means of the senses is true. The upshot will be that all human knowledge will be destroyed, though for no good reason. (AT VII 150–1)

What is this matching? For the immediate purpose of this passage it seems that it merely requires that if something 'does not conflict with our human concepts' then it should have that possibility which 'relates to the object itself'. This is all that is required for the move from 'there is no contradiction in our concept of God' to 'the nature of God is possible'. And this way round 'matching' parallels the move from 'possible$_1$' to 'possible$_2$' which we had no reason to deny to Descartes. The question is whether Descartes intends to allow that the converse implication—for the notions in this passage—fails: as it does between possibility$_2$ and possibility$_1$. Only if Descartes can allow that something is possible in the 'way which relates to the object itself' while, nevertheless, 'involving a contradiction in our concepts' can the two dichotomies match up.

But Descartes surely cannot allow this. The 'matching'—without which 'all human knowledge will be destroyed'—has to be both ways (co-extensiveness). Consider the first non-theological example. What would lead us 'just as well (to) deny that the angles of a triangle are equal to two right angles', that is, to deny that triangles are Euclidean? It would have to be that although a non-Euclidean triangle did (as Descartes thought) 'conflict with our human concepts' (that is, was *im*possible in the first sense) this did not guarantee that the object itself—a triangle—could not be non-Euclidean. In other words, the possibility of the thing—a non-Euclidean triangle—would not be ruled out by the fact that the notion—*non-Euclidean triangle*—did 'conflict with our human concepts'. And this *would*, for Descartes, destroy all human knowledge. So, for Descartes, the possibility of human knowledge requires that the two notions of possibility mentioned in (29) match both ways. They cannot, therefore, coincide with the notions postulated from the reading of the letter to Mesland.

We can put the point rather differently. We know, from *Meditations V*, that the necessity attaching to statements of essence is not 'imposed by his mind' but concerns the object itself. That is, the *im*possibility (for Descartes) that e.g. the angles of a triangle not add up to two right angles, concerns the thing itself. And it is knowledge of such impossibilities, i.e. of such necessities, which would be destroyed if he could not infer them from 'conflicts with our human concepts', in other words, if the possibility of the object itself did not entail the possibility defined in terms of lack of conflict with our concepts. Passage (29), with its view of a possible abyss of scepticism, far from supporting the idea that the modalities asserted in Cartesian science are dependent on the nature of our minds or our concepts, presupposes that they are not. What is the case is that the only kind of *ground* we have for modal assertions is the knowledge we have of what we can and cannot conceive: of what does, or does not, involve a contradiction in our conception. It is the fear that these grounds might not match what they are used to ground which generates the possibility of scepticism. The point emerges very clearly if we put together a passage from the letter to More of February 1649 with one from the letter to Gibieuf of 19 January 1642. In the former he writes:

> True, our mind is not the measure of reality or of truth; but it certainly should be the measure of what we assert or deny (PL 242).

The latter makes very clear what this dual claim involves:

> You will say perhaps that the difficulty remains, because although I conceive the soul and body as two substances which I can conceive separately, and which I can even deny of each other, I am not certain that they are in reality such as I conceive them to be. Here we have to recall the principle already stated, that we cannot have any knowledge of things except by the ideas we conceive of them; and consequently, that we must not judge of them except in accordance with these ideas, and we must even think that (i) whatever conflicts with these ideas is absolutely impossible and involves a contradiction. Thus we have no reason to affirm that there is no mountain without a valley, except that we see that the idea of the two things cannot be complete when we consider them apart. . . . Someone may tell me that though I can conceive [two halves of a part of matter] apart I have no reason to deny their inseparability because I do not know that God has not united or joined them so tightly that they are entirely inseparable. I would reply that however he may have joined them, I am sure he can also disjoin them; so that (ii) absolutely speaking I have reason to call them divisible, since he has given me the faculty of conceiving them as such. I say the same about the soul and the body and in general all the things of which we have distinct and complete ideas; that is, I say that their being (iii) inseparable involves a contradiction. But I do not deny that there can be in the soul or the body many properties of which I have no ideas; I only deny that there are any which are inconsistent with the ideas that I do have, including the idea that I have of their distinctness; for otherwise God would be a deceiver and we would have no rule to make us certain of the truth. (PL 124–5)

Descartes, unlike some of his commentators, keeps sharply apart the *content* of his modal assertions, which does not concern his ideas, or what he can or cannot conceive, and the grounds for these assertions which, for him, can only concern these matters. The second passage makes very clear (i) that he needs 'matching' to go both ways: that is, from what he can conceive to what is (really) possible, and from what conflicts with his ideas to what is (absolutely) impossible; (ii) that his guarantee of such 'matching' is that God is not a deceiver; and (iii) that without such a guarantee knowledge, as he conceives it, would be impossible.

VII

In this section I try to reach a clearer formulation of what is at issue between those who do, and those who do not, think that for Descartes necessity is, in some sense 'mind-dependent': and to adjudicate that issue. I shall proceed by first looking at the formulations of some of these who appear to hold versions of the view that Cartesian modality *is* 'mind-dependent'.

1. *Margaret Wilson*

After discussing two other interpretative issues about the 'creation' doctrine, Wilson makes the following remarks:

> (A) It is clear enough, in any case, that Descartes did regard the 'necessity' we perceive in mathematical propositions as *in some sense and degree a function of the constitution of our minds* (my emphasis)—themselves finite 'creatures'.[41]

And Wilson thinks Descartes should be congratulated for anticipating later views.

> (B) From Hume and Kant onward it has been widely held that alleged perceptions of 'necessity' cannot be taken for granted, and that we must in some sense or other have recourse to the structure and workings of our own minds to give an account of these 'perceptions'.[42]

Both these formulations, especially the underlined phrase in (A), are rather vague. Even so, I think, they point to different doctrines. (B) merely says that in giving an account of our (alleged) *perceptions* of necessity, we need to say something about the human mind. (A) points to the different claim that, in giving an account of the (alleged) object of these perceptions—necessity—we are to allude to the constitution of our minds.

Descartes certainly holds a version of (B). Our minds are such that certain things cannot be conceived by us to be the case. They involve 'a contradiction in our conception'. It is in virtue of such facts about our minds that we judge (rightly, Descartes holds) certain things to be impossible, their negations to be necessary. But that Descartes holds a version of (B) is not something for which he could conceivably be congratulated.

[41] *op. cit.*
[42] *ibid.*

He is offering an answer to the question: why do we judge that certain things are possible, others impossible, others necessary? As it is a question about why *we* make certain judgments, *any* answer, whatever else it contains, *must* say something about those aspects of us, of our minds, which lead us to make these judgments. How else could it explain why we make these judgments? Putting it rather differently: if we also hold that these judgments are of the sort which can constitute *recognition* of necessity, then Descartes' remarks about the limits of our powers of conception constitute his answer to the second of Dummett's two questions about necessity: how do we recognise it? Again, evidently, *any* answer to that question must say something about us, about that aspect of our minds which enables us to recognize necessity.

The more interesting claim (A) should rather be seen, first, as commenting on Descartes' answer to something like Dummett's first question about necessity: what is its source? And, secondly, as suggesting that in answering a version of this question Descartes is bringing in materials which concern 'the constitution of our minds'. But to what precise form of this question is Descartes supposed to be offering an answer? And how, exactly, is this answer supposed to bring in matters of 'the constitution of our mind'?

We know that if the question is 'Why are certain things necessarily, eternally, immutably so?' then his initial response makes no mention of our minds. The official, much-repeated, answer is that they are necessarily etc. so because God has willed that they be necessarily etc. so. But perhaps facts about the character of our minds enter even into this answer. The suggestion might be that Descartes' position is that the necessity of a truth *p* is constituted by the fact that we cannot conceive of its negation's being the case. Thus God's making it necessarily the case that *p* would be constituted by God's making our minds such that we cannot conceive of *p*'s not being the case. If asked 'why are certain truths necessary?', the necessary that *p*. That is, if asked 'what is it for it to be necessary that *p*?', Descartes' answer is that this consists in a fact about our minds *viz.* that we cannot conceive of not-*p*'s being the case. If asked 'why are certain truths necessary?', the answer is that it is because God has willed that they be, that is, has willed that our minds be so constituted that we cannot conceive of not-*p*'s being the case. This appears to be part of the position which Hidé Ishiguro ascribes to Descartes. I now turn to an examination of her account.

2. *Hidé Ishiguro.*

Ishiguro begins her account with some remarks on the important passage from *Meditations* V we have already looked at ((9), p. 161). She comments:

> . . . . he has made clear that *even if no triangular figure were to exist outside his consciousness and never did exist* the triangle he imagines has a determinate nature, or form, or essence, which is unchangeable and eternal.
>
> . . . . This nature of the triangle is no figment of his own. It does not depend on his (individual) mind. . . . We see that this nature or essence is not an empirical property of things either, since it exists even were no figure to exist outside our minds. . . .
>
> These (eternal) truths concern the immutable forms of the internal objects of our imaginings and thinkings, and of which we can have clear and distinct ideas. . . . They are laid down by (God) not in the form of a code, but in the constitution of our mind. In creating our mind, he creates the eternal truths. . . . Our mathematics and geometry, for Descartes, would be the way they are because of God's creation of our minds—*even if there were no external physical world to which we would apply them*. They are not special capacities that enable us to enter into a privileged relation with physical things in the world also created by him. . . .

There is much that I find disputable in this. Let me make some detailed points. (i) Her translation '. . . . even if no triangular figure *were* to exist' is tendentious. Cottingham has: 'even if perhaps no such figure exists, or has ever existed, anywhere outside my thought'. The point may just be an epistemic one. He does not know, at this stage in the *Meditations*, whether there are any extended things. Of course there are difficulties in Descartes' thought (as in anyone's), about the relation which the ('ideal') objects of geometry have to the physical world, even when he knows that such a world exists. But, despite this, two points should be made. The first is that he gives non-geometrical, indeed non-mathematical, examples of the points he is making here.

> From the fact that I cannot think of a mountain without a valley, it does not follow that a mountain and valley exist anywhere, but simply that a mountain and a valley, whether they exist or not, are mutually inseparable. But from the fact that I cannot think of God except as existing, it follows that existence is inseparable from God, and hence that he really exists. It is not that my thought makes it so, or imposes any necessity on any thing; on the contrary, it is the necessity of the thing itself, namely the existence of God, which determines my thinking in this respect. (*Meditations* V, AT vii 66–7)

When later he does know that mountains and valleys do exist, he is surely going to say that the eternal truth concerning them *does* concern 'physical things in the external world also created by him'. They do not merely concern the 'immutable forms of the internal objects of our imaginings and understandings'.

Secondly, whatever that latter claim, applied to the eternal truths of mathematics, means, Descartes appears to repudiate it. In the letter to Clerselier, appended to the *Fifth Replies*, he responds to certain critics who:

> . . . . think they see clearly that mathematical extension, which I lay down as the fundamental principle of my physics, is nothing other than my thought, and hence that it does not and cannot have any subsistence outside my mind, being merely an abstraction which I form from physical bodies. And they conclude that the whole of my physics 'must be imaginary and fictitious, as indeed the whole of pure mathematics is, whereas real physics dealing with the things created by God requires the kind of matter that is real, solid and not imaginary'. Here is the objection of objections and the epitome of the entire doctrine held by these 'people of great intelligence' who are cited here. All the things that we can understand and conceive are, on their account, only imaginings and fictions of our mind which cannot have any subsistence.

Descartes' scorn for this position makes it quite clear that he does not think that physics, and 'indeed the whole of pure mathematics' relates merely to 'imaginings and fictions of the mind'.

(ii) Ishiguro makes great use of passages in which Descartes talks of the eternal truths being 'laid down in our mind'. But in most such passages, he also says, though she doesn't quote this, that God (also) laid them down in nature. Thus, in the very first statement of the 'creation' doctrine:

> Please do not hesitate to assert and proclaim that it is God who has laid down these laws in nature just as a king lays down laws in his kingdom. There is no single one that we cannot understand if our mind turns to consider them. They are all inborn in our minds just as a king would imprint his laws on the hearts of all his subjects if he had enough power to do so. (PL 11)

This dual idea occurs also in the *Discourse*

> What is more, I have noticed certain laws which God has so established in nature, and of which he has implanted such notions in our minds, that after adequate reflection we cannot doubt that they are exactly observed in everything which exists or occurs in the world. (DM V AT VI 41)

My own view would be that what constituted God's creation of the eternal truths was his laying them down in nature as eternally and immutably true. He did also implant them in our minds. But that he did so is part of Descartes' epistemology of modality, not its metaphysics. God, being benevolent, implanted in us the means, after adequate reflection, to *know* these truths. The 'metaphysical' doubt can be put: until we know that there is a benevolent God we have no assurance that the laws imprinted in our mind, and the limitations they impose on our conceivings, match the laws laid down in nature. If the (necessary) truth of the eternal truths were constituted by God's laying them down in our minds, the 'metaphysical' doubt could not get even the grip it does.

That the point is essentially epistemological emerges, I believe, even in that passage in which Descartes says the eternal truths have their 'seat' in our mind (*Principles* I, 49) (without any reference to their being laid down in the world). It occurs in the context of a series of explicitly epistemological articles—an extended discussion of 'clear and distinct perception'. I, 49 itself ends:

> we cannot fail to know (the eternal truths) when the occasion for thinking about them arises, provided that we are not blinded by preconceived opinions. (AT VIIIA 24)

And the next article is headed:

> *Eternal truths are clearly perceived; but because of preconceived opinions, not all of them are clearly perceived.*

This muddling of the constitutive and the epistemological, which I noted in Wilson, emerges very clearly in a later remark of Ishiguro's:

> The reason why when we add two and three we cannot but get the sum of five is because eternal truths, according to Descartes, have their seat in the mind.

This is right. That is a case of Descartes' explanation of why, if we free ourselves of preconceptions, we can 'clearly and distinctly perceive' the eternal truths. But Ishiguro is trying to argue for the quite different claim that the reason why, when a group contains two objects and three others it necessarily contains five overall, is constituted by something to do with our mind. None of the passages she quotes supports this idea in the least.

(iii) Indeed there is something very bizarre in trying to support the idea that the necessity of the eternal truths, the essentiality of essences, is constituted by facts about our minds, by quoting *Meditations* V, which, after all, explicitly says that 'there is a determinate nature, or essence, or form of a triangle which is immutable and eternal, and not invented by me or dependent on my mind'. This must have struck Ishiguro. Hence, presumably, the bracketed 'individual' in 'the nature of the triangle . . . does not depend on his (individual) mind'. And she later writes:

> (The eternal) truths do not, it is true, depend on how particular individual minds are made—for example, to be cleverer or to perceive better.

But this simply makes the whole position even more unCartesian. The idea that a view which Descartes clearly rejects when phrased in terms of 'his' mind, might be a view he does accept when reference is made to 'our minds' ('What is at issue is the universal validity of these eternal truths in our mental constitution') goes against the most explicit statement of Descartes' methodology in the *Meditations* (See *Second Replies* AT VII 142–3 quoted as (22) p. 167).

Moreover, the claim that 'In creating our mind, he creates the eternal truths' must, for a believer in a dateable event of the creation of Adam, be literally false. (And undermine all Descartes' motives (à la Curley) for holding the doctrine.) I think there is little hope of defending *this* version of the 'mind-dependence' thesis. Let us turn to:

3. *Frankfurt*

Frankfurt's view on the modal content of the 'creation' doctrine is that it holds that no truths are (ultimately) necessary. God could have made contradictions true. He puts the central difficulty as one of understanding this 'could'. He notes that Descartes' reply is to hold that we should not expect to comprehend this, as it concerns God's infinite power, which we cannot grasp. Frankfurt, in turn, objects:

> Now a person's assertion that there is something that he cannot understand is often entirely comprehensible, and there may be quite good evidence that it is true. In the present instance, however, the assertion is peculiar and problematical. That there is a deity with infinite power is supposed by Descartes to entail the possibility of the logically impossible. But if it must entail this, then the assertion that God has infinite (and hence unintelligible) power seems itself unintelligible. For it appears that no coherent meaning can be assigned to the notion of an infinitely powerful being as Descartes employs it—that is, to the notion of a being for whom the logically impossible is possible. And if this is so, then it is no more possible for us to know or to believe that God *has* infinite power than it is, according to Descartes, for us to understand that power. If we cannot understand 'infinite power', we also cannot understand, and hence cannot believe or know, the proposition that God's power is infinite.[43]

It is hard to relate Frankfurt's deployment of 'unintelligible', 'understand' and 'know' to Descartes' terminology. Descartes says that we cannot 'comprehend' (grasp, conceive of;

[43] *op.cit.* p. 44.

comprehendere, concipere) those states of affairs which, given God's power, could have been the case: *e.g.* (on the 'no necessity' view) that 2 and 3 not be 5, (on the 'iterated modality' interpretation') that 2 and 3 not necessarily be 5. Hence we cannot 'comprehend' (ditto) the possibilities that *e.g.* God bring it about that 2 and 3 not be 5, or that God bring it about that 2 and 3 not necessarily be 5. But there is no licence, in Descartes or in truth (as I argued), for the move from that to the conclusion that we do not understand (*intelligere*) the propositions which describe these possibilities. There has to be a notion of conceiving in which it is not valid to go from: we cannot conceive of *p*'s being the case, to: we cannot understand the proposition that *p*. For there has to be a notion of conceiving, if it has any connection with possibility, in which we cannot conclude from our understanding a proposition that we can conceive of what it describes as being the case.

Descartes' position, I argued, does entail that the notion of possibility in which these are possibilities is not that in which the possible and the conceivable are at least co-extensive. In other words we have to do with possibility$_2$. I shall later argue that any position which shares a certain (very plausible) structure with Descartes' will have a structurally similar consequence. We can move towards this by noting certain views which Frankfurt ascribes to Descartes as a response to the objection he has just outlined. (It is unclear exactly which step in that objection they are a response to.) What will emerge, I believe, is that the positions which Frankfurt ascribes to Descartes, and sees as distinctive responses by him to a difficulty in his own, odd, position, are no such things. They are what anyone who understood a certain dialectical situation would have to say.

The first view that Frankfurt ascribes to Descartes is that what we can and cannot conceive is a contingent matter. But how could anyone deny this? If the notion of what we can or cannot conceive is meant to play the rôle it does, in Descartes and others, of explaining what aspect of the human mind determines its judgments of modality, how could it fail to be, like any other feature of the human mind, a contingent notion? Frankfurt writes as if the following position were one which Descartes distinctively holds, and which could be rejected:

> The inconceivability of (the) falsity of (the propositions we find to be necessary) . . . is not inherent in them. It is properly to be understood only as relative to the character of our minds.

But what would it mean to say that the 'inconceivability' of the falsity of a proposition was 'inherent in it'? This seems only to make sense if one takes 'inconceivability' just to mean 'impossibility'. So that to say that the falsity of a proposition is 'inconceivable' is just to say that the proposition is necessarily true. But *that* notion of 'inconceivability'—not 'relative to the character of our minds'—has no rôle to play in the epistemology of necessity. There is not even the hope of an explanation of why we regard certain propositions as necessary in saying that—in this sense—their falsity is 'inconceivable'. This is just to say that we regard them as necessary because they are necessary. It says nothing about what, in us, leads us so to regard them. And it is hard to see how any features of us which might be so invoked could fail to be contingent features of us.

Editor's Conclusion:

None of the manuscripts from which this paper has been derived extend beyond this point. However, remarks appearing elsewhere in McFetridge's papers (some of which can be found in this volume) indicate that he might have concluded his discussion along the following lines:

Neither Wilson, nor Ishiguro nor Frankfurt is able to resolve the difficulties for Descartes, who is committed to the view that there are two notions of possibility, while being unable to provide a coherent epistemology for the second of them. Descartes believes that there are things which are possible, in the second sense, of which we cannot conceive. But he is unable to distinguish, among the things which we can 'understand' but of which we cannot 'conceive', those which do represent possibilities and those which do not. In effect he has located modal distinctions within a certain metaphysical space—God's creation of possibilities—and a certain epistemological space—our powers of conceiving. But his theory requires us to make modal distinctions which are not confined to those spaces, and in the making of which we have neither metaphysical nor epistemological guidance. The difficulty arises from the fact that what is contained within those spaces is only a contingent matter, so that the search for necessities inevitably takes us beyond their limits.

This difficulty, McFetridge would have argued, recurs for many, perhaps all, theories which try to explain why certain truths are necessary by invoking matters which are themselves contingent—for instance, the view that necessary truths are 'true by convention' or 'true by virtue of the meaning of the words used to express them'. And there is no simple solution to the difficulty, since to give a theory of necessary truths which grounds those truths in necessities is to give no theory at all. His view, therefore, was that Descartes' discussion, for all its 'scattered' character, showed a sensitivity to what is perhaps the most fundamental problem of modality: the problem as to how modal thinking is possible at all.

(RS)

[The following draft of an introduction to McFetridge's intended book on modality, while very short, serves to put the themes of preceding papers in historical context, and offers interesting suggestions of a possible systematic treatment. (RS)]

Appendix

Demonstration, Necessity and Logic in Early Modern Philosophy

Many discussions of epistemology by seventeenth- and eighteenth-century philosophers are organised around a technical concept of demonstrative knowledge (also put: demonstrative science or, simply, science), which derives, at several removes, from Aristotle. More precisely, such discussions centre on a disjunctive concept of demonstrative or *intuitive* knowledge, the formulation of which owes much to Descartes. (I shall ignore this complication until we come to his views.) For these philosophers' views on necessity we must turn to their treatment of demonstrative knowledge. What, then, *is* demonstrative knowledge? Why is it central to the epistemology of this period? What is its connexion with necessity? No single answer to these questions will fit the views of all the philosophers of these centuries, but some preliminary generalizations may be of help in the examination of particular viewpoints.

To the second question an answer is this: for most of the writers of this period—'empiricists' no less than 'rationalists'—knowledge was paradigmatically, often exclusively, of that which could be *demonstrated*. Thus Descartes, at the start of this period, remarks that 'science in its entirety is true and evident cognition'; hence we must 'reject all merely probable knowledge';[1] and in the work in which he most fully carried out this programme he equates this ambition with that of writing

[1] Descartes, *Rules*, II.

'.... nothing ... of which I do not possess very exact demonstrations'.[2] The same connexion between science, knowledge and demonstration persists in Hume, writing at the end of this period. After claiming to show that the opinion that whatever has a beginning has also a cause of existence is 'neither intuitively nor demonstratively certain' he re-expresses that conclusion as the claim that this opinion is not derived from 'knowledge or any scientific reasoning'.[3] The knowable, that which can constitute science, is that which is capable of demonstration. But what is demonstration?

Here, there is considerable disagreement among the philosophers of this period. A preliminary outline of the issues can be given by tracing some of the historical strands which informed their conception of the topic.

1.1 *Aristotle*

First, Aristotle's *Posterior Analytics* provided a philosophy of scientific knowledge which continued to be enormously influential even on those many philosophers who were explicitly anti-Aristotelian. Central to that philosophy was the idea that a key mode of achieving such knowledge was *via* demonstration. Of course, then as now, Aristotle's cryptic notes were open to very varied interpretation. But a crucial passage runs:

> We think we know a thing *simpliciter* . . . whenever we think we are aware both that the explanation because of which the object is its explanation, and that it is not possible for this to be otherwise.[4]

And he goes on to remark that one way in which this knowledge can be achieved is by what he calls 'demonstration'. These two thoughts provide a preliminary answer to our third question—how the topic of demonstration connects with that of necessity. For Aristotle is connecting scientific understanding with knowledge that something could not possibly be otherwise, that something must be so; and remarking that at least one way of achieving such knowledge is through demonstration. Much

[2] Descartes, *Meditations*.
[3] Hume, *Treatise*, Selby-Bigge Edn. p. 82.
[4] *Prior Analytics* 71b 10.

of the rest of Book I of the *Posterior Analytics* is an account of what a demonstration is, and how it brings about scientific knowledge or understanding. Central to the complex account is that a demonstration that *p* consists in a syllogism, *i.e.* a necessarily truth-preserving inference, the conclusion of which is *p*, and the premisses of which are themselves necessarily the case. A demonstration enables us to know that and why it is the case that *p*, in part by revealing that and why *p* is necessarily the case.

One inherited strand in the seventeenth century's conception of scientific knowledge is, then, that it will be knowledge that certain things must be so, together with the idea that such knowledge is to be obtained, or presented, by means of demonstrations approximating to (some interpretation of) Aristotle's account. An important second contribution to the conception of demonstrative knowledge was an imposing paradigm of such knowledge—geometry as presented in Euclid's *Elements*. The juxtaposition of Aristotle's account and Euclid's practice was neither arbitrary nor unproblematic. It was not arbitrary for various reasons. First, many of Aristotle's own illustrations of his account of demonstrative knowledge are geometrical ones. Secondly, the three kinds of premisses which serve as starting points in Euclid's demonstrations—definitions, postulates and 'common notions' ('axioms': often, in the seventeenth century, 'maxims')—are explicitly identified by Aristotle as elements in a demonstrative science, and the examples in Euclid seem to fit fairly closely Aristotle's account of these matters. The seventeenth century, then, inherited a philosophical account of demonstrative science which appeared largely to fit that which it took to be the paradigm of such science.

But problems can, and did, appear in this apparently neat picture, problems which were to plague seventeenth-century and later views of these topics. The first, and perhaps the major one, is this: on Aristotle's account, the necessarily truth-preserving inferences by means of which the theorems of a demonstrative science were to be deduced from the definitions, axioms and postulates should be those studied by logic (*dialektike*): and that, for Aristotle and most subsequent writers for over two thousand years, meant those inferences codified in Aristotelian 'syllogistic' logic. But those pious Aristotelians who attempted to present Euclid's argumentation syllogistically soon found that the task was hopeless. The simple fact is that Euclidean geometry, like most serious mathematics or other science, deploys forms of propositions and inferences which were not covered by Aristotelian logic. The standard seventeenth-century response—Leibniz was the great exception—was the misprisal of logic. Rather than thinking that there must be logical inferences of a kind not codified in received logic they concluded—ironically accepting Aristotle's logic as the only logic there could be—that logic was a worthless discipline. It is, therefore, comparatively rare to find seventeenth-century discussions of necessity focusing on the deployment of that concept in the central idea of logic—the idea of a valid argument.

A second consequence of the concatenation between the Aristotelian account and the Euclidean paradigm of demonstrative knowledge was the intrusion of epistemic notions into the philosophy of modality. The starting points of Euclidean geometry appear to have not merely the Aristotelian requirement of necessity—things could not be otherwise—but the epistemological features (which scholars assure us are not among Aristotle's demands on such starting points) of being knowable with certainty, perhaps even being 'self-evident'. (It is, of course, unclear what these features amount to.) Such epistemological features came increasingly to be demanded of the starting points of demonstrative science. Once built into the account of such science, these epistemological features became almost the central defining criteria of demonstrative knowledge. And this had profound consequences on the rôle, in seventeenth- and eighteenth-century thought, of the two historical roots of its conception of demonstrative science—Aristotle's prescription and Euclid's example. For, in this period, non-geometrical mathematics developed apace and in a manner quite unlike the axiomatized model prescribed by Aristotle (for science in general) and exemplified (in geometry) by Euclid. Thus for the seventeenth century an account of the apparently distinctive features of a demonstrative science—that its truths could not be otherwise, and that we could have certain knowledge of them—often proceeded on a basis divorced both from Aristotle's prescription and Euclid's example, while being continually distorted by their unavoidable background presence.

Much of the complexity of seventeenth-century discussions of these matters springs from this tension between background and foreground.

1.2 *Descartes*

Central to the accounts of demonstrative knowledge offered by Descartes and others of the period is a distinction between intuition and deduction. Descartes explains *intuition* in his early *Rules for the Direction of the Mind* thus:

> By 'intuition' I do not mean the fluctuating testimony of the senses or the deceptive judgment of the imagination as it botches things together, but the conception of a clear and attentive mind, which is so easy and distinct that there can be no room for doubt about what we are understanding. Alternatively, and this comes to the same thing, intuition is the indubitable conception of a clear and attentive mind which proceeds solely from the light of reason.[5]

Further on he writes:

> .... two things are requisite for mental intuition: first, the proposition intuited must be clear and distinct; second, the whole proposition must be understood all at once, and not bit by bit.[6]

And after the first passage he gives some examples of what can be known in this way:

> Thus everyone can mentally intuit that he exists, that he is thinking, that a triangle is bounded by just three lines, and a sphere by a single surface, and the like.[7]

We have here at least two elements. First an alleged psychological phenomenon: that there are certain propositions which we cannot doubt to be true when attended to appropriately. Secondly, an apparent explanation of what it is about these propositions and our grasp of them which produces this assurance: *viz.* that the propositions are 'clear and distinct' and grasped 'in their totality'.

Intuition, then, involves a single act of a kind of mental

[5] *Rules*, 3, C I 14, H&R I 7.
[6] *op.cit.*, Rule 11, C I 37, H&R I 33.
[7] *op.cit.* Rule 3.

'vision' and it is in this respect that it contrasts with another mode of knowing *viz. deduction*. This Descartes explains as 'the inference of something as following necessarily from some other propositions which are known with certainty'. Descartes is typically thinking of cases where a proposition is believed as the result of a series of inferential moves, taking one through intermediate propositions, from 'first principles'. He insists at each stage it is by intuition that we know that the proposition there inferred does follow necessarily from one or more earlier propositions.

> The self-evidence and certainty of intuition is required not only for apprehending single propositions, but also for any train of reasoning whatever. Take, for example, the inference that 2 plus 2 equals 3 plus 1: not only must we intuitively perceive that 2 plus 2 make 4, and that 3 plus 1 make 4, but also that the original proposition follows necessarily from the other two.[8]

But in a chain of such inferences we may not be able to connect the initial propositions with the final conclusion by a single mental act. Rather we need to remember that we have successively intuited both the starting points and the necessary connexions between the intermediate propositions. Deduction, then, involves a temporarily extended movement of the mind, requiring memory in order to confer certainty on its deliverances.

Intuition, from the examples above, appears sometimes to yield knowledge of merely contingent truths. I mentally intuit that I exist: although I might not have existed. But I also know by intuition that $2+2=4$, which Descartes thinks is necessarily true. Moreover intuition itself yields knowledge *of* necessity, most centrally in our grasp that certain propositions are necessary consequences of others. How, according to Descartes, can intuition yield such knowledge of necessity?

In the *Rules*, Descartes appears to sketch a theory of the source of necessity which connects it very closely with its epistemology. In the second half of *Rule* 12 he is considering what 'things' are appropriate objects of knowledge. The notion of 'thing' here is very broad, including properties ('natures') and propositions. (Descartes has an elaborated dichotomy into

[8] Descartes, *Rules* IV: AT X 369.

'simple' and 'composite' things, which need not enter here.) He writes

> . . . . the conjunction between these (simple) things is either necessary or contingent. The conjunction is necessary when one of them is somehow implied (albeit confusedly) in the concept of the other so that we cannot conceive either of them distinctly if we judge them to be separate from each other. It is in this way that shape is conjoined with extension, motion with duration or time, etc., because we cannot conceive of a shape which is completely lacking in extension, or a motion wholly lacking in duration. Similarly, if I say that 4 and 3 make 7, the composition is a necessary one, for we do not have a distinct conception of the number 7 unless in a confused sort of way we include 3 and 4 in it.[9]

Descartes here appears to be giving an account of the *source* of (some?) necessities which makes our knowledge of them quite unproblematic. Suppose we ask the author of the *Rules*: what *makes* it necessary that whatever has shape has extension? The answer appears to be something about *us*. Our concept of shape includes that of extension, in such a way that we cannot conceive of something having shape but lacking extension. And that we cannot so conceive would apparently be, for Descartes, something of which, like other first-person psychological facts (*e.g.* that I am thinking), I could have 'intuitive' knowledge. Knowledge of necessity, on this sketched account of its source, would seem to be a kind of self-knowledge. (Note how this picture explains the apparently bizarre grouping together of such psychological knowledge with knowledge of logical relations.)

But this sketchy psychologistic account of the source of necessity was not Descartes' full and considered opinion. This can be brought out by the following consideration. Let us note first that the previous quotation applies these ideas to elementary propositions of arithmetic. Now Descartes, early in his major mature work, the *Meditations* notoriously argues that doubt can be cast on our knowledge of such truths (*a fortiori* on our knowledge of their *necessary* truth) by the following consideration: that for all we know there may be a

[9] Descartes, *Rules*, C I 45–6.

powerful and malicious demon who is deceiving us in our most firmly held beliefs even about such 'simple' things. But if it was Descartes' view that the necessity (and *a fortiori* the truth) of such propositions depended simply on what I could, or could not, conceive, then it is unclear how the malicious demon could so deceive me. He would need to be able to deceive me concerning my own concepts. But Descartes holds that I cannot be deceived concerning the 'contents' of my own mind, which is what 'concepts' appear to be for Descartes.

Moreover, and more importantly, Descartes himself writes as follows:

> . . . . I find within me countless ideas of things which even though they may not exist anywhere outside me still cannot be called nothing; for although in a sense they can be thought of at will, they are not my invention, but have their own true and immutable natures. When, for example, I imagine a triangle, even if perhaps no such figure exists, or ever existed, anywhere outside my thought, there is still a determinate nature, or essence, or form of the triangle which is immutable and eternal, and not invented by me or dependent on my mind. This is clear from the fact that various properties can be demonstrated of the triangle, for example that its three angles equal two right angles, that its greatest side subtends its greatest angle, and the like; and since these properties are ones which I now clearly recognize whether I want to or not, even if I never thought of them at all when I previously imagined the triangle, it follows that they cannot have been invented by me.[10]

[10] *Meditations* V.

X

Explicating '*x* knows *a priori* that *p*'

1. Problem-situation

Kant's classic definition of the notion of *a priori* knowledge is, or ought to be, notorious for its brevity and unclarity. It runs: '. . . we shall understand by *a priori* knowledge . . . knowledge absolutely independent of all experience'.[1] Its brevity is obvious. One might begin to note its unclarity by asking: what exactly is meant by 'experience'; and more importantly, what is the force of 'independent'? I shall not directly confront these questions. I shall rather consider the following: can we give any more precise and illuminating account of the notion of *a priori* knowledge than Kant's? The recent literature contains, to my knowledge, only two worked-out accounts, those of Kitcher and McGinn.[2] These are very different: they are couched in terms of quite different concepts and are (in a sense shortly to be made precise) of very different forms. What lies at the root of the differences? Is either analysis adequate? How are they to be appraised? It is perhaps worth noting that these questions arise even for those philosophers, like Mill and Quine, whose only use for the notion of *a priori* knowledge is in the claim that there is none. Like the atheist, such a philosopher owes us a precise account of what it is that he thinks there isn't.

2. *Criteria of adequacy*

How can we tell if a proposed explication of '*x* knows *a priori* that *p*' is acceptable? It is no good to require that the explication match our 'intuitions' concerning which knowledge

[1] *The Critique of Pure Reason*, (trs) Norman Kemp Smith (London: Macmillan, 1964), B3, p. 43.

[2] See Philip Kitcher, 'A Priori Knowledge', *Philosophical Review*, 1980, and *The Nature of Mathematical Knowledge* (Oxford: Oxford University Press, 1984) Ch 1; Colin McGinn, '*A Priori* and *A Posteriori* Knowledge', *Proceedings of the Aristotelian Society*, 1975–1976.

is *a priori* and which is not. There is no philosophical agreement about such intuitions. As we have noted, some deny that there is any *a priori* knowledge. We cannot build it into our requirements that such views come out wrong.

Let us ask: what is the presupposition of being *interested* in an alleged distinction between *a priori* and *a posteriori* knowledge? Why might epistemology need or want such a distinction? I suggest that the presupposition is that these notions constitute something like 'epistemological natural kinds'. And I suggest that this is so only if the alleged distinction corresponds to a *natural division* in answers to epistemological questions. That is, there has to be an important epistemological question which requires a different answer when addressed to cases of, respectively, *a priori* and *a posterior* knowledge. Let me amplify.

A central question of epistemology might be phrased: what makes a true belief knowledge? This question is ambiguous.

(a) It might be a request for a definition or analysis of '*x* knows that *p*'. Agreeing that '*x* knows that *p*' (*Kxp*) entails 'It is true that *p*' (*Tp*) and '*x* believes that *p*' (*Bxp*), then the form of such an analysis is agreed, *viz.*

x knows that *p* iff *Tp* and *Bxp* and *Exp*

where '*Exp*' ('*E*' for '*episteme*') stands for — '*x*'s belief that *p* has the knowledge-conferring feature'. The aim of the analysis, is to spell out what *that* comes to.

One way, then, in which there could be an important *a priori/a posteriori* distinction would be if distinct '*E*'s' were involved in the two cases. That is, if we had to offer a different *analysis* of '*x* knows that *p*' where the knowledge was *a priori* or *a posteriori*. But this highly implausible. Even the believer in *a priori* knowledge, is hardly going to claim that 'know' is *ambiguous* as between (say) '*x* knows that 2+2=4' and '*x* knows that it is raining'.[3]

(b) Alternatively, the question 'What makes a true belief

[3] Although one might note that there are in the literature purported analyses of knowledge the proponents of which explicitly limit them to the case of *a posteriori* knowledge, *e.g.* David Armstrong in *Belief, Truth and Knowledge* (Cambridge: Cambridge University Press, 1973). This I am suggesting, *en passant*, is quite misguided.

knowledge?' might rather be directed at *particular* true beliefs, asking what *gave them*, in particular, the knowledge-conferring feature '*E*'. The idea, then, would be that there is a single feature '*E*' which beliefs could have in importantly different 'ways'.

We might put this slightly less abstractly by presupposing something about '*E*' *viz.* that what is crucial to a belief's being knowledge is something about the process by which it was acquired. That is, read '*Exp*' as: 'the process by which *x*'s belief that *p* was acquired has the knowledge-generating feature'. The suggestion then would be that there is an important *a priori/a posteriori* distinction only if these relate to means of acquiring beliefs which, if they possess '*E*', do so in importantly different 'ways'.

But what does that mean? When are 'ways' in which a belief-generating process has '*E*' importantly different? We might make a suggestion by considering the general problem 'How is knowledge possible?' In the present framework, this might be put: how *can* belief-producing processes have '*E*'? We can then say that there is an interesting *a priori/a posteriori* distinction if we can distinguish 'empirical' and '*a priori*' belief-producing processes in such a way that the questions:

(i) How can an 'empirical' belief-producing process possess '*E*'?

(ii) How can an '*a priori*' belief-producing process possess '*E*'?

have a significantly different force, or require significantly different answers.

We can put this differently. Question (ii) is, of course, simply a way of expressing the classical question 'How is *a priori* knowledge possible?'—a question which even believers in *a priori* knowledge have found pressing, and not answerable simply on the basis of materials adequate for answering 'How is *a posteriori* knowledge possible?'. (Kant, though, we may recall, despite pressing the problem of *a priori* knowledge, ultimately holds that the materials needed to give an account of *its* possibility were also needed to account for the possibility of *a posteriori* knowledge.) We can say then: there is a significant notion of *a priori* knowledge *only* if there is a 'distinctive' problem about how it is possible.

I suggest, therefore, that the central constraint on an adequate elucidation of '*x* knows *a priori* that *p*' (if such is to be found) is that it serve to show why there is a distinctive problem about the possibility of *a priori* knowledge, and exactly what that problem is.

Perhaps it might be retorted that we need no very deep investigation of the concept of *a priori* knowledge to explain the force of that problem: that we can be content with Kant's brief—'knowledge which is independent of all experience'; and that the strong undertow we all feel to empiricism—crudely put, the doctrine that all knowledge needs to be grounded in experience—will then serve to explain the force of the problem 'How is *a priori* knowledge possible?' This retort is silly. For—sticking to these terms—the strong undertow towards 'empiricism' just *is* the expression of the idea that there is something distinctively problematic about *a priori* knowledge. An exact understanding of what is problematic is what we need in order to understand the undertow. Moreover, the brevity and unclarity of the above formulation of empiricism exactly matches those features of Kant's definition of *a priori* knowledge. Until we understand what we should mean, exactly, by '*a priori* knowledge' we do not so much as know what empiricism *is*.

3. *The form of an account of 'x knows a priori that p'*

A priori knowledge is, obviously, a species of knowledge. In the first instance, then, an analysis of '*x* knows *a priori* that *p*' (*APKxp*) ought to look like:

APKxp iff *Kxp* and *APxp*

where *APxp* stands for that feature which is peculiar to *a priori* knowledge. Our task is to spell out what '*APxp*' comes to.

Now, we assumed, *Kxp* ought to be analysable by something of the form:

Kxp iff *Tp* and *Bxp* and *Exp*

Putting the two schemata together, a completely analysed account of *a priori* knowledge would look, in the first instance, like:

APKxp iff *Tp* and *Bxp* and *Exp* and *APxp*

But now a question will arise concerning any proffered account of '*APxp*' *viz.* whether by entailing one or more of the other components of '*APKxp*' it renders possible a simplification. In full generality there would be eight possibilities. But I shall first presume that, whatever it comes to, *APxp* always entails *Bxp*. I am presuming, that is, that the condition which serves to differentiate an instance of *a priori* knowledge is a condition which can only be applied on the presumption that the putative *a priori* knower at least believes the proposition in question. (We can thus read '*APxp*' as '*x* has acquired the belief that *p* by an *a priori* route'.) The interesting contrast is now between those analyses of '*APxp*' which do, and those which do not, entail the other two features of knowledge *viz. Tp* and *Exp*. Call these, respectively, accounts of *Kind I* and *Kind II*.[4] We can now suggest that the question 'How is *a priori* knowledge possible?' will look importantly different depending on whether the analysis of *APxp* is of *Kind I* or of *Kind II*.

Kind II

The key feature of accounts of this kind can be put like this: we can pick out a class of beliefs in terms of the kinds of routes (*a priori*) by which they have been acquired which are illuminatingly grouped together and contrasted with another class of beliefs—those acquired by empirical or *a posteriori* routes. And we can do this, and hold the class of such *a priori* beliefs to be non-empty while still, if we wish, denying that there is any *a priori knowledge*. For, on an account of this kind, that a belief is acquired by an '*a priori*' route does not entail that that belief is knowledge. For it does not entail either that the belief is true or that it has the epistemic feature. So the question 'How is *a priori* knowledge possible?' can here take the form: how can it be that any belief which has the differentiating feature *APxp* *also* have the features '*Tp*' and (crucially) *Exp* which are required for it to be *knowledge*? And the problem will be a

[4] An account is of *Kind I*, then, if it has the consequence that '*x*'s belief that *p* was acquired by an *a priori* process' (*APxp*) entails 'It is true that *p*' (*Tp*) and 'the process by which *x*'s belief that *p* was acquired has the knowledge-generating feature' (*Exp*). In other words, an account is of *Kind I* if it has the consequences that '*x*'s belief that *p* was acquired by an *a priori* belief producing process' (*APxp*) entails '*x* knows that *p*' (*Kxp*).

In contrast, an account is of *Kind II* if it has the consequence that *APxp* does not entail *Tp* and *Exp*: if it has the consequence that *APxp* does not entail *Kxp*.

serious one if *APxp* not only does not entail *Txp* and *Exp*, but also *appears* to stand in tension with one of these: or if it stands in tension with something we are at least inclined to think is involved in *Exp*.

In short, because on accounts of this form *APxp* does not entail *Kxp*, there can be a real question: how can any belief which has feature *APxp* (which is arrived at by an *a priori* route) also be knowledge?[5]

Kind I

On the first approach, however, we cannot drive a wedge between a belief's being acquired by an *a priori* route, and that belief's being knowledge. It is thus not clear what acceptable form a *general* problem 'How is *a priori* knowledge possible?' can take on this approach.

More could be said on this. But I shall here briefly remark that Kitcher, who offers an account of Kind I, clearly does not think there is any such *general* problem. His account thus violates the general adequacy condition I proposed. It also suffers from other defects. To that account we shall now turn.

4. *Kitcher's account: motivation and exposition*[6]

Basic to Kitcher's account of '*x* knows *a priori* that *p*' is a view about the correct *form* of an account of '*x* knows that *p*'. It will, he claims, be 'psychologistic'; but all he means by this is that whether or not a true belief is knowledge will depend on the nature of the process which produces the belief. Knowledge will be true belief produced in 'the right way'. (Kitcher is thus opposed to those accounts of knowledge which ignore the nature of a belief's genesis and which focus instead on the logical relations among propositions believed. His 'psychologism' can thus be seen as part of the project of 'naturalizing' epistemology. With this aspect of Kitcher's thought I am in complete agreement.)

The central task for an account of '*x* knows that *p*' will thus be, on the present view, to say *what* feature a belief-producing

[5] In *Ways of Paradox* (New York: Random House, 1966) p. 122, Quine suggest that although there might be no *a priori* knowledge, there might nonetheless be a distinction between the *a priori* and *a posteriori* grounds for holding a belief (though he thinks both factors may be operative everywhere).

[6] See Kitcher, *The Nature of Mathematical Knowledge*, pp. 22–24.

process must have for it to produce belief 'in the right way' to be knowledge. Competing contemporary accounts of knowledge —causal theories, reliability theories, Nozick's 'tracking theory' —can be seen as offering different views on this question. Kitcher wishes to remain neutral as between such accounts. (Understandably, given the controversy surrounding them, one would not wish one's view of *a priori* knowledge to depend on which detailed proposal, if any, was acceptable. To what extent an account of *a priori* knowledge can remain neutral concerning *knowledge* is a question to which we shall return.) He thus introduces as a primitive notion that of a 'warrant' which is to apply to all and only those token belief-producing processes which produce belief 'in the right way'. The *form* of an account of knowledge is, for Kitcher, thus:

> *x* knows that *p* iff *p* and *x* believes that *p* and *x*'s belief that *p* was produced by a process which is a warrant for it.

A priori knowledge, he wants to say, will be knowledge produced by a particular *kind* of warrant—an *a priori* warrant. His central task, then, is to say what is distinctive of *a priori* warrants. The brief, traditional, account of *a priori* knowledge is knowledge that is independent of experience. Kitcher's account of an *a priori* warrant can be seen as offering a particular explication of that idea by construing 'experience' as the totality of a subject's sensory states; and construing 'independent' counterfactually: the knowledge could have been obtained by a process of the same type that actually produced it, no matter what the course of the subject's experience, provided it was sufficient to allow him to acquire the concepts required to grasp the proposition in question. Such a course of experience Kitcher calls a 'life sufficient for *p*'. This, given his proposed form for an account of knowledge, requires that, in any such life, a process of the type in question would, were it to produce the belief that *p*, produce a true and warranted belief. Overall, then, Kitcher proposes:

> (1) A person's experience at a particular time will be identified with his sensory state at the time. . . . The total sequence of experiences *x* has had up to time *t* is *x's life at t*. A life will be said to be *sufficient for x for p* just in case *x* could have had that life and gained sufficient understanding to believe that *p*.

(2) x knows *a priori* that p iff x knows that p and x's belief that p was produced by a process which is an *a priori* warrant for it.
(3) $\propto$ is an *a priori* warrant for x's belief that p iff $\propto$ is a process such that, given any life e, sufficient for x for p:
(a) some process of the same type could produce in x a belief that p
(b) if a process of the same type were to produce in x a belief that p, then it would warrant x in believing that p
(c) if a process of the same type were to produce in x a belief that p, then p.

5. *Kitcher's account: objections*
a) *A Kind I Account*
It will immediately be seen that Kitcher's account is of *Kind I* in the sense of section 3: the differentiating feature of *a priori* knowledge—the belief that p's being produced by an *a priori* warrant—is such that, given clauses (b) and (c) in the account of '*a priori* warrant', any belief so produced is *ipso facto* knowledge (is true and warranted). This being so, Kitcher's account of *a priori* knowledge does not allow him to make sense of the problem 'How is *a priori* knowledge possible?' along the lines: how can beliefs with the differentiating feature—beliefs held on *a priori* grounds—be knowledge? Rather, if Kitcher *were* to pose a general problem it would have to be: how can there be beliefs with the differentiating feature *viz.* produced by *a priori* warrants in Kitcher's sense?

It *might* be thought obvious that there *is* a problem here: how can there be belief-producing processes which remain available, warranting, and truth-guaranteeing under such a wide range of counterfactual circumstances concerning the subject's sensory states? But it is unclear that this is a general problem. There are two ways to make this point. The first is *ad hominem*. Kitcher's interest in explicating the notion of *a priori* knowledge is to provide a clear analysis of the central claim of his book: *mathematical* knowledge is not *a priori*. But Kitcher does not defend this view on the basis of any *general* difficulty about the idea of *a priori* knowledge, and clearly feels none. His approach is piecemeal: arguments are produced to show that particular processes invoked to explain the formation of our mathematical beliefs—mathematical 'intuition', proofs *etc.*—do not meet Kitcher's conditions on *a priori* warrants. Another way to make this point is implicit in my second line of objection, to which I shall immediately turn; his account, far from revealing why there is a problem about the very possibility of *a priori* knowledge, makes it all too *easy* for there to be such knowledge.

(b) *Self-knowledge*

Kitcher himself notes that his account may be thought too 'liberal', allowing as cases of *a priori* knowledge which are 'intuitively' no such thing. One example is a certain kind of self-knowledge—knowledge of one's own present psychological states. Kitcher suggests that this 'risk' springs from the 'psychologistic' (in his sense) form of an account of knowledge. But it springs from no such thing, but rather from the fact that on his account, *a priori* knowledge is just a special case of incorrigible knowledge.[7]

Kitcher's own discussion of this difficulty is tortuous.[8] He lacks the perspective from which to explain why this possible consequence of his account *is* a problem. (Saying it is 'counterintuitive' explains nothing.) The risk that certain kinds of self-knowledge will come out as *a priori* on his analysis might be put like this: suppose there are certain propositions which ascribe to oneself a kind of experience where (i) these propositions can only be understood in a life which contains such experiences; (ii) the process which leads from the experience to the belief in the experience-ascribing proposition cannot fail to produce a true and warranted belief. (Propositions of the kind 'I am in pain' might be an example.) Now, of course, both (i) and (ii) might be denied for such propositions. So Kitcher's account *might* escape this consequence. But my basic criticism is this: self-knowledge is correctly classified as *a priori* only if it exemplifies a special case of the general problem 'How is *a priori* knowledge possible?' But I take it that, although there are problems about how the present kinds of self-knowledge are possible, they are not the same problems as *e.g.*

[7] For a perceptive discussion of this feature of Kitcher's, and others', account of *a priori* knowledge see A. Edinin, '*A Priori* Knowledge for Fallibilists', *Philosophical Studies*, 1984, pp. 189–198. Edinin, however, provides no *diagnosis* of the nature of the failing.

[8] *Ibid*, pp. 27–31.

how following a mathematical proof (traditionally alleged to be a type of process generating *a priori* knowledge) can produce knowledge. More importantly, the question whether or not such self-knowledge *is* illuminatingly grouped with *e.g.* mathematical knowledge as traditionally conceived *should not depend on whether or not (i) or (ii) hold of such self-knowledge.* But on Kitcher's account, the question whether or not self-knowledge is *a priori does* depend on whether (i) or (ii) hold of such knowledge.

(c) *Universally empirical knowledge*

Kitcher raises the worry that on his account certain kinds of knowledge gained by perception will be counted *a priori.* These will be knowledge of propositions which '. . . are true in any world of which we can have any experience, and given sufficient experience to entertain those propositions . . . we could always come to know them on the basis of experience.'[9] A Kantian example might be 'There is an external world'. He calls such cases *universally empirical knowledge*, concedes that there could be such, and raises the objection that they are labelled '*a priori*' on his account. His response is that '. . . . the classical notion of a priority is too vague to decide such issues'.[10] If by the 'classical notion' one means Kant's brief attempt at an explicit analysis, one can agree. So if the central aim of an account of *a priori* knowledge was to be faithful to such analyses, then one could agree they here leave room for 'discretion'. But, as I argued, the key constraint on a contemporary account of *a priori* knowledge should not be the (admittedly vague) classical formulations but rather the sense of the problematic nature of *a priori* knowledge. And from that point of view, Kitcher's 'universally empirical knowledge' should clearly *not* be judged *a priori*; being based on perception it simply does not raise the traditional problems about the possibility of *a priori* knowledge.

(d) *Knowledge produced by 'non-empirical processes'*

My final objection to Kitcher may move us in the direction of a more adequate account.

[9] *Ibid*, p. 31.
[10] *Ibid.*

As noted, a central aim of Kitcher's book is to argue that mathematical knowledge is not *a priori.* And his central strategy is, given that his account is of *Kind I*, piecemeal: examining various processes which, it has been thought, generate *a priori* mathematical knowledge and arguing that they do no such thing—that they fail to come up to Kitcher's (stringent) standards for being *a priori* warrants. A diagnostic question then arises: why have philosophers (mistakenly, in Kitcher's view) thought that these processes *do* generate *a priori* knowledge?

On at least two occasions Kitcher offers a diagnosis. The first concerns a notorious proposal of Gödel's: that mathematical knowledge can be generated by a form of non-sensory apprehension—'mathematical intuition'—directed on the (Platonistically conceived) abstract subject-matter of mathematics. Now why might someone who believed that we had such a faculty be led to think that the knowledge which it generated was *a priori*? Kitcher comments briefly: 'mathematical intuition is a non-empirical process. Hence anyone who confuses non-empirical processes which actually warrant belief with *a priori* warrants will read Gödel as upholding *a priorism*' (*i.e.* the view that mathematical knowledge is *a priori*).[11] Again, commenting on the less *recherché* proposal that following a proof or computation generates *a priori* knowledge, he remarks 'one can easily go astray here by conflating *a priori* knowledge with knowledge obtained by a non-empirical process'—and agrees that in the case of following a proof or computation 'a non-empirical process engenders belief'.[12]

But this gives the game away. Although Kitcher never explains what he means by a 'non-empirical process' in these passages he seems to commit himself to the following ideas:

1. Certain belief-producing processes (of which 'mathematical intuition', if it exists, and following a proof, are examples) are significantly grouped together as 'non-empirical' processes which engender belief; and may be significantly contrasted with 'empirical' processes which engender belief.

2. Some of these non-empirical belief-producing processes

[11] *Ibid*, p. 59.
[12] *Ibid*, p. 43.

can generate knowledge (*i.e.*, on Kitcher's account, produce true warranted belief).

3. Some mathematical knowledge is generated by such 'non-empirical' processes.

Now, as a first move, the mathematical *a priorist* could simply give Kitcher *his* notion of *a priori* knowledge, granting that mathematical knowledge is not *a priori* in *that* sense, but restate his position as: mathematical knowledge is (typically, at least) generated by 'non-empirical' processes. We have already argued that Kitcher's account is ill-suited to be an analysis of the notion of *a priori* knowledge, because it fails to say what the general problem 'How is *a priori* knowledge possible?' comes to. If we can make clear sense of the notion of a 'non-empirical' belief-producing process, a genuine problem might be posed as: how can a belief produced by a non-empirical process be knowledge? But then, given our central constraint, it would look as if 'knowledge produced by a non-empirical process', and not Kitcher's notion of *a priori* knowledge, would be the concept of genuine epistemological interest.[13]

6. *McGinn's account: motivation and exposition*[14]

The paradigm 'empirical' belief-producing process is, I suppose, perception. We might now ask: in virtue of what feature do perceptually generated beliefs count, when they do, as knowledge? A natural first thought might be this: in simple cases, they count as knowledge because the fact that makes the belief true *causes*, *via* perception, the belief in question. I see the cat and know that there is a cat in front of me. I know because the cat, or the fact that there is a cat there, causes me to have that belief. As a first shot, then, we might say that knowledge is *a posteriori* when the belief which constitutes the knowledge is caused by the fact which makes it true. *A priori* knowledge, then, would be knowledge where the belief in question is *not* caused by the fact which makes it true.

This simple account has two merits. The first, and for

[13] We might see McGinn's account as, in part, motivated by following out this line of thought. This said, however, in his paper: '*A Priori* and *A Posteriori* Knowledge', *op.cit.*, McGinn himself offers no such motivation.

[14] In addition to the '*A Priori* and *A Posteriori* Knowledge' essay, see C. McGinn, 'Modal Knowledge' in R. Healey (ed) *Reduction, Time and Reality* (Cambridge: Cambridge University Press, 1981).

present concerns the *central*, merit is that it is an account of *Kind II*. That is, the differentiating feature of *a priori* knowledge, *viz.* that the belief not be caused by the fact which makes it true, does not entail that the belief in question is knowledge. Indeed it seems to stand in some tension with the idea that the belief is knowledge. For, we might ask, if the belief in question is *not* caused by that which makes it true how can it be anything but an accident that, so acquired, the belief acquired is true? But it is a familiar thought that for a true belief to be *knowledge* it must be 'no accident' that, given the way the belief was acquired, the belief is true. So this account very nicely explicates what the problem of *a priori* knowledge is: how can beliefs which are acquired without being caused by that which makes them true nevertheless be 'non-accidentally' true, *i.e.* knowledge?

Secondly, and as McGinn notes, an account along these lines avoids the apparent implication of Kant's account (and, as we saw Kitcher's) that certain cases of knowledge of one's own mental states come out as *a priori*. Some such knowledge is *of* experience, but is not, as perceptual knowledge is, *based* on experience. Still, intuitively it is not *a priori*. It is not *a priori* on the present simple account. For such beliefs about one's mental states *are* caused by the mental states themselves (or the fact that one has them). And the present account can *explain*, as Kitcher's did not, why it is 'counter-intuitive' to call such knowledge *a priori*. Precisely because the beliefs in question are caused by their subject-matter, there is not the above problem as to how they can be knowledge.

Unfortunately, although the simple account seems acceptably to label 'non-inferential' perceptually based knowledge as *a posteriori*, it appears to go wrong with cases of *inferential* perceptually based knowledge.[15] Consider: I see a flock of birds hurriedly fly off. I believe, indeed know, that there is a cat in the vicinity. My knowledge is *a posteriori*. But my belief that there is a cat is not caused by the cat, or the fact that there is a cat

[15] Some of the complexities here mirror difficulties in simple causal theories of knowledge. Not that the present view is any such thing. On the contrary, precisely because it locates causal notions in the differentia of *a posteriori* knowledge, it involves denying that causation enters into the analysis of the general notion of *knowledge*.

there. So this knowledge would be labelled *a priori* by the present simple account.

McGinn thus introduces a complication. What crucially makes this case still a case of *a posteriori* knowledge, he suggests, is that here there is a grounding belief *s*—that the birds are flying off—which *is* caused by its subject-matter. The suggestion then is that one knows *a posteriori* that *p* if one knows that *p* and there is an *s* which is one's ground or reason for believing that *p*, and the subject matter of *s* causes one (*via* one's belief that *s*) to believe that *p*. (In the case of non-inferential knowledge $s=p$.) We get the definition of *a priori* knowledge by putting a 'not' in the third clause. *viz.*

(4) *x* knows that *p a priori* iff
 (i) *x* knows that *p*
 (ii) (∃*s*) (*s* is *x*'s ground or reason for believing that *p*, and
 (iii) it is *not* the case that the subject-matter of *s* causes *x* to believe that *p*).

This more complex account is obviously still of *Kind II*. It appears, therefore, to meet the central constraint we are imposing. But I shall argue that it wrongly labels as *a posteriori* certain cases which ought to be labelled as *a priori* because they raise exactly the same epistemological problems raised by those cases which the account *does* label '*a priori*'.

7. *McGinn's Account: Criticism: 'inferential' a priori knowledge-yielding faculties*

We saw that the complication in McGinn's account was introduced in order to label correctly certain cases of inferential *a posteriori* knowledge. I wish now to argue that there are certain putative cases of knowledge which ought to be construed as *a priori* knowledge—because they are problematic in the way it is beginning to appear that *a priori* knowledge is. But that *if* such cases of knowledge are construed as *inferential* knowledge then McGinn's account labels them as *a posteriori*. That is, McGinn's account fails because being *a priori* according to his account does not coincide with being problematic in the way (according to that very account) *a priori* knowledge is meant to be.

To make this argument less abstract, I shall illustrate it by a particular view of the ontology and epistemology of mathematics which we have already alluded to in section 5 above, *viz.* Gödel's. On this view the subject-matter of mathematical statements are abstract objects, conceived as mind-independent entities, not existing in space and time and (hence?) not entering into causal relations with the spatio-temporal world. And we are supposed to acquire mathematical knowledge by means of a quasi-perceptual faculty of 'mathematical intuition' directed somehow on the abstract realm.

Let us first suppose that this faculty yields non-inferential knowledge, that is, it directly produces, without an intermediary grounding belief, the knowledge-constituting mathematical beliefs. This then is a case where, in McGinn's terms, $p = s$. And any knowledge that *p*, yielded by such a faculty, will come out, appropriately, as *a priori*; for the subject-matter of *p*, the abstract realm, being causally inert, cannot cause the belief that *p*. This is a result that suits McGinn:

> On any view according to which the subject-matter of mathematical discourse, and of mathematical grounds, consists of abstract entities—on any Platonist view, that is—(4) confers apriority upon mathematics and knowledge thereof.[16]

There is, though, an old debate in the philosophy of perception concerning whether perceptually acquired knowledge of the external world is or is not *inferential* knowledge. One camp says no: when, in broad daylight *etc.*, looking at a pig, I acquire the belief that there is a pig in front of me, that belief is not inferred from any other, more basic grounding belief. The inferentialist camp says rather that the belief acquired non-inferentially is merely that I am having a visual (or olfactory) experience as of a pig's being in front of me. If I then go on to believe that there *is* a pig there, then that belief is inferred from the initial one.

Now if that debate makes sense in the philosophy of perception, why should there not be a similar one in the philosophy of quasi-perception, the philosophy of Gödelian 'intuition'? Suppose, as a result of 'mathematical intuition' I acquire the belief that the cumulative hierarchy ascends into the transfinite. Is this belief inferred or not? One camp says no:

[16] '*A Priori* and *A Posteriori* Knowledge', p. 201.

the faculty of intuition directly yields the mathematical belief in question. The other, mirroring the inferentialist position in the philosophy of perception, says that my non-inferential belief is about my own mental state—that I am having a mathematical intuition as of the cumulative hierarchy transcending into the transfinite from which I then infer the mathematical belief. And clearly even if mathematical intuition *sometimes* directly yields a mathematical belief, one could hold that at other times, say when one was in a cautious mood, it operated inferentially. The point now is that mathematical beliefs yielded *inferentially* by mathematical intuition will—if they are knowledge—be *a posteriori* knowledge by McGinn's account. For the grounding belief—that I am having a mathematical intuition as of . . . *will* be caused by its subject-matter, *viz.*, by the workings of the faculty of intuition. But it is clearly wrong for the status—*a priori* or *a posteriori*—of putative knowledge yielded by mathematical intuition thus to depend on whether the knowledge is yielded inferentially or non-inferentially. For the putative knowledge is problematic *in precisely the same way* on both the inferential and the non-inferential picture. In each case the question is: how can we see it as non-accidental that the beliefs yielded by mathematical intuition should be true of the realm of abstract objects?

The foregoing argument can clearly be generalised. Consider any knowledge-yielding faculty of which it is problematic how it non-accidentally yields true beliefs, *i.e.* any *a priori*-knowledge-yielding faculty. Either it is inferential in the sense that it first yields a belief about the subject's own mental state, e.g., 'I am having a mathematical intuition as of *p*'—and then yields the *a priori* belief that *p*; or it directly yields the *a priori* belief that *p*. But if the *a priori*-knowledge-yielding faculty is inferential then McGinn's account wrongly labels the knowledge it produces as *a posteriori*. And if the faculty is non-inferential then we can render the knowledge it yields as *a posteriori* on certain occasions by exercising it inferentially (perhaps when in a cautious mood). But we should not be able to change the status of the knowledge the faculty yields from *a priori* to *a posteriori* in this manner: exercised non-inferentially or inferentially it is equally problematic how the faculty non-accidentally yields true beliefs, for the facts which make true the beliefs it ultimately yields play no part in causing those beliefs.[17]

8. *Towards an alternative: knowledge and non-accidentally true belief.*[18]

My suspicion is that any account of '*X* knows *a priori* that *p*' will have to be more committed about the analysis of '*X* knows that *p*' than the two we have looked at so far. But familiarly, in the literature, detailed accounts come and go with great rapidity. One would not wish one's account of *a priori* knowledge to be too committed to any one such account. What follows is the start of an attempt to steer between Scylla and Charybdis.

It has been a common-place of post-Gettier discussions of '*x* knows that *p*' that one cannot know that *p* if it is, in some sense, 'an accident' that one believes truly that *p*. The notion of non-accidentally true belief is not, in itself, any more perspicuous than that of knowledge. So it would, I believe, be an error to offer it as itself an analysis of '*x* knows that *p*'.[19] Different recent accounts of knowledge might be seen as attempts to say, specifically, what 'non-accidentally true belief' comes to, by offering accounts of '*x* knows that *p*' which, they hope, will not allow 'accidentally true beliefs' to count as knowledge.

Such approaches do not, though, proceed via any *general* account of the notion of non-accidentality. An alternative approach to the analysis of knowledge, and one which I believe has not been followed, might have the following two stages: (1) a general account of the place of the notion of 'non-

[17] Another example would be *modal* beliefs (taken as having realistically construed possible worlds as their subject matter) yielded by the faculty of sensory imagination. Such a faculty might operate non-inferentially: directly yielding modal beliefs; or it might operate inferentially: first yielding (non-modal) beliefs such as 'I am having a sensory image as of a pink elephant' from which the modal belief 'there could be a pink elephant' would be inferred.

[18] This section should be regarded as more provisional than any of the preceding.

[19] For someone who does offer an analysis of knowledge in terms of non-accidentally true belief see P. Unger, 'An Analysis of Factual Knowledge', *Journal of Philosophy*, Vol 1968. For sensible comments on this see A. Goldman, 'Discrimination and Perceptual Knowledge', in G. Pappas and M. Swain (eds) *Essays on Knowledge and Justification* (Ithaca, N.Y: Cornell University Press, 1978), p. 123, and C. McGinn, 'The Concept of Knowledge' in P. French *et al.* (eds) Causation and Causal Theories, *Midwest Studies in Philosophy*, Vol IX, (Minneapolis: University of Minnesota Press, 1984) footnote 13.

accidentality' in the account of knowledge; followed by (2) a general analysis of the notion 'It is no accident that'. The idea would then be that the two stages would together yield an account of '*x* knows that *p*'. And the second stage is surely of interest in its own right: there are other areas of philosophy, *e.g.* in discussions of causation, and of explanation where it would help to be clear on what it was for something to be 'accidentally' the case. There seems to be almost no work on this topic.[20]

When I did some work on stage 2, I found it hard to make progress. But for present concerns that does not matter. The suggestion I wish to make is that, for the purpose of explicating '*x* knows *a priori* that *p*', we need only commit ourselves to a view on (1)—the role of the notion of 'non-accidentality' in the explication of '*x* knows that *p*'. We should stay largely neutral on (2) (which is where the major disagreements among analysists of knowledge occur).

Dogmatically, then, I suggest the following view on (1). The role of the notion of 'no accident' in an account of '*x* knows that *p*' is in the following schema:[21]

> (K) *x* knows that *p* only if (*not* iff) it is true that *p*, and *x* has come to believe that *p* by means of process *M*, such that it is no accident (in the circumstances) that *x*'s coming, *via M*, to believe that *p* is his coming, *via M*, to believe truly that *p*.

I now presume something about a general analysis of 'it is no accident that . . .'. I shall assume that if it was no accident that, for example, the robbers arrived at the well at the same time as the rich man, then there will be some *explanation*, some *account* of why it was no accident that they were at the well at the same time. Applied to schema (K), then, I am assuming that if it is no accident that by coming *via* means *M* to believe that

[20] The only recent writing I know of is Sorabji's discussion of Aristotle on coincidences; see R. Sorabji, *Necessity, Cause and Blame* (London: Duckworth, 1980) Chapter 1. (But see also G.E.M. Anscombe, 'Causality and Determination' in *Metaphysics and the Philosophy of Mind: Collected Philosophical papers, Vol II* (Oxford: Blackwell, 1981), and R. Hambourger, 'The Argument From Design' in C. Diamond and J. Teichman (eds) *Intention and Intentionality* (Brighton: Harvester Press, 1979), (J.H.)).

[21] One might compare this with Bernard Williams' final remarks on the nature of knowledge in his *Descartes: The Project of Pure Enquiry* (Harmandsworth: Penguin Books, 1978) Ch 1.

p, *x* came to believe truly that *p*, then there will be some *account*, some *explanation* of why it was no accident that by coming by these means he ended up truly believing that *p*.

The next suggestion would be that significant differences between *kinds* of knowledge—in particular between *a priori* and *a posteriori* knowledge—should be based on differences in the *kind* of account that can be offered of why it is no accident that beliefs acquired by different means are true.

Compare and contrast this schematic suggestion with McGinn's. On his account (recall his definitions), the contrast between *a priori* and *a posteriori* knowledge that *p* is based in different kinds of account of how the belief that *p* has been acquired. On mine it would be based on different kinds of account of why, having acquired the belief in a certain way, it is no accident that the belief acquired is true. What I suggest *may* work is to take over McGinn's stress on the causality of the grounding of belief and embed it in an account of my structure.

The crude idea would be that in the case of *a posteriori* knowledge the causal origin of the belief did, while in the case of *a priori* knowledge it did *not*, explain why it was no accident that the belief thus acquired was true. But this is too simple. For any belief which constitutes knowledge, the causal origin of the belief must have a part to play in explaining why it is no accident that the belief is true. (For it seems that any knowledge-constituting belief could have had a different causal origin by which it would not have been knowledge—by which it *would* have been an accident that the belief thus acquired was true.) Thus the present crude idea would trivially have the consequence that there is *no a priori* knowledge. But what *may* work is to take over more of the details of McGinn's account and embed them in the structure I have been suggesting, as follows:

x knows *a posteriori* that *p* iff
i) *x* knows that *p*
ii) there is an explanation of why it is no accident that *x*'s belief is true which makes essential appeal to the fact that
iii) $(\exists s)$ (*s* is *x*'s ground or reason for believing that *p* and the fact that *s* causes *x* to believe that *p*.

and

x knows *a priori* that *p* iff

i) *x* knows that *p*

ii) there is no explanation of why it is no accident that *x*'s belief is true which appeals to the fact that

iii) (∃*s*) (*s* is *x*'s ground or reason for believing that *p* and the fact that *s* causes *x* to believe that *p*).

Bibliography of Ian McFetridge

Previously Published Articles and Reviews

Articles

1) 'Propositions and Davidson's Account of Indirect Discourse', *Proceedings of the Aristotelian Society*, Vol 76, 1975–6, pp. 131–145.
2) 'Are Moral Requirements Hypothetical Imperatives?', *Proceedings of the Aristotelian Society*, Supplementary Volume, 52, 1978, pp. 31–42.
3) 'Supervenience, Realism, Necessity', *The Philosophical Quarterly*, Vol 35, 1985, pp. 246–258.
4) 'Realism and Anti-Realism in an Historical Context', in J. Haldane & C. Wright (eds) *Realism, Reason and Projection* (Oxford: Oxford University Press, 1991).

Reviews

1) *Essays in Analysis.* Bertrand Russell (ed. D. Lackey), *British Journal for the Philosophy of Science*, 26, 1975, pp. 83–5.
2) *Deviant Logic*. (Susan Haack), *Philosophy*, Vol 51, 1976, pp. 114–115.
3) *Proofs and Refutations: The Logic of Mathematical Discovery*. (Imre Lakatos), *Philosophy*, Vol 52, 1977, pp. 365–366.
4) *Treatise on Basic Philosophy*, Vols I & II. (Mario Bunge), *Mind*, Vol 87, 1978, pp. 144–146.
5) *Paradoxes: A Study in Form and Predication*. (James Cargile), *Philosophy*, Vol 55, 1980, pp. 421–423.
6) *Rational Action*. (Ed. Ross Harrison), *Mind*, Vol 92, 1983, pp. 626–629.
7) *An Introduction to Philosophical Logic*. (A.C. Grayling), *Philosophical Books*, Vol 24, 1983, pp. 164–165.
8) *Quality and Concept*. (George Bealer), *Mind*, Vol 93, 1984, pp. 455–458.

9) 'Recent Work on Wittgenstein', *The Philosophical Quarterly*, Vol 34, 1984, pp. 70–73. (Multiple Review Article):
Perspectives on the Philosophy of Wittgenstein. (Ed. Irving Block).
Wittgenstein: Language and World. (John Canfield).
Wittgenstein: To Follow a Rule. (Eds. Steven H. Holtzmann & Christopher M. Leich).
Wittgenstein and his Times. (Ed. Brian McGuinness).
Wittgenstein's Tractatus: An Introduction. (H.O. Mounce).
Ludwig Wittgenstein: Personal Recollections. (Ed. Rush Rhees).
Wittgenstein. (George Henrik von Wright).

10) *Fundamentals of Ethics*. (John Finnis), *Mind*, Vol 94, 1985, pp. 158–160.

11) *The Nature of Mathematical Knowledge*. (Philip Kitcher), *Mind*, Vol 94, 1985, pp. 321–323.

12) *Sense and Content: Experience, Thought and their Relations.* (Christopher Peacocke), *Philosophical Books*, Vol 26, 1985, pp. 101–105.

13) *Exercises in Analysis: Essays by Students of Casimir Lewy*. (Ed. Ian Hacking), *Philosophical Books*, Vol 27, 1986, pp. 158–161.

14) *Morality and Objectivity: A Tribute to J.L. Mackie.* (Ed. Ted Honderich), *Philosophy*, Vol 61, 1986, pp. 542–544.

Index